PREPARATION FOR LICENSING AND BOARD CERTIFICATION EXAMINATIONS IN PSYCHOLOGY

The Professional, Legal, and Ethical Components

Second Edition

BRUNNER/MAZEL CONTINUING EDUCATION IN PSYCHIATRY AND PSYCHOLOGY SERIES

Series Editor: Gene Usdin, M.D.

This series provides comprehensive, state-of-the-art study guides to help those who are preparing for advanced examinations in psychiatry and psychology. Written by experts representing various areas of specialization, the guides are designed to be accurate, current, and accessible.

1. PSYCHIATRY SPECIALTY BOARD REVIEW
William M. Easson, M.D., and Nicholas L. Rock, M.D.

2. NEUROLOGY FOR THE PSYCHIATRY SPECIALTY BOARD REVIEW
Leon A. Weisberg, M.D.

3. CHILD AND ADOLESCENT PSYCHIATRY FOR THE SPECIALTY BOARD REVIEW
Robert L. Hendren, D.O.

4. PREPARATION FOR LICENSING AND BOARD CERTIFICATION EXAMINATIONS IN PSYCHOLOGY: The Professional, Legal, and Ethical Components, *Second Edition*
Robert G. Meyer, Ph.D.

Brunner/Mazel Continuing Education in Psychiatry and Psychology Series No. 4

PREPARATION FOR LICENSING AND BOARD CERTIFICATION EXAMINATIONS IN PSYCHOLOGY

The Professional, Legal, and Ethical Components

Second Edition

Robert G. Meyer, Ph.D.

University of Louisville

BRUNNER/MAZEL Publishers • New York

Note: With dramatic advances continually being made in the clinical sciences, it is a challenge for physicians to keep abreast of both modifications in treatment that such advances require and of new drugs being introduced each year. The author and publisher of this volume have taken care to make certain that the doses of drugs and schedules of treatment are correct and compatible with the standards generally accepted at the time of publication. However, it is essential for the reader to become fully cognizant of the information on the instruction inserts provided with each drug or therapeutic agent prior to administration or prescription.

Further, as most of the topics are by nature ambiguous, it is suggested that the reader consult further reference sources or an attorney for clarification should there be a question regarding a specific clinical or legal case.

Library of Congress Cataloging-in-Publication Data

Meyer, Robert G.
    Preparation for licensing and board certification examinations in
psychology : the professional, legal, and ethical components /
Robert G. Meyer.—2nd ed.
        p.   cm.
    Includes bibliographical references and index.
    ISBN 0-87630-767-5
    1. Psychology—Certification—United States. 3. Psychologists—
Licenses—United States.   I. Title.
    BF80.8.m48   1995
    150'.76—dc20   94-23369
                                                            CIP

Published by
BRUNNER/MAZEL, INC.
19 Union Square West
New York, New York 10003

Manufactured in the United States of America

10 9 8 7 6 5 4 3 2 1

To Christopher Robert Hubbard
(with a big thanks to Monika and David)

CONTENTS

SERIES EDITOR'S NOTE

This book, by Robert G. Meyer, Ph.D., Professor in the Department of Psychology at the University of Louisville, is superbly written and an excellent review for mental health professionals, including not only psychologists but also psychiatrists. The title emphasizes its usefulness for psychologists in preparing for licensing and board certification examinations. The author's obvious effort to make the volume as current as possible is exemplified by the up-to-date content as well as 1994 references and citations, e.g., comments regarding the O. J. Simpson incident of June 1994, discussions of psychopharmacologic agents released in the latter half of 1994, and clinical diagnoses noted that are based on the recently published DSM-IV.

In this day and age when the various mental health specialties are identifying their core identities, the inclusive nature of this volume makes a strong claim for the broadening interests and involvement of psychologists.

There is a strong focus on and considerable attention is paid to legal–ethical and professional issues, areas of markedly increased recent interest to all mental health professionals.

This second edition of Meyer's book constitutes a ready reference to and update of the dramatic developments and changes in the delivery of mental health services and their relationship to societal factors. This volume is a credit to Brunner/ Mazel's Continuing Education in Psychiatry and Psychology Series.

GENE USDIN, M.D.
Senior Psychiatrist, Ochsner Clinic
Clinical Professor of Psychiatry
Louisiana State University School of Medicine
New Orleans, Louisiana

SECTION I:

General Examination Issues

Chapter 1

INTRODUCTION

This book is designed to help candidates pass the professional practice and legal-ethical issues components of a state licensing exam and/or a board certification exam in the various practice subspecialties of psychology, e.g., clinical, counseling, school, child, and forensic psychology; neuropsychology; and psychological hypnosis. After this introductory chapter, Chapter 2 presents the heart of this book, an overview of professional issues and relevant legal cases and related ethical issues. Chapter 3 deals with special considerations in professional case presentation for the office or in the courtroom. Chapter 4 deals with the assessment of those special populations and conditions that present professional and/or legal-ethical issues across most psychological subspecialties, e.g., substance abuse, dangerousness to others, suicide, etc. Chapter 5 focuses on malingering and deception. Chapter 6, coauthored by Harvey A. Tilker, Ph.D., Theodore Feldmann, M.D., Jean D. Tilker, R.N., B.S.N., and this author, discusses psychopharmacology as it relates to psychology.

A primary goal of this book is to provide you with information on procedures and strategies that will help you pass those components of board certification and licensing exams that focus on professional issues, which by the present definition include practice issues, legal and ethical issues, and related informational content. References will be provided only where they are essential. In most cases, amplification of content issues, as well as the more detailed referencing, can be found in my other related books, such as *Law, Behavior and Mental Health* (Smith & Meyer, 1987), *Abnormal Behavior and the Criminal Justice System* (1992), and *The Clinician's Handbook* (1995).

This book presents a significant, indeed intimidating, number of legal cases. However, no candidate for any exam would need to be familiar with anywhere near all of them. The best strategy would be to know at least one or two critical cases (along with the important concepts) in any area you can reasonably expect that you might discuss or be questioned about. You should know the full range of cases in an area you will indicate is a strength or specialty.

It is, of course, appropriate to experience some anxiety. If you didn't, you probably would not prepare adequately. Licensing boards and those certifying boards that are concerned with quality naturally want to maintain proper standards. But, for the most part, they will help you to understand how to meet those standards, and will not unnecessarily hinder you. Hopefully, the discussion of issues and strategies in this book will reduce some of your dysfunctional anxiety.

There are a number of workshops available that can help you prepare for either a licensing or a board certification exam. It is recommended that you take one (especially for board certification preparations or if you are taking a licensing exam after being away from school for a number of years), and it is obviously ideal if you can take one sponsored by or recommended by that particular board.

As early as possible in the process, you should familiarize yourself with the specific supervision requirements of the board to which you are applying. There are guidelines for various components that you might be examined in, as well as for the specialty area as a whole. For example, the American Psychological Association (*APA Monitor*, March 1992) has published a set of guidelines on how to carry out a child custody case. It is also important to be familiar with any Specialty Guidelines that are relevant to your subdiscipline of psychology, as in clinical psychology or neuropsychology. For example, guidelines for forensic psychology were published in 1991 in *Law and Human Behavior*, *15*(6), 655–665.

The Work Sample is usually a critical component in the board certification process. An important issue is how to choose one potential work sample over another. My primary recommendation is that you not choose an unusual, nor an especially interesting or controversial, case. Rather, choose one that demonstrates the approach and procedures you typically employ. If you choose an unusual case, you are likely to introduce a variety of issues with which you may be less familiar, while providing an agenda for your examination committee that may focus questions on an area you are not used to dealing with.

A case that you perceive as especially interesting can bring similar problems. For example, I have seen a number of submitted work samples that include a multiple personality. These cases are interesting, but they inevitably lead to difficulties during the examination. For one thing, I've never seen an examination committee agree on the controversial aspects of "multiples," even as to whether multiples occur rarely or relatively commonly. As a result, it always seemed as if at least one committee member developed a negative view of the examinee because of his or her responses related to these cases.

For board certification, any required work sample should a) reflect your typical practice; b) show care in preparation, e.g., in details like an absence of typos and misspellings; c) have been proofread by a colleague for both content and readability; d) fit all the guidelines provided by your board (or have an explanation why it doesn't); e) contain a brief self-critique section, if that is allowed; f) include all the critical information a reader will need, without being unnecessarily lengthy; g) include subheadings and other means of organizing the material; and h) deal with direct or implied issues of confidentiality.

GENERAL POINTERS FOR EXAMS

(1) Get as much information ahead of time about the process as you can. Seek counsel from others who have taken the exams or who are familiar with the exam process. Then, plan out your preparation—and do it. It's amazing how many people go into these exams with only minimal preparation.

(2) Expect your committee to be collegial and respectful of you. In many face-to-face exams, there are three examiners. This allows a "tiebreaker" and provides some control over the possibility of a "rogue examiner." However, to be effective, any committee has to be probing and wide-ranging, which may at times seem adversarial. Be prepared, but it is likely that you will experience some anxiety in any event.

(3) To the degree feasible, know your committee. For example, read their writings if they have published anything at all (and, of course, read any materials your board recommends). Some boards allow you to veto a member if you have a reasonable concern that he or she may be biased against you. Don't be reluctant to immediately bring forth such a concern. If you raise no objection, then happen to fail the exam and subsequently raise an objection, it will have far less impact.

(4) Be proactive—not pushy! By this I mean provide as much information as you can, as long as you know that it is accurate. Examiners have typically been provided guidelines about how long the exam is supposed to last. If you are doing the talking, you are influencing the exam's agenda. The fewer questions they ask, the less they are likely to drift into areas about which you feel less confident.

(5) Go beyond your stated areas of competence. For example, if you are being examined or boarded in one area, e.g., clinical, but can show some expertise in another area, such as neuropsychology, this is usually going to impress your committee and at the same time further structure your exam time (but, be careful—see 6a).

(6) Typical problems (aside from a lack of depth in preparation) include the following:

  a. Examinee thinks he or she is "expert" because of regularly working in a limited portion of the broader area in which certification or licensing is being granted. This is more likely to be a problem in specialty areas like forensic psychology or neuropsychology.

  b. There is an inadequate work sample.

  c. Examinee does not use tests, or does not use the appropriate tests, where they are needed.

  d. Examinee is not active in his or her profession or appears to have a weak identification with the field. A psychologist should at least be a member of APA and of his or her state association and, better still, have an active role in some sector of the profession.

e. Examinee does not keep up with the field. It doesn't look good if a psychologist subscribes to no journals, seldom reads journals, etc.

f. Examinee is too naive and/or defensive about ethical issues. Examining committees often ask candidates if they have ever encountered an ethical dilemma. A surprising number reply, "No." This will be seen as a "failing" answer by many committees. Be prepared to provide some discussion to such questions.

g. It is possible that the examinee may inadvertently challenge the pet peeve of one of the examiners. For example, in one forensic board exam I sat on, a colleague-examiner believed that "any forensic psychologist should know John Monahan's original eight correlates of dangerousness." The candidate knew only a couple of them, and this apparently resulted in a borderline rating by this examiner. Fortunately, this was changed (as was the attitude of this examiner—it was his first exam) after discussion, and the candidate passed.

h. On occasion, candidates run into trouble because they somehow elicit personal upset or hostility from an examiner. Fortunately, such violations by examiners are rare. Most boards provide a) for colleague ratings that help to eliminate "bad" examiners, b) somehow record the procedures so that such violations can be detected, and c) are supportive of appeal procedures that are designed to correct any such violations.

Chapter 2

LEGAL-ETHICAL-PROFESSIONAL ISSUES

ETHICAL PRINCIPLES

The first meeting of the American Psychological Association took place in 1892, the first constitution was adopted in 1894, and incorporation occurred in 1925. A committee to develop an ethical code was formed in 1925, and the first ethics code was formally adopted in 1953. Several revisions have occurred since then. Professional psychologists are now guided by both an ethics code and a set of guidelines specifically developed for each specialty area.

A new code was put into effect December 1, 1992, and published in the December 1992 edition of the *American Psychologist*. The APA Ethics code consists of a Preamble, six general principles (A—Competence; B—Integrity; C—Professional and Scientific Responsibility; D—Respect for People's Rights and Dignity; E—Concern for Others' Welfare; F—Social Responsibility) and eight overall ethical standards (1—General Standards; 2—Evaluation, Assessment, or Intervention; 3—Advertising and Other Public Statements; 4—Therapy; 5—Privacy and Confidentiality; 6—Teaching, Training, Supervision, Research, and Publishing; 7—Forensic Activities; 8—Resolving Ethical Issues).

Some standards that are noteworthy because they are new in some fashion, or are a stronger focus in many cases, are as follows:

1.11—prohibits sexual harassment (1.12 extends it to other types of harassment);

1.17—discusses cautions against conflicts of interest in multiple relationships;

1.18—barter for services, which has traditionally been prohibited, is something that psychologists "ordinarily refrain" from but can now do if it is the only option, is not clinically contraindicated, and is not "exploitative";

1.19—prohibits sexually exploitative relationships of all sorts;

1.25—may use "collection agencies or legal measures" if first informs the client, and then provides an opportunity to make prompt payment;

1.27—may not receive payment for a referral that "is not based on the referral itself" (see *Edenfield v. Fane* [1993], and related material for possible qualifications);

2.08—psychologists retain responsibility even when they use automated services (score, interpret, etc.);

4.01—if a psychologist is being supervised, that must be communicated to the client;

4.03—"couple and family relationships"—roles must be clarified up front;

4.05—"psychologists do not engage in sexual intimacies with current patients or clients";

4.06—or accept as clients persons with whom they have had sexual intimacies;

4.07—no sexual intimacies may occur with any former client within two years; they may be allowable after two years, but only in unusual circumstances and where the psychologist bears the burden of proof that it is acceptable;

4.08—"psychologists do not abandon patients or clients" (other standards seem to say you can terminate as long as you facilitate alternative services and/ or immediate transfer if needed);

6.23—"mere possession of an institutional position, such as Department Chair, does not justify authorship credit";

8.07—(the last standard listed)—prohibits filing or encouraging the filing of frivolous complaints.

The latest ethics code did not directly address the issue of retention of records. However, this was later addressed, and in the September 1993 issue of the *American Psychologist, 48*(9), 984–986, it was stated that where no federal, state, or local laws govern the situation, complete records must be kept for at least three years after the date of the last contact; essential records or a summary must be kept for an additional 12 years. If the client is a minor, the record period is extended until three years after the client attains the age of majority. These rules were based on rules in some of the specialty guidelines. If these were to be revised, the rule would revert to seven years for the complete file, which is more stringent than any existing state statute.

You may be asked why we have codes of ethics. For two reasons: (a) to protect the consumer and serve the public good; (b) to provide guidelines, or rules (depending upon how they are to be applied in practice) for professional practice. The reader is advised to not only be aware of the ethical principles and specialty guidelines that affect his or her practice, but also consult with casebook examples (e.g., July 1988, *American Psychologist*, 557–563) that will help elucidate such principles.

The most common cause of an ethics complaint is a dual relationship (usually including sexual involvement), thus a violation of 4.07. Other common causes are functioning outside one's area of competence, false or misleading public statements, a misuse of tests, and problems stemming from child custody cases. Surprisingly, in light of the intense public debate and polarization over research with animals, APA very seldom even receives a complaint in this area, let alone adjudicates against a psychologist-researcher.

In 1994, APA had approximately 77,000 fellows, members, and associate members (every one a potential target of ethics complaints). Out of every two original inquiries, approximately one develops into a formal complaint. Based on an estimate of 143 complaints received, complaints are being filed at approximately a 0.22% rate. Though there is no evidence of an increase in per capita complaints, over the years there is some evidence of a higher percentage of complaints being carried through to a formal resolution within APA and, increasingly, in the legal arena.

> Marshall v. American Psychological Association (1987) provides clear support for APA's right to monitor the ethics of its members, to expel a member and to publicize that expulsion because of an ethics violation, and to not permit a member to resign once his ethical conduct comes under scrutiny.

AN OVERVIEW OF THE LEGAL SYSTEM

The legal system is a dominant entity in our modern society. This may reflect the lessening of confidence in such traditional socializing institutions as church, neighborhood, and family, or a diminishment of their power. It certainly includes an inequity of power that in part explains society's fondness for "attorney-bashing." That is, attorneys totally dominate state and federal judicial systems. But, they also have attained significant power, and in some cases a clear dominance, in both the legislative and executive branches of government as well, at the federal, state, and local levels. Attorneys are among the first to defend the concept of separation of church and state. Yet, they blithely ignore the fact that, as minions of the "cathedral of the law," they have been able, by way of their dominant influence throughout the three branches of government, to establish their preferred status and the present imbalance of power in favor of the legal profession.

In any case, the professional standards or ethical initiatives of any profession are ultimately subsumed or changed by legal precedents. This is why this chapter weaves ethical-professional issues into the context of legal cases. As noted in Chapter 1, the reader may find the number of cases to be a bit intimidating. But, they do provide the appropriate framework for discussion, and no candidate for any exam would need to know anywhere near all of these cases per se.

Our legal system in the United States is complex, composed of many different types of courts in the 50 states and at the federal level. Any given legal transaction may be governed solely by state law, or solely by federal law, or perhaps by both. The federal and state court systems are composed of various trial and appellate courts.

Jurisdiction, a term that describes a court's power to hear and decide a case, is defined by statute or constitutional provision. There are several types of jurisdiction, the most important of which include original jurisdiction and appellate jurisdiction. Original jurisdiction implies that a court has authority to hear and decide a case, usually when first filed. Appellate jurisdiction means that a court has authority to review a case already decided in a lower court. After the generally assumed first right of appeal, appellate review is generally discretionary; while one may always attempt to appeal lower court decisions, the appellate court may refuse review. Subject matter jurisdiction means that the court is qualified by statute or the Constitution to hear a particular type of case. For example, state family courts have jurisdiction in divorces, delinquency matters, and probate proceedings, while the criminal courts do not.

Understanding jurisdictional matters may be very helpful in gaining insight into the nature of a court proceeding and how to cope with it. Unfortunately, state court systems differ greatly. Generally, there are justice and trial courts, courts of appeal, and one highest court. Justice courts have limited original jurisdiction and usually process minor civil and criminal cases, such as routine traffic violations or small personal claims. Trial courts are a state's general court of original jurisdiction. Most serious matters are heard here. Many states find it useful to have specialized trial courts to hear only civil or criminal matters. Some further establish subject matter jurisdiction for courts that will serve highly specialized roles. Appellate courts primarily serve as discretionary courts of review with very limited original jurisdiction, while all appeals can theoretically be channeled to a state supreme court of some type.

The general courts of original jurisdiction in the federal system are district courts. Each state may have one or more districts, and large districts even have more than one division. Each district is administered by a chief federal magistrate and a federal district court judge. Appeals from federal courts are handled by 14 circuit courts of appeal, plus one for the District of Columbia. These courts may review decisions by district courts within their jurisdiction, review orders of many administrative agencies, and issue some original writs in appropriate cases. The United States Supreme Court has limited original jurisdiction and may exercise appellate jurisdiction over district and circuit courts and the highest courts in each state.

The effect of appeals may seem to be straightforward: if dissatisfied with a lower court ruling, appeal to a higher one. In practice, the legal maneuvering is much more complicated. Often, appeals merely lead to orders that a court of original jurisdiction hold a new trial, reconsider some matter under new guidelines, or refrain from some action. Also, when appeals under one rationale no longer seem likely to succeed, it is sometimes possible to start with new appeals at a lower level. An example would be asserting that new evidence had come to light that had not been available in an earlier proceeding. Thus, many cases weave a tangled web through a tortuous process of appeals. This makes for many decisions and much writing. And, unfortunately, an observation made by F. Rodell in 1936 (*Virginia Law Review, 23,* 38) still has some truth value: "There are two things wrong with almost all legal writing. One is its style. The other is its content."

While the preceding discussion of legal matters and systems is vastly oversimplified, it does provide a toehold for understanding some of the following issues.

PROFESSIONAL-LEGAL ISSUES

Frye v. U.S. (1923)   the "Frye Rule"—a federal Court of Appeals asserts that a technique or procedure, in this case the "systolic blood pressure deception test," has to be "sufficiently established to have gained general acceptance in the particular field in which it belongs" to be allowed into evidence. (For an update on the specific admissability of the polygraph, see Honts and Perry [1992].) There does appear to be an emerging consensus that the polygraph may be admitted as a rebuttal when the individual's character is called into question.

Daubert v. Merrell Dow Pharmaceuticals (1993)   this case resolved the above issue as the Supreme Court justices were firmly in support of the thrust of the Federal Rules of Evidence (1987), which emphasize a "helpfulness standard," rather than "scientific acceptance."

Daubert involved the question of whether Bendectin caused serious birth defects when it was ingested by a woman during pregnancy. The trial court refused to consider expert testimony for the plaintiffs that Bendectin could cause such injuries because the work of these experts had not been subject to peer review and had not been shown to be "generally accepted as reliable" by the scientific community. In effect, the Supreme Court in *Daubert* eliminated the *Frye* rule that has dominated consideration of expert testimony in many courts for nearly 70 years.

Rule 702 of the *Federal Rules of Evidence*, which deals with expert testimony, provides, "If scientific, technical, or other specialized knowledge will assist the trier of fact to understand the evidence or to determine a fact in issue, a witness qualified as an expert by knowledge, skill, experience, training, or education may testify thereto in the form of an opinion or otherwise." The federal rules do not permit the admission of information *claiming* to be scientific knowledge, however. The Court noted that the rule requires that the information be "scientific," which "implies a grounding in the methods and procedures of science," and that it must be "knowledge," which means more than "subjective or unsupported speculation." It also noted that the information must "assist the trier of fact," which suggests that the testimony of the expert must "have a reliable basis in the knowledge of the discipline."

The majority of the Court emphasized that it is the responsibility of federal judges to review expert evidence to insure that it rests on a reliable foundation and is relevant to the case. As part of this function, the Court suggested that the following factors should be used in considering the admissibility of expert testimony: (1) whether it has been tested using some accepted scientific methodology; (2) whether it has been subject to peer review and publication; (3) whether the known or potential rate of error of the scientific technique justifies its use; and (4) whether it has achieved a degree of acceptance within the scientific community. The Court emphasized that these were *factors* to be considered and that the essential question is scientific validity within the context of the issues presented by a particular case. The Court also recognized that this is a "flexible" standard and explained, "there are important differences between the quest for truth in the courtroom and the quest for truth in the laboratory. Scientific conclusions are subject to perpetual revision. Law, on the other hand, must resolve disputes finally and quickly." Finally, the Court expressed its view that "vigorous cross-examination, presentation of contrary evidence, and careful instruction on the burden of proof" are sufficient to deal with bad scientific evidence that is presented to a judge or jury.

This case does have something in it both for those who support the expansive admission of expert testimony and for those who want to limit it. On the whole, however, the case came down on the side of the broad admission of expert opinion even when it has not achieved in large measure an acceptability within the profession itself. In that sense, it is the end of the *Frye* rule. It will permit the admission of a wide range of highly speculative "syndrome" mental health testimony. At the same time, judges should be encouraged to provide some limits on the admissibility of such evidence consistent with the Court's caution to trial judges. Psychologists involved in cases in which unreliable expert opinion is being presented may be called upon to help demonstrate to the judge that the proposed testimony does not meet the four factors identified by the Court in *Daubert*.

Unfortunately, the Court did not directly consider another option for coping with questionable scientific evidence, i.e., the appointment of independent experts, which is allowed by Federal Rule 506. It solves many of the problems.

Jenkins v. U.S. (1961) often cited as the basis for admissability of testimony by psychologists, but its importance is probably not that great as it held that (1) psychologists are qualified in the area of mental disorder if it aids the trier of fact; (2) qualifying depends on the nature and extent of the knowledge base, not upon the title of psychologist; (3) the qualification of specific experts is up to the specific trial judge.

Funk v. Commonwealth (Virginia, 1989) affirmed the *Ake v. Oklahoma* (1983) holding (discussed later) that psychiatric assistance must be provided to indigents in capital cases where mental condition is at issue, but further held that the *Ake* requirement is satisfied by the appointment of a clinical psychologist.

Blue Shield of Virginia v. McCready (1982)   the Supreme Court allows antitrust laws to be successfully employed by psychologists against a practice that limits reimbursement through a physician.

CAPP v. Rank (1990)   a California Supreme Court case wherein it was held that psychologists may have hospital privileges independent of psychiatrists.

Morris v. Chandler Exterminators (1991)   a Georgia Appeals Court first finds psychologists are competent to testify about the physical causes of nervous disorders, but the Georgia Supreme Court then unanimously overturns this (May 12, 1992), a difficult precedent for neuropsychologists.

Patrick v. Burget (1988)   the Supreme Court held that professional peer review committees are not exempt from antitrust laws, in this case, regarding attempts to prevent psychologists from obtaining hospital privileges.

Supreme Court of Virginia v. Friedman (1988)   the Supreme Court holds that a state may not require a professional to be a state resident in order to be admitted to practice by reciprocity.

Shapero v. Kentucky Bar Association (1988)   the Supreme Court recognizes the right of attorneys (and, by implication, other professional groups) to aggressively advertise to specific groups.

Two developments have amplified this issue. First, in a consent agreement between APA and the Federal Trade Commission, finalized on December 27, 1992, APA agreed that it *may not prohibit* its members from making public statements about the desirability of offered services, or statements that imply or express unique, unusual, or one-of-a-kind abilities, or statements likely to appeal to a person's emotions or anxieties concerning the possible results of obtaining or failing to obtain offered services products or publications. They also may not prohibit testimonials regarding the quality of services, soliciting individuals while they are being serviced by other like professionals, or paying referral services (even some apparent kickback situations). Essentially, it limits APA to formulating principles controlling deceptive practices, uninvited in-person solicitation, or use of undue influence. This agreement appears to be further strengthened by the following Supreme Court decision.

> Edenfield v. Fane (1993) this case focused on a Florida Board of Accountancy rule that CPAs could not engage in "direct, in-person, uninvited solicitation." The Supreme Court struck down the Florida rule because it violated freedom of speech (First Amendment).

This case is particularly interesting because the Court earlier upheld a ban on in-person solicitation by lawyers. The Court distinguished these two cases in a way that will provide important rules regarding in-person solicitation by psychologists and other professionals.

In determining whether a state may preclude certain in-person and telephone solicitation of prospective clients, the Court said that it must consider "whether the state's interests in proscribing [the solicitation] are substantial, whether the challenged regulation advances these interests in a direct and material way, and whether the extent of the restriction on protected speech is in reasonable proportion to the interests served." The Court emphasized that the ban on personal solicitation will depend on "the identity of the parties and the precise circumstances of the solicitation." The Florida board claimed that the restriction was necessary to protect consumers from fraud or overreaching by CPAs and to maintain the appearance of CPA auditing independence. The Court found that these interests were substantial, but that the board had not demonstrated that these risks were real and that its restriction actually reduced the risk substantially. It pointed to the fact that the board presented no studies that suggested personal solicitation by CPAs created dangers of fraud or overreaching or compromised independence. Nor had the board presented any reason to believe that CPAs who engage in in-person solicitation are more inclined to compromise professional standards than are others.

The Court contrasted the prohibition on attorney in-person solicitation (which it upheld) with the prohibition on CPA solicitation (which it struck down). The Court noted that unlike lawyers, CPAs are not "professionally trained in the art of persuasion" and are therefore less likely to overwhelm a potential client. Second, the typical client of the CPA is "far less susceptible to manipulation" than are accident victims whom a lawyer might solicit. Third, lawyers may solicit accident victims "at a moment of high stress" unlike the more typical business solicitation of the CPA. This reduces the vulnerability of the potential client, but also reduces the level of invasion of privacy from the solicitation. Finally, CPAs seek long-term, continuing contracts with clients, which are not likely to result from high-pressure sales techniques, unlike the attorney who may be seeking a one-time personal injury representation from a prospective client.

It is, of course, impossible to know with certainty how the Court would apply these principles to a psychology board's rule that precluded in-person and telephone solicitation by psychologists. In part, the answer may depend on the nature of the rule and what was precluded. Solicitation of business entities (e.g., test validation services or efforts to be added to an approved provider list for insurance or health care purposes) probably could not be prohibited. A very strong argument can be made, however, that the Court would uphold a rule that precludes in-person or telephone solicitation by psychologists of individual clients. First, psychologists are trained to be experts in manipulation. Second, the prospective clients would be expected to be solicited during a period of high stress and this may make them more prone to the manipulation. Third, the opportunity for invasion of privacy would be significant.

Licensure and Certification

Mental health professionals may be licensed, or certified, or both. Licensure is granted by a state, to protect the public, not to enhance the profession. In essence, it is a permit to practice, and it establishes that the professional has met at least minimal standards.

> Dent v. West Virginia (1889)   by upholding the constitutionality of the West Virginia Medical Practice Act as an exercise of the state's legitimate police powers, the Supreme Court establishes that the authority to regulate health professionals is within the purview of state government.

Certification is typically granted by an independent board. When it is working well, i.e., when a board emphasizes high standards and rigorous evaluation procedures, it enhances the quality of that profession, and provides the public a means of identifying a level of quality above that of licensure. At the same time, the truth is that you could get a group of your friends together and decide to certify people as "Really Good Therapists," since in most states the term "therapist" would not be controlled by licensure. You could make up fancy diplomas and charge outrageous fees to become certified, and frankly, that appears to be about the quality level you will find in at least a few very impressive-sounding boards that certify in the mental health field. So the quality of board certification is only as good as the board's qualification and examination procedures. Medicine has the best system of board certification, as they have somehow managed to eliminate "outlaw" boards. So, the truth is that, in some instances, board certification may dupe the public as much as it facilitates good practice in other situations.

> Peel v. Attorney. Registration and Disciplinary Commission (1990)   the Supreme Court holds that a state cannot prohibit professionals from advertising a certification process by a legitimate private organization, even if is not the "best" or "highest" certification available (or, in some cases, one that has very minimal standards).

The Eleventh Circuit U.S. Court of Appeals (in *Abramson v. Gonzalez*), basing its 2–1 decision on First Amendment free speech rights, ruled on January 3, 1992, that Florida's psychology licensing law prohibiting unlicensed psychologists from calling themselves psychologists is an unconstitutional restriction on free speech. The decision was based largely on the fact that Florida's law has been a title protection act rather than a protection of practice act. That is, while it prohibits unlicensed individuals from using the title "psychologist," it does not prevent these persons from engaging in the practice of psychology. The issue may eventually reach the Supreme Court because this Eleventh Circuit decision is at odds with a Fourth Circuit decision that says use of a protected title by an unlicensed individual can be prohibited as misleading the public.

Related Cases

Canton v. Harris (1989) the Supreme Court finds that police departments may be liable for a failure to provide officers with adequate training to care for mentally ill "clients," allowing a precedent for more mandated training by psychologists and other professionals for public servants who deal with the mentally ill.

West Virginia University Hospital v. Casey (1991) the Supreme Court holds that an award of attorney fees does not include the cost of those expert witness fees that the prevailing party paid in pursuing its claim.

Austin v. United States (1993) in this rather technical decision involving the calculation of reimbursement to health care providers under Medicare, the Supreme Court gave great latitude to the government in determining what method of calculation of reimbursement should be permitted. The notable part of this case was the degree to which the majority of the Court deferred to the federal agency in setting reimbursement policies. This decision at least implies that there will be limited review of reimbursement regulations by federal courts in a national health plan.

ETHICAL-LEGAL ISSUES

In any case that involves a potential legal issue, you have the ethical obligation to inform the client of 1) the purpose of the evaluation, 2) who employed you, 3) the limits of confidentiality, 4) the use of the results and who will receive the report, and 5) any legal rules that apply. You'll need to define who is the "client."

Be prepared to discuss how you should respond: 1) to a request to perform a type of evaluation that a) you usually don't do, b) you don't believe is the correct procedure, and c) for some reason you morally oppose; 2) if the law conflicts with any ethical principles or "guidelines"; 3) to a push or request to be an "advocate" for one side; 4) to a request to accept a contingency fee; and/or 5) to a request that could lead to a dual relationship.

You should know the common reasons for possible malpractice actions, such as: 1) sexual involvement with clients, or other forms of dual relationships; 2) negligent or incorrect treatment or diagnosis; 3) a breach of confidentiality; 4) a failure to prevent suicide or assault; 5) a breach of duty to warn. At the 1991 APA meeting in San Francisco, Margaret Bogie of the APA Insurance Trust reported that during 1976–91 there were 2,622 claims against psychologists for some form of malpractice. Some were dropped, some were proven to be unfounded, but the following breakdown reflects the percentage of claims made and of the eventual settlement costs.

Classification	% of Claims	% Cost
Sexual Involvement	19.0 (about 500)	49. (32 million)
Incorrect Treatment	14.9	12.5
Loss from Evaluation	10.6	10.5 (police-fire test)
Breach of Contract	6.9	5.5
Incorrect Diagnosis	6.1	4.8

Based on some of the above statistics, Ms. Bogie suggests (tongue-in-cheek, I presume) the following risk management tip—"if you have sex with a client, kill him or her." It is noteworthy that one-third of the claims in the first category (sexual involvement) surfaced five or more years after the actual incident(s). The APA Insurance Trust can be reached at 750 1st Street, N.E., Suite 605, Washington, DC 20002-4242; Phone 800-477-1200.

> Riley v. Presnell (1991) demonstrates that the "discovery rule" is the reason why such suits occur so much later, and are allowed, i.e., it stops the statute of limitations clock until the injury is "discovered" by the plaintiff. Riley asserted that his psychiatrist had seduced him into homosexual activity after plying him with alcohol and marijuana. Riley filed the suit seven years after he had stopped seeing Dr. Presnell, though he would normally have three years under Massachusetts law. The Massachusetts Supreme Judicial Court upheld Riley's claim that filing was delayed because the harm from Dr. Presnell's behavior had rendered Riley unable to recognize his deterioration.

This case and concept (delay of the "discovery rule") also has strong relevance to child abuse cases.

Dual Relationships

Because therapist-client sexual contact is explicitly disapproved by all major professions and because it is demonstrably harmful to clients, it is not surprising that it is a fertile ground for malpractice litigation.

> Zipkin v. Freeman (1968) in this widely cited precedent case for tort action in this area, Dr. Freeman, a licensed psychiatrist, accepted Mrs. Zipkin on referral from her general physician. She complained of recurrent headaches and gastric upset that could have been attributed to anxiety. At Dr. Freeman's instigation, she left her husband, filed lawsuits against both her husband and brother, and subsequently burglarized their homes. "Treatment" consisted of nude swimming parties and overnight trips with the doctor for the purpose of sexual trysts. Mrs. Zipkin was also persuaded to move into an apartment above the doctor's office and to supply him with financial capital for speculative business ventures. At trial, Dr. Freeman's behavior was found unprofessional, and the Zipkins eventually received the rather underwhelming total indemnity of $5,000.

The Zipkin case involved obviously outrageous conduct by the therapist, and it is unusual in that the perpetrator was a guru-type who set out to exploit his patient. It is far more common for therapists to report that they become sexually involved with a client due to feelings of depression, loneliness, need, or vulnerability, and most are separated, divorced, or experiencing marital problems at the time.

> Roy v. Hartogs (1976) defendant was seduced into sexual intercourse as part of her prescribed therapy. Trial court awarded $153,679.50, but upon appeal, award of punitive damages was stricken and $25,000 was allowed for compensatory damages. Dr. Hartogs then sued his insurance company to have them pay the $25,000. The company refused, saying the intercourse was not "treatment" as covered by the policy, and the court agreed with the insurance company.

There is now a clear recognition of the impropriety of sexual involvement with a client after the termination of therapy. Debate now centers more on whether there should be a time period after which such behavior is allowed. For example, consider a possible question such as, "Assume you saw a client for two sessions, and the referring problem was resolved to everyone's satisfaction. Assume you meet this client three years later at a cocktail party and you sense a mutual attraction. Would it be ethically acceptable to pursue a romantic relationship?" You can press the issue by making it one session, and 10 years later.

APA, as noted earlier, has now clarified this issue in the Ethical Principles, asserting a two-year rule with the burden of proof clearly remaining with the therapist even for those situations beyond two years. Also, realize that some states have statutes that prohibit such contact for a certain period of time, e.g., Florida forbids it for perpetuity, and state law could extend it, though probably not shorten it.

To avoid a sexual involvement with a client, therapists must be sensitive to their own vulnerabilities. Any indication that matters could get out of hand requires immediate action. Consultation with a trusted colleague should be the first course of action, and the therapist should strongly consider entering treatment himself. Also, see the section on dual relationships in Chapter 3 for detailed advice on coping with this issue.

> | Morra v. State Board of Examiners of Psychologists (1973) | the first clear recognition, here by the Kansas Supreme Court, of a licensing board's right to revoke the license of a psychologist who either attempts to become or does become sexually involved with a client.

> | St. Paul Fire and Marine Insurance Co. v. Mori (1992) | a malpractice insurer is not liable for physicians' (and by implication, psychologists') sexual conduct with a client when it does *not* arise out of an act of treatment designed to induce a transference.

Be prepared to discuss the difference between "claims made" and "occurrence" insurance policies. Occurrence policies pay for claims made under terms at the time of the alleged act and apply to acts during the policy dates, no matter when they are reported. "Claims made" policies usually apply the terms in force at the time the claim is made, and pay only for claims made and reported during the policy period (thus, they require a "tail" to cover delayed claims). As a local insurer advertises, "Be wise, be insured," or be prepared to discuss why you are not insured.

Improper Treatment

Suits for improper treatment do not necessarily refer to applying the wrong type of procedure. They can refer to negligence during the course of an intervention that might otherwise be proper and helpful to the patient.

> | Abraham v. Zaslow (1972) | Dr. Zaslow's "Z therapy" was aimed at reducing "primal rage." Zaslow would attempt to break through resistance by applying "tactile stimuli" whenever the client was not being fully open and honest. The tactile stimuli actually included tickling, poking, and beating administered while the client was forcibly held. One patient who received over 10 hours of this procedure suffered such severe bruising of the upper half of her body that kidney failure ensued. Although the proceedings employed might arguably have been proper

for an adherent of "Z therapy," they do not comport with the proper conduct of psychotherapy as a general treatment. The client recovered $170,000 in damages.

The Standard of Care

It is noteworthy that within the psychological therapies, as opposed to medical practice, there is usually a less clear "standard of care," i.e., a consensus treatment(s) generally accepted as appropriate for a specific disorder. Hence, it is more difficult to argue that the treatment employed was not appropriate. The flip side is that there are less clear guidelines for the mental health clinician in the first place.

Battery

Even normal, widely used therapeutic procedures may lead to liability for battery if the client has not consented to the procedures. Generally this is true only for methods that employ touching or application of some physical procedure, such as giving injections or using biofeedback equipment. It is normally unlawful to touch another person's body without his or her consent.

Webster's defines battery as the "unlawful beating or use of force on a person without his consent." While this does not sound like any activity common to psychotherapy, suits for battery or assault have been brought against various practitioners, some of whom, like Dr. Zaslow in the above case, are hardly in the mainstream.

> Hammer v. Rosen (1960) John Rosen, M.D., a proponent of "direct analysis," was a theorist-therapist who was considered to be more in the mainstream. He believed that regressed and psychotic patients require aggressive means to establish contact. In the case of at least one client, this involved punching, slapping, and hitting to the face and upper body. The client later successfully sued. Note that this case did not involve malpractice per se; the actions and injuries sustained had nothing to do with professional conduct. Dr. Rosen's attack was unlawful under any circumstances and was litigated as an intentional tort.

It is possible that other therapy methods could lead to liability when proper consent is not obtained, e.g., flooding or implosion techniques that are quite aversive and intentionally create very high levels of anxiety. If the client does not clearly understand and agree to the procedure in advance, he or she might successfully sue for assault, which does not require actual bodily injury.

Confidentiality—Duty to Warn

Because the potential information lost to the courts may be significant, important public policy reasons are required to grant an extension of privilege to a new group. It has to be shown that the professional's work (and therefore society) would be greatly harmed by allowing the courts to compel breaches of confidentiality.

How is this to be assessed? The most widely recognized test of the appropriateness of testimonial privilege derives from the thinking of the eminent legal scholar, John H. Wigmore. Wigmore proposed a cost-benefit analysis from society's perspective, as follows:

(1) The communications must originate in a confidence that they will not be disclosed.
(2) This element of confidentiality must be essential to the full and satisfactory maintenance of the relation between the parties.
(3) The relation must be one which in the opinion of the community ought to be sedulously fostered (actively encouraged).
(4) The injury that would inure (occur) to the relation by the disclosure of the communications must be greater than the benefit thereby gained from the correct disposal of the litigation.

Privilege itself is not the absolute shield it appears to be. Even if the professional has a statutory right to privilege, the interpretation of when it applies is left to the courts, and to legislatures. As noted elsewhere in this book, the right to claim the privilege belongs to the client, not to the therapist. If the client waives the right to privilege, the therapist must testify. Additional failures of privilege arise due to the presence of third parties (e.g., group psychotherapy?). Courts have interpreted the Wigmore criteria to mean that if information is given to a third party there is no expectation of confidence and hence no privilege.

Be prepared to discuss the problems of confidentiality as they relate to Employee Assistance Programs (EAPs), and so far in a lesser fashion, to managed care programs in general. Though employees are often assured of total confidentiality when referred to an EAP program, there are several ways that employers can legally obtain information: a) if the supervisor, even casually, suggested that the client contact the EAP, the supervisor is entitled to know what visits were made (though not the contents of such visits); b) if the employee sues for wrongful termination, discrimination, breach of contract, or virtually anything else; or c) if the client is suicidal or threatens violence or reports the abuse of a child. Also, if the client files a workplace injury claim, EAP records are often turned over to claims adjustors.

In re Lifschutz (1970) a California case that first clearly recognized that a constitutional right to privacy includes a psychotherapist-patient privilege (which the *patient owns*), but it does not prevent the patient-litigant exception.

Caesar v. Mountanos (1976) the United States Court of Appeals for the Ninth Circuit held that the constitutional right of privacy protects the confidentiality of psychotherapist-patient communications. In this case, a case factually similar to *Lifschutz*, Dr. Caesar refused to answer questions about one of his patients and was held in contempt of a California state court. Dr. Caesar then took the federal privacy claim to federal court. The patient had filed suit against third parties alleging that two separate automobile accidents had caused her "pain and suffering not limited to her physical ailments." Although the Ninth Circuit agreed that confidentiality is essential to psychotherapy and that the very nature of the communications brings them within the constitutional right of privacy, it rejected the argument that the privilege was absolute. Instead, the court held that the privilege may be limited when necessary to advance a compelling state interest.

In re Zuniga (1983) a Sixth Circuit court case that found a federal, limited common law psychotherapist-patient privilege.

Pennsylvania v. Ritchie (1987) a Supreme Court case that can be seen as eroding privilege, as the judge was allowed to subpoena a state agency's confidential mental health file, over the defense's objections, to decide which material in this criminal case would be revealed.

Buchanan v. Kentucky (1987) a Supreme Court case in which the defendant used a defense of "extreme emotional disturbance." The prosecutor was allowed to procure an earlier report that the psychiatrist had prepared as part of an earlier determination as to whether a pre-trial detainee was appropriate for transfer to a hospital setting for psychiatric treatment. The defendant had never been informed that this could occur. The fact that the defendant had raised the issue of mental state in his homicide trial was a factor in the decision.

Doe v. Roe and Poe (1977) Roe, a psychiatrist, and Poe, her psychologist-husband, wrote a book about plaintiff Doe, eight years after treatment was terminated. It included verbatim fantasies, thoughts, statements, etc., and sold 220 copies. Defendants claimed that plaintiff had given her oral consent while in therapy. The trial court (this is a lower court decision, so has value primarily as a precedent case) held the alleged oral consent was worthless. Plaintiff obtained an injunction against further publication, and $20,000 damages. Defendants could not show a legitimate scientific value that might have allowed such disclosure.

U.S. v. Moore (1992) the IRS, in an action against a psychiatrist, was permitted by the Fifth Circuit to obtain that psychiatrist's list of patients, how much each one owed, and the insurance company name of other third-party payers.

Cheatham v. Rogers (1992) a decision by the Texas Court of Appeals that could be extremely disruptive to mental health professionals if it is taken as precedent in other jurisdictions. During preparation for a trial on a custody hearing, the father sought the mental health records of a court appointed "counselor." The trial court quashed the subpoena, but the Court of Appeals supported the subpoena, saying: a) the state statute allowing confidentiality does not apply to lawsuits affecting the parent-child relationship, as it makes no discrimination between parties and nonparties to such actions; b) the emotional health of counselor could provide evidence for impeachment through bias; and c) this "compelling state interest" allowed breaching her admitted privacy rights.

Dangerousness

The concept of dangerousness, especially as it applies to involuntary civil commitment, is ambiguous and problematic. Specifying the concept as "imminent dangerousness" is an improvement, but problems still exist. Does dangerousness include emotional harm, cognitive harm, or economic harm, as well as physical harm? What about harm to property? How severe or frequent must harm be to justify intervention? Although some experts suggest limiting dangerousness to acts intended to do physical harm to self or others, the courts have not always concurred, and positions on this matter vary from state to state.

Even if an acceptable definition of dangerousness were found, only part of the problem would be solved, since the accurate prediction of dangerousness is still required. There is a strong tendency to overpredict dangerousness. This is not surprising. A professional who fails to protect a community or a specific person by not detecting the dangerousness of a person who then engages in violent behavior pays a heavy professional and social price.

Tarasoff v. Regents of University of California (1976) the California Supreme Court allows the Tarasoff estate to sue the student health clinic at U.C.-Berkeley. At first (1974) finds a "duty to warn"—on rehearing amends it to a "duty to protect," i.e., "duty to exercise reasonable care to protect the foreseeable victim."

A psychologist at the University of California-Berkeley mental health clinic determined that one of his patients, Mr. Poddar, was dangerous and had probably meant it when he said he intended to kill a woman, Ms. Tarasoff, who he thought was avoiding his romantic approaches. Indeed, she probably was avoiding him—and as it turned out, with very good reason. The clinic called the campus police, told them about the situation, and requested that they pick Poddar up for further evaluation. The police went to Poddar's house, talked to him, decided there was no problem, and left. Two months later Poddar did kill Tarasoff, and the university health service was sued for failure to take appropriate action to protect Tarasoff from Poddar. Ironically, the campus police were the first group to be dropped from the suit as not legally liable. Poddar later returned to his native India, married, and is reportedly living a contented middle-class existence.

An almost unending series of subsequent cases from California (e.g., *Bellah* and *Thompson*, following) and other states further refined the duty to protect. The following highlight critical points or provide important precedents.

Bellah v. Greenson (1978) in this case, a therapist's juvenile patient committed suicide and the family alleged that they should have been warned of this potential. Apparently sticking to the "public peril" justification for breaching confidence, the court held that the therapist had no duty to warn unless there was a risk of "violent assault to others." The possibility of suicide did not require the therapist to violate confidentiality. This ruling does not imply that therapists cannot give such warnings if they view them as advantageous to the patient in the long run.

Thompson v. County of Alameda (1980) in this case, an incorrigible juvenile sex offender revealed to authorities that he intended to murder whatever child he next accosted. Nonetheless, on the recommendations of a juvenile counselor, a licensed therapist, he was released from custody and carried out his threat. When the parents of the murdered youngster sued the county authorities, the California court further narrowed the duty to protect others by saying that a duty arises only when there are "specific threats to identifiable victims."

Although the cases cited above tend to confine therapist liability to narrow circumstances, some states have actually expanded the basis for liability in several ways. These include requiring therapists to accurately predict dangerousness even in the absence of overt threats, as well as requiring various active intervention efforts designed to prevent violence.

McIntosh v. Milano (1979) New Jersey courts hold that therapists could be sued for failing to protect even when there were no threats communicated. The plaintiff alleged that the therapist should have inferred both dangerousness and the identity of the potential victim from other information available.

> Jablonski v. United States (1983) in a case similar in reasoning to *McIntosh*, several therapists at a Veterans Administration hospital were sued. Their patient had been convicted of rape many years earlier and had recently threatened the mother of his girlfriend, but their assessment indicated that he did not meet civil commitment criteria. The primary therapist and his supervisor each warned the girlfriend that she might not be safe in the apartment she shared with the patient and that she should move out, which she eventually did with additional encouragement from her minister and others. However, she subsequently visited the apartment, where the patient killed her. The victim's estate sued for negligence on several grounds. The court ruled, in part, that the therapists were negligent because they did not forecast the homicide based on the "psychological profile" of the patient.

Yet, again:

> White v. U.S. (1986) in this D.C. Circuit Court case, emanating from St. Elizabeth's Hospital, a duty to warn is acknowledged, but then rejected on the facts in this case, as there was no actual threat—so the case follows the "specificity" rule; it also held that a careful assessment and evaluation that concludes there was no real danger precludes a "duty to warn."

So, the critical issues in these and other cases remain "specific threat" to "specific victim" and "foreseeable danger."

Suicide

> Meier v. Ross General Hospital (1968) firmly established a basic duty of therapists to exercise adequate care and skill in diagnosing suicidality, based on a duty to protect the client from his or her own actions.

> Dinnerstein v. State (1973) a case that clearly establishes the principle that the clinician can be held liable if the treatment plan overlooks/ neglects a patient's suicidal tendencies.

Bellah v. Greenson (1978) also cited earlier; holds there is no Tarasoff "duty to warn" significant others of the possible suicidality of a client, especially since this case refers to outpatient setting.

Addictions

Alcohol and other drugs have been an issue in innumerable cases in both the civil and criminal law.

Robinson v. California (1962) the Supreme Court holds that it is unconstitutional to convict on the "status" of being addicted. Robinson had needle marks and a scab and discoloration on his forearm, and admitted that he used narcotics. He was convicted under a California statute designed to get addicts into rehabilitation, that read "No person shall…be addicted…" The judge in that trial instructed the jury that the accused could be convicted if they found him to have either committed the act or be of the status in violation of the statute under which the offense was being considered.

However, the Supreme Court's decision, delivered by Justice Stewart, held that Robinson could not be convicted on the basis of his *status* as an addict. They noted that he would still retain the status of "addict" even if he were "cured," in which case the indictment, if upheld, would allow for his repeated arrest. In addition, it was held that to punish an individual because of such a status would be cruel and unusual punishment, in violation of the Eighth Amendment.

Powell v. Texas (1968) the Supreme Court holds that a person may be convicted on *behaviors* stemming from addiction. Powell, who had been arrested for being intoxicated in a public place, was found guilty and fined $20 in Austin, Texas. Throughout subsequent appeals, his attorney argued that he was a chronic alcoholic (a fact that was not really disputed), and that his appearance in public was not of his own free will, thus seeking to bring this under the cruel and unusual punishment aspect of the Eighth Amendment. However, Justice Marshall, who delivered the majority opinion, stated that this would not come under the *Robinson* holding since Powell was not convicted for the status of being a chronic alcoholic, but rather for the *behavior* of being in public while drunk on a specific occasion. As such, it was asserted that there was no attempt to punish a status or even a condition, but simply to regulate behavior. They also note that to find Powell innocent would open the floodgates for other types of criminal defendants going free on the basis of other "compulsions."

Much of the reformists' thinking in *Robinson*, and also in the testimony provided in *Powell*, reflects the disease model of substance abuse. This disease model generally assumed that: (1) substance abuse disorders, particularly alcoholism, reflect a physiological disorder, possibly genetically determined; (2) abusers have virtually no control over their intake of the substance because of this dysfunction, and; (3) with some substances, especially alcohol, they permanently retain their status, even when they are able to abstain.

The assumptions in the disease model of substance abuse have been shown to be not entirely true in their implications. For example, some alcoholics are able to return to a pattern of social drinking even after many years of chronic alcohol abuse. There is also clear evidence that many alcoholics, even while in the status of chronic alcoholism, can refrain from the first drink (a bedrock assumption in Alcoholics Anonymous). A case holding to the extreme in this direction is the following.

Traynor v. Turnage (1988)   the Supreme Court upholds allowing the VA definition of primary alcoholism as "willful misconduct," (that is, not the result of other psychological disorder) following the ideas of theorist-researchers like Stanton Peele.

Skinner v. Railway Labor Executives Association (1989)   the Supreme Court upheld the railway's right to drug-test employees who violated particular safety rules, without a warrant and without evidence that the person was under the influence of drugs at the time of the accident/event. In contrast, in 1994, in the case of *University of Colorado v. Derdeyn*, the Supreme Court upheld David Derdeyn's suit to find unconstitutional a random urinalysis, required of student athletes, trainers, managers, and cheerleaders. It was held that the school-state's interest in maintaining drug-free athletic teams did not override Derdeyn's privacy interests, and that this testing program was a violation of the Fourth Amendment as an "unreasonable search."

Harmelin v. Michigan (1991)   a first-time offender possessing 650 grams of cocaine was given life without parole, and appealed on grounds that it was cruel and unusual punishment, but the Supreme Court said this was not prohibited by the Eighth Amendment. The moral: "Buy retail."

Chapman v. U.S. (1991)   the convicted defendant in a drug possession case appealed, saying that the relevant statute was based on weight of LSD-laced substance in its entirety, e.g., the whole sugar cube rather than just the substance itself, and thus led to disproportionate weight, but the Supreme Court said no to appeal. The moral: "Don't buy the add-ons."

There have been some cases in which persons have ingested substances inadvertently. For example, certain individuals who unknowingly ingested substances like LSD (e.g., "spiked punch" cases) have committed acts destructive to themselves or to others. It has been consistently held by the courts in such a case that the person who was responsible for the ingestion of the substance is the one legally responsible for any resulting destructive acts.

Post-Traumatic Stress Disorder (PTSD)

Persons involved in the legal arena commonly encounter or offer diagnoses of post-traumatic stress disorder (PTSD) (see Chapter 4). The difficulty with this is that it is hard to establish the link between the current alleged disorder and a previous situation. The "face valid" nature of the symptomatology, such as nightmares about the prior incident, is often the only clear support for the diagnosis. Hence, PTSD is amenable to conscious and unconscious faking.

> Pard v. U.S. (1984) offers a clear example of faking and PTSD in the legal arena. Mr. Pard had been charged with two counts of attempted manslaughter and one count of attempted murder, stemming from an attempt to kill his ex-wife and a consequent shoot-out with police officers. He received a verdict of not guilty by reason of mental disease or defect. The jury accepted his assertion that he was suffering from a PTSD, generated by alleged extensive combat experiences in Vietnam. After the criminal trial, Mr. Pard lodged a civil suit for related damages against the U.S. government and the Veterans Administration. During that trial, the defendants provided extensive evidence that, at most, Mr. Pard had only been marginally exposed to combat.

The early use of PTSD in the legal arena focused on the victim as severely disordered, almost psychotic-like at times, as a result of the trauma. Later applications, particularly in battered spouse and racial or sexual discrimination cases, presented the PTSD as an expected or even "normal" response to a trauma by a "normal person."

> Ibn-Tamas v. United States (1979) the first use of the "battered woman" (spouse) syndrome in the legal arena.

PTSD became popular in the legal arena because it allowed a face-valid conduit from the trauma to the compensation for damages. The following is an interesting case in that it allows recovery without a showing of damage.

Harris v. Forklift Systems (1993) Teresa Harris alleged that sexually derogatory comments by her employer at a Nashville trucking company forced her to quit. She sued under Title VII of the 1964 Civil Rights Act, alleging discrimination by sex. She asserted that her employer had requested her to retrieve coins from his front pants pocket, suggested they go to a local motel to negotiate her pay raise, and asked if she had gained a sales contract by providing sexual favors.

The critical finding by the Supreme Court was the support of a "hostile or abusive" standard under the "reasonable person" doctrine, unanimously ruling that a person who was sexually harassed on the job need not prove she was psychologically damaged in order to recover damages.

In *Saxton v. AT&T* (1993), a U.S. Appeals Court affirmed and applied the Harris standard, i.e., no need to prove psychological injury, but denied Saxton's claim, based on two incidents: one where her supervisor put a hand on her leg and forcibly kissed her in a nightclub, and then a few weeks later, in a park, when he attempted to grab her. The court asserted that these incidents were not serious or frequent enough, i.e., the new standards.

Syndromes

The difficulty with syndromes in the legal arena, including the "battered spouse syndrome" (see *Ibn-Tamas v. United States* [1979] above) is embedded in the "syndrome" component. A syndrome is defined in *Webster's Third International Dictionary* as "1: a group of symptoms or signs typical of a disease, disturbance, condition or lesion in animals or plants 2: a set of concurrent things: concurrent." Various other definitions of syndrome contain most of the same elements, with the general idea being that a syndrome is a group of behaviors or events that are reported or observed with consistency. For the specific issues here, syndromes are reported or observed patterns of behavior that are predictably precipitated by some event.

But there are difficulties conceptually. First, there is the clear implication that in some fashion and/or to some degree, a consequent critical behavior has been compelled. For example, when establishing the battered spouse syndrome in an assault or murder case the clear purpose is to void some degree or even all of the perpetrator's responsibility for the behavior. The standard argument, at least by implication, is that the establishment of the syndrome's existence "de facto" mutes or voids responsibility. At the same time, it is evident that a) only a minuscule percentage of battered spouses ever criminally assault or murder their abuser; b) there is no variable or set of variables that differentiates those who do from those who don't; and c) if there is a valid case for the behavior as self-protection, the availability of the more legally acceptable self-defense claim negates the need for the establishment of a syndrome.

To highlight this in lectures and workshops, I often argue for the validity of the "estranged spouse syndrome." One of the clearest, and most well-known, examples apparently demonstrating this syndrome is the case of O. J. Simpson, as all of the essentials of the syndrome apparently are found there: one spouse (A) is evidently still in love with or emotionally dependent upon the other (B); B is disengaging from A, but because of ambivalence, concern for A's feelings, fear of A, etc., B provides mixed messages; some event or series of events transforms A's intellectual understanding into an emotional or "gut-level" awareness; A becomes severely emotionally disrupted by a sense of loss, often confounded by feelings of shame, humiliation, betrayal, jealousy, etc.; depression, anxiety, and anger grow in a variable admixture; in some cases, personality predispositions of A (and to some degree B) combine with a catalytic event—possibly facilitated by easy access to the means and the use of disinhibiting substances—emotional arousal, and disruption peak and spill into homicidal and/or suicidal ideation and behavior.

Why is this pattern more common in men? First, I believe the data clearly establishes a greater overall biological propensity toward aggression in males. Second, since in our society females are still much more likely to retain the majority of control and contact in child custody, the threatened and real loss is often far greater for males.

Why is this defense not available? The answer seems to lie with our sociopolitical choices, as relative to the battered spouse syndrome, the estranged spouse syndrome has at least equally predictable consistency and probably a statistically greater likelihood of cycle completion into homicidal or suicidal violence. In fact, a greater percentage of cycle completion along with the greater biological propensity toward aggression in males would support the argument that the behavior of a male who acts within the estranged spouse syndrome is actually more "compelled" than a female who acts within the battered spouse syndrome.

The potential points for discussion are whether any, or which, syndromes should be available as legal defenses, the related sociopolitical issues, the voiding or mitigation of responsibility, and the concepts of "concurrence" and "compelled."

COMPETENCY

The concept of competency underlies many of the legal and ethical issues that confront psychologists in their everyday duties. Virtually any psychological evaluation involves the issue of competency in its most general sense. Thus, the following discussion has implications on a number of fronts. Within the legal arena, there are a number of specific competencies that are evaluated, e.g., to stand trial, to be executed, to make a will, to handle one's affairs, as under guardianship laws.

To Stand Trial

Our predecessor, the English system of criminal justice, incorporated a requirement that the defendant plead to the charge prior to the trial. It is believed that the concept of "competency" first arose as a reaction by the English courts to defendants who, rather than making the required plea, stood mute. The court in such a case then tried to ascertain whether the defendant was "mute by malice" or "mute by a visitation by God." If "mute by malice," the court sought to force a plea by use of a process in which increasingly heavier weights were placed upon the individual's chest until they provided the required testimony (not surprisingly, it was also often the desired testimony). If "mute by a visitation of God," he or she was spared the ordeal. This latter category initially included the literally deaf and mute, but over time was expanded to include the "lunatic." Of course, the requirement that the defendant be competent also has roots in the more general concern that it was simply unfair to subject certain types of people to trial.

Early American courts periodically utilized the competency doctrine. In 1835, for instance, the man who attempted to assassinate President Andrew Jackson was declared unfit to stand trial (*United States v. Lawrence*, 1835). Then, in 1889, a federal court of appeals gave the doctrine of competency constitutional status, observing that "it is fundamental that an insane person can neither plead to an arraignment, be subjected to a trial, or, after trial, receive judgment, or after judgment, undergo punishment; …to the same effect are all the common-law authorities…It is not 'due process of law' to subject an insane person to trial upon an indictment involving liberty or life" (*Youtsey v. United States*, 1889, pp. 940–941). Over the years, the doctrine has retained this constitutional status, with the United States Supreme Court more recently finding that the principle that an incompetent defendant may not be tried is "fundamental to an adversary system of justice" (*Drope v. Missouri*, 1975, p. 172).

> Dusky v. U.S. (1960) the Supreme Court established standards under which due process would be satisfied in competency-to-stand trial matters. The Court then held that the test must be whether the accused has a) sufficient present ability to consult with an attorney with a reasonable degree of rational understanding, and b) whether he has a rational as well as factual understanding of the proceedings taken against him.

Though this test could hardly be described as specific, it does help to define two broad areas (cognitive and cognitive-interpersonal) of competency to stand trial. The first centers on the ability to know and understand the charges and legal processes taken against the defendant. The phrase "rational as well as factual" has been widely interpreted to mean that the accused must understand not only the specifics of the allegation, but also the potential consequences of trial (i.e., a sentence, possible imprisonment), the relative merits of basic legal strategies, and so forth. The second broad requirement is that the accused be able to consult with an attorney. Given that many laypeople do not understand legal procedures or the advice of their attorneys, "reasonable" understanding may be considerably less than perfect. Also, note that what is required is "capacity" rather than willingness to assist one's attorney. If it is determined the client "can, but won't," she is likely to be found competent, even if some mental disorder is involved in the "won't."

Several specialized instruments have been developed to aid in assessing components of competency, but they do not necessarily simplify the process of deriving a final opinion, and as a case discussed later (*Godinez v. Moran*, 1993) at least suggests, such specialized instruments may be superfluous. Perhaps the most widely used and accepted methods were originated by the Laboratory of Community Psychiatry at Harvard by Louis McGarry and his colleagues. The Competency Assessment Instrument (CAI) (Laboratory of Community Psychiatry, 1973) is their attempt to structure and standardize a formal competency interview (see Table 2A). It is based upon a group of 13 separate facets of criminal competency, with the subject rated on each dimension.

There are continuing efforts to refine assessment instruments such as these. For example, the Fitness Interview Test (FIT) is a revision and expansion of the CAI that aims to give a broader assessment of all possible grounds for a finding of incompetency to stand trial (Roesch et al., 1984).

The Competency Screening Test (CST), developed primarily by Paul Lipsitt, was designed as a screening device intended to identify those who are clearly competent before commitment for evaluation. It consists of 22 sentence stems such as, "When I go to court the lawyer will _____"; "If Jack has to try his own case, he _____"; "If the jury finds me guilty, I _____." Answers are scored 0, 1, or 2, with higher scores indicating greater certainty of competency.

> Higgins v. McGrath (1951)   this case sets forth a reasoned argument that competency to stand trial is not to be equated with the presence or absence of a psychosis (or even delusions per se). In this case, Higgins was accused of using the mail for obscene purposes. He was evaluated by several psychiatrists, who all testified that he was a paranoid schizophrenic with persecutory delusions. The psychiatrists concluded that Higgins was incompetent and he was committed under the incompetency statute. Higgins filed a writ of habeas corpus for a redetermination of competency. The court replied that Higgins's delusions were not sufficient to bar his trial.

The decision first clarified the concept that a defendant may have a diagnosable severe mental disorder and still may possess sufficient capacity to "understand and assist." In actual practice, a great deal of sophistication about the criminal process is not required for defendants to be adjudged competent, and later decisions have held that the Constitution does not even require a "meaningful relationship" between a defendant and his attorney.

Pate v. Robinson (1966) the Supreme Court rules that the trial court must order an inquiry into competency if a "bona fide doubt" exists as to the defendant's competency. The confusion that typically emerges in applying the Pate standard is how "bona fide" doubt is interpreted.

Jackson v. Indiana (1972) the Supreme Court rules that individuals found incompetent for trial cannot be held indefinitely if there is no real chance of recovering competency. Mr. Jackson was a mentally retarded individual who was also deaf and mute. An Indiana court found that he was incompetent to stand trial for two counts of robbery totalling nine dollars, and ordered him sent to a state hospital where he spent the next four years. Because of the intractability of his problems, it was likely that he would have remained incarcerated for the rest of his life. Not only was Jackson never convicted of a crime, but he was also never given an opportunity to challenge the allegations against him. The Supreme Court found that such confinement violated his Fourteenth Amendment rights to due process, since he had not in fact been convicted of any crime yet was forcibly incarcerated by the state. They decided that confinement following an incompetency determination must "bear some reasonable relation to the purpose for which the individual is committed." That is, it must be aimed at restoring competency, not just warehousing a mentally disordered defendant. If competency cannot be expected within a reasonable period of time, "then the State must either institute the customary civil commitment proceeding that would be required to commit indefinitely any other citizen or release the defendant."

The Supreme Court failed to define a "reasonable" period of time, and since the *Jackson* decision various criminal jurisdictions have adopted a range of procedures. States typically allow from one to five years of treatment to restore competency.

Medina v. California (1992) unless the state automatically puts the burden of proof on the prosecution as to whether a criminal defendant is competent to stand trial, it falls upon the party making that assertion, usually the defendant. Preponderance of the evidence is the standard of proof.

Godinez v. Moran (1993) the Supreme Court has held in other cases that due process requires that a defendant have the ability to consult with an attorney "with a reasonable degree of rational understanding" and that the defendant have "a rational as well as a factual understanding of the proceedings against him." This means that a person may not be "subjected to a trial if the person's mental condition is such that he lacks the capacity to understand the nature and object of the proceedings against him, to consult with counsel, and to assist in preparing his defense." What had not been clear is whether the same competency standard would apply to other elements of criminal trial decision making, notably the decision to plead guilty or to waive counsel and act as one's own attorney. This decision finds a very low standard for competency to plead guilty or waive the assistance of counsel, i.e., mental competency for pleading guilty or waiving the right to counsel is the same as it is for competency to stand trial. It is the *decision* to waive counsel, not the *ability* to act in one's own defense, that is the issue.

It is also noteworthy that the Court here clearly rejected the consensus of the field that competence is tied to specific functions to be performed, and is situation-based. This may call for some reassessment of competency assessment instruments.

It should be noted that, in contrast to criminal responsibility, competency is considered to lend itself to more adequate measurement because 1) the issue is based on mental status in the here and now, rather than at the time of the crime, and 2) the more specific and behavioral requirements of competency are easier to operationalize.

TABLE 2A
Components of Competency Assessment Instrument

1. Appraisal of available legal defenses.
2. Unmanageable behavior.
3. Quality of relating to attorney.
4. Planning of legal strategy, including guilty plea to lesser charges where pertinent.
5. Appraisal of role of: a) Defense counsel; b) Prosecuting attorney; c) Judge; d) Jury; e) Defendant; f) Witnesses.
6. Understanding of court procedure.
7. Appreciation of charges.
8. Appreciation of range and nature of possible penalties.
9. Appraisal of likely outcome.
10. Capacity to disclose to attorney available pertinent facts surrounding the offense, including the defendant's movements, timing, mental state, and actions at the time of the offense.
11. Capacity to realistically challenge prosecution witnesses.
12. Capacity to testify relevantly.
13. Self-defeating versus self-serving motivation.

From McGarry et al., 1983.

What Disorders Are Usually Associated with Plea of Incompetency?

(1) Mental Retardation—it is unusual to find a lack of intellectual ability in the more sophisticated crimes. But sometimes that at least appears to be the case, from a de facto perspective. In September 1991 in Madison, Wisconsin, Michael Stohr was arrested for counterfeiting after clerks at a printing supply store tipped off federal investigators about a man who had been browsing around. Clerks said the man lingered in the store holding dollar bills up to a color chart and finally putting in an order for a particular shade of green ink.

(2) Psychosis—as noted earlier, this cannot be equated with incompetency, though it is often a factor. It is also a pattern that the courts often consider the patient/defendant "cured" for a long enough period of time for the trial to proceed.

(3) Amnesia—attempted on occasion, usually without much success.

| Wilson v. U.S. (1968) | held that amnesia in and of itself is not grounds for incompetency.

Incompetency to stand trial is prone to a variety of abuses. One of the most troubling issues centers on the defendant's right against self-incrimination and the nature of examinations for competency. Courts have held that the defendant cannot object to a motion by the prosecution or the judge to initiate competency hearings. Because the information discussed with the examiner is usually not privileged, and because it may be useful to the prosecution in the event of an insanity plea or in the penalty phase of the trial, the defendant may unavoidably aid in his own prosecution. This possibility was vividly illustrated in the following case.

| Estelle v. Smith (1981) | Ernest Benjamin Smith and a friend, Howie Ray Robinson, robbed a Dallas convenience store. Robinson shot a clerk during the course of the offense, and both men were indicted for capital murder. While they were awaiting trial, a judge asked Dr. James P. Grigson, a psychiatrist, to assess Smith's competence to stand for trial. Dr. Grigson spoke to Smith for about 90 minutes and concluded that he was competent. He filed no report with the court, but forwarded a letter stating his conclusions. Smith's attorneys were not informed that their client had been examined by a psychiatrist.

Smith was found guilty on the evidence, and at the sentencing hearing Dr. Grigson was called to testify and was admitted over the objections of Smith's attorney. He offered the opinion that Smith was "a sociopathic personality...on the far end of the sociopathic scale." He went on to state that "We don't have anything in medicine or psychiatry that in any way at all modifies or changes this behavior.... There is no treatment.... Mr. Smith is going to go ahead and commit other similar or same criminal acts if given the opportunity to do so." The jury promptly sentenced Smith to death.

Smith's attorneys filed an appeal that was subsequently heard in a federal appeals court. The court found that failure of the prosecutor to notify the defense that Smith would be evaluated by an expert who could be called to testify against him violated his rights against self-incrimination and to effective counsel, as provided by the Fifth and Sixth Amendments. It thus emphasized several points: a) the unreliability of psychiatric testimony; b) the need to inform a client that statements can be used against him to predict future dangerousness; c) the right to consult an attorney before submitting to such an examination and to have an attorney present during the examination in capital cases.

Although the court held that Smith could not be compelled to undergo examination and have the results used against him, it did not specify how the results of incompetency evaluations could be used. Dr. Grigson's conduct would raise serious ethical concerns for most practitioners. But what of the responsible practitioners who try to aid the court in competency determinations? Can they be compelled to reveal any or all of the information they obtain, even though they did not intend to participate beyond the competency hearing?

Competency to Plead Guilty

North Carolina v. Alford (1970)   the Supreme Court allows the basis of the "Alford plea," which says that since "it appears there is enough evidence to convict me, I plead guilty, but don't admit guilt."

Competency to Be Executed, and the Death Penalty

Ford v. Wainwright (1986)   the Supreme Court reaffirmed the position of many state courts that the Eighth Amendment prohibition of cruel and unusual punishment is violated when severely disturbed individuals are subjected to capital punishment. This is part of a more general principle that offenders must be competent at all stages of their involvement in the criminal justice system. On October 19, 1992, the Louisiana Supreme Court ruled 5–2 that an insane inmate (in this case as a result of schizophrenia), Michael Owen Perry, could not be forced to take medication (in this case, Haldol) to make him competent to be executed. Earlier, he had twice been found incompetent to stand trial, but then was found competent in a third hearing. You may be asked whether it is ethical for you to treat such an individual, thus making him qualified for the death penalty. The obvious answer is no. But it may be argued you are treating to get him back into the process, including appeals, etc. Persons with a specific interest in this issue should consult K. Heilbrun, M. Radelet, and J. Dvoakin (1992), "The Debate on Treating Individuals Incompetent for Execution," *American Journal of Psychiatry, 149*, 596–605.

Ake v. Oklahoma (1983)   the Supreme Court orders that indigent defendants must be provided psychiatric expertise at the point of sentencing in a capital case where mental condition or dangerousness is at issue. As noted earlier, *Funk v. Commonwealth* (1989) extends this to psychologists.

Colorado v. Connelly (1986)   this Supreme Court opinion from the same year as *Ford v. Wainwright* appears to be inconsistent with the general thinking in that case. The Court held here that individuals can be convicted of crimes on the basis of confessions prompted by severe mental illness (in this case, command hallucinations representing the voice of God). This opinion seems to suggest that there are no competency requirements prior to initiation of formal legal proceedings in criminal cases.

You may be asked about your views on the death penalty, or what arguments can be made for or against the death penalty. Typical arguments *against* capital punishment include:

- Executing someone is an irreversible step; thus, the execution of an innocent person cannot be undone.
- Even though there may be good reasons to support an execution, the state functions as a killer, and, in turn, society can become dehumanized.
- The death penalty has not been proven to deter others from committing similar crimes.
- The processing of cases involving the death penalty is more costly than life imprisonment because of long delays and appeals. A mandated death-penalty sentence may raise difficulties in finding juries willing to find defendants guilty.
- For many years, the enactment of capital punishment was discriminatory. In the United States, the majority of those executed have been black.

Typical arguments *in favor of* the death penalty include:

- Employing the death penalty where appropriate discourages private revenge and vigilantism.
- The death penalty is sanctioned in religious traditions, such as the Bible,

as well as by historical tradition, as a culturally approved manner of dealing with heinous offenders.

- There is no good evidence that the death penalty is not an effective general deterrent.
- The death penalty could easily be made more economical than the permanent, lifelong warehousing of the most dangerous criminals.
- The death penalty clearly deters the person who is executed from doing any more damage to individuals or society.
- As regards retribution, it is reasonable to say that those who kill innocent persons in cold blood deserve similar punishment.

See also the later section on juvenile death penalty cases.

> Furman v. Georgia (1972) the strength of philosophical and legal disagreements engendered by the death penalty is illustrated by the opinions of the Supreme Court here. The Court did not decide that the death penalty itself was unconstitutional, only that the way it was being applied was unconstitutional. At the time of this decision, there had been no executions in the United States for five years even though the death penalty existed in 41 jurisdictions at the time.

After *Furman*, states began adopting new capital punishment statutes, as the Court held that the death penalty was not *per se* unconstitutional. The Court subsequently decided a number of cases that established a narrow road for states to follow. First, states cannot allow juries or judges complete discretion in imposing death. Second, mandatory death penalties are unconstitutional. Third, the defendant must be permitted to present any aspect of his or her character in mitigation. Fourth, the Court permits states to allow judges rather than juries to impose death sentences after considering special mitigating and aggravating circumstances. Lastly, the Court also held that imposing the death penalty for a rape or kidnapping in which the victim was not killed violates the Eighth Amendment because it is disproportionately severe to the crime.

> Payne v. Tennessee (1991) reversing earlier decisions, the Supreme Court holds that states may present victim impact statements to juries in death-penalty cases.

Other Competencies

Guardianship—refers to specific functions rather than presence of mental disorders.

Competency to work—usually comes under Social Security and Workman's Compensation jurisdictions.

To Make a Will

Although there are numerous legal grounds upon which the validity of a will or codicil (amendment to an existing will) may be challenged, those with the clearest a priori relation to mental disorder are the claim that 1) the testator lacked *testamentary capacity* at the time the disputed will or codicil was signed and 2) that specific contents of the will or codicil resulted from *undue influence* exerted upon the testator by one or more persons. Often, both allegations are made simultaneously. If lack of testamentary capacity is proven, the entire will or codicil is invalid; if undue influence is proven, those portions of the will or codicil that either result from or cannot be separated from the results of influence are invalid.

As noted, when the courts find that the deceased did not possess testamentary capacity, the will is ignored. The law of testamentary capacity is fairly straightforward, at least in its statement. The testator must be able to do the following:

(1) Understand the nature and extent of his or her property.
(2) Realize the persons who are the natural objects of his bounty (e.g., relatives and friends).
(3) Understand the distribution of the property contained in the will.
(4) Understand the nature of a will and be able to form an intent to make a disposition of property that will be carried out after death.
(5) Generally know how these elements relate to each other and form an orderly scheme for the distribution of property.

It is important to note that neither eccentricities, mistaken beliefs, old age, nor unreasonable provisions in the will establish incompetence. The cognitive abilities described above generally require only limited understanding of basic information. As with all the "competencies," any tests used have to be relevant to function. Videotaping and/or psychological evaluation at the time the will is made, then filed with the will, provide a strong bulwark against any future challenges.

CIVIL COMMITMENT, RIGHT TO TREATMENT, AND CONSENT TO INTERVENTION

Since any psychologist may be called upon to commit someone, you should: a) know how to do it in your state, i.e., the actual procedures that you would have to do to carry it out; b) know the essence of the relevant statutes; and c) know the standard criteria, which typically are mental disorder or defect, a formal hearing, a need to take out a petition, and a finding of dangerousness to self or others.

Historically, the concept of commitment came out of the traditional concept of *parens patriae*. It was furthered in the 1950s by the development of antipsychotic medications, which allowed additional and more effective treatment. The civil rights movement also contributed by its devaluation of the parens patriae concept.

Then, in 1967, in the case of *In re Gault* (discussed in more detail later), due process was operationalized for juveniles, but the effects generalized to some degree to the area of civil commitment.

> In re Oakes (1845)   this case is the first articulation of the basis for civil commitment in America. Mr. Oakes was an elderly Cambridge, Massachusetts, man, whose family, over his objections, delivered him to the McLean Asylum in Belmont. His behavior was somewhat unusual, but in retrospect it is difficult to know whether it was pathological or just socially unacceptable. Oakes was held at the asylum against his will and with no prior trial or judicial action. Ultimately, he petitioned for release. His request was eventually heard by the Massachusetts Supreme Court, which deliberated two full days before issuing its opinion and subsequent order that Oakes remain confined. At least five important precedents were established by *Oakes*, including: 1) that the state has a right to confine mentally disordered persons if they are perceived as dangerous; 2) that "insane" persons lack free will; 3) that caretakers should have the major role in decision making for the mentally disordered, including length of treatment; 4) that civil proceedings do not require the same due process considerations as criminal matters; and 5) that involuntary treatment is justified not only by the detainee's dangerousness, but also for his or her own welfare.

Though the opinion noted the issues of both dangerousness and humanitarian concern for the afflicted, *Oakes* has been widely regarded as a precedent for *parens patriae* justification for commitment. Parens patriae, which essentially means "the state as parent," is a doctrine that can be traced from ancient Roman law through the Anglo-Saxon tradition until its adoption by the American legal system. It refers to a duty of authorities to function as benevolent guardians for those who cannot fend for themselves, particularly if their incapacity is due to mental disorder.

Several precedents established by this case served to lessen the rights of those who were considered for commitment. First, the notion that mentally disordered individuals lack free will provided a rationale for not giving due consideration to their wishes. Additionally, the court's opinion established a precedent for "paternalism," the idea that family and professional caretakers will make decisions for an impaired individual based solely on that person's best interests.

Unfortunately, the effects of involuntary commitment rarely matched expectations. Individuals were confined, at least on occasion, for arbitrary reasons, and were not afforded their constitutional right to due process.

Know that the rights generally included in civil commitment include: a) right to an attorney; b) notification of charges and when hearings occurred; c) hearings on the issue with a statement of charges; d) the standard of proof is stated; and e) commitment procedures follow rules of evidence.

Addington v. Texas (1979) this Supreme Court decision placed the burden of proof on the petitioner and the state, who must demonstrate by "clear and convincing evidence" that the detainee meets the statutory criteria for commitment. This level of proof is a compromise between mere "preponderance" of the evidence, used in other civil matters, and "beyond a reasonable doubt," the standard in criminal proceedings. It is noteworthy that states can adopt a more stringent level of proof if they wish. Kentucky, for example, requires proof of commitment criteria beyond a reasonable doubt (at least in theory), largely because its courts view commitment as a "quasi-criminal" proceeding.

Heller v. Doe (1992) the Supreme Court upheld Kentucky's use of "beyond a reasonable doubt" as the standard for commitment of the mentally ill and "clear and convincing" for the commitment of the mentally retarded (MR), holding it constitutional and not in violation of the Fourteenth Amendment "equal protection" clause. The rationale for the lower standard for MR was that 1) the diagnosis of MR was viewed as usually more specific and accurate, and 2) treatment for MR was usually less invasive (thus offers a lesser loss of liberty interest). (See also Bersoff et al., 1994.)

Barefoot v. Estelle (1983) the Supreme Court held that there are no constitutional barriers for mental health experts to testify in capital cases about long-term dangerousness. "The suggestion that no psychiatrist's testimony may be presented with respect to defendant's future dangerousness is somewhat like asking us to disinvent the wheel.... It makes little sense, if any, to submit that psychiatrists, out of the entire universe of persons who might have an opinion on the issue, would know so little about the subject [of dangerousness] they would not be permitted to testify."

Paradoxically, the psychiatric testimony presented in *Barefoot* also demonstrates how a jury can be misled. Barefoot was convicted of murdering a police officer. He had five prior arrests for nonviolent offenses. Although neither of the two psychiatrists who testified for the prosecution had examined Barefoot, both diagnosed him as a sociopath. Most importantly, both also told the jury that such a person would commit violent acts in the future. One of the psychiatrists, Dr. Grigson, claimed that his predictive accuracy was "100% and absolute," and the other claimed accuracy within a reasonable psychiatric certainty. The jury found it probable that Barefoot would commit acts of violence in the future. Consequently, he was sentenced to death, and executed.

Satterwhite v. Texas (1988) the Supreme Court disallowed the testimony of Dr. Grigson because he had no clinical interview or even any significant face-to-face contact with the patient, Mr. Satterwhite. The Court concluded that his opinions were not admissible, as they were not based on anything that could be reasonably interpreted as acceptable psychiatric practice. Please note that Dr. Grigson, also known as "Dr. Death," was one of the psychiatrists who provided testimony in *Estelle*, and in *Barefoot*.

Jones v. U.S. (1983) held that it is constitutionally acceptable to hold a defendant who has been acquitted NGRI (Not Guilty by Reason of Insanity) until the defendant proves he or she no longer needs to be held, and there is no real time limit.

You should know how to define dangerousness. Terms typically used are: a) to others; b) to self; c) to property (no, dangerousness to property alone is not adequate grounds); d) gravely disabled (occasionally, e.g., in *Washington v. Harper*, 1990). Indeed, "gravely disabled" is being used more commonly today, and the longer a person is hospitalized, the more likely this concept will be used.

Risk Assessment and Containment

Be prepared to discuss issues of both risk assessment and risk containment in relationship to potentially violent individuals. For example, in risk assessment, present such components as directly questioning the person and other relevant individuals; obtaining any available, relevant records; know relevant policies and laws; thoroughly document all information you obtain as well as the stimulus-rationale for your concern. Your risk management should at least consider intensified and/or more controlled treatment, communication with all concerned, clear follow-up and compliance procedures, use of consultations, and commitment. (See also Assessments of Dangerousness to Self and Others in Chapter 4.)

The variables usually relevant to this issue are: a) history, especially history of having experienced and/or committed violence; b) the person's overall level of functioning, including alcohol or drug use; c) the present sources of stress and their levels of severity; d) the individual's available coping techniques; e) the individual's access to any means to make any attempt; and f) access to proposed or potential victims.

Know some of the literature on the prediction of dangerousness (see Chapter 4), e.g., John Monahan (1981) is the pioneer in this area, and cites the following eight correlates (actually nine, as the eighth would appear to be two separate factors) as basic in such predictions: 1) young—there is a high correlation with age, beginning around age 15–18 and continuing up to age 30–35 (after age 35–40, statistically speaking, there is little or no correlation); 2) male; 3) lower socioeconomic class; 4) disadvantaged minority; 5) less educated; 6) lower IQ; 7) unstable school and/or vocational history; 8) history of juvenile violence and/or a drug-alcohol history. However, overall, as noted, the critical variable is a personal history of violence—has the person "done it, felt it, or seen it?"

Know that socioeconomic factors and even media publicity can be factors, e.g., that homicide rates have been found to rise on the third day after a heavyweight championship fight.

Know something about Megargee's Overcontrolled Hostility (O-H) scale, embedded in MMPI-2 (see Chapter 4).

Know the relationship of mental disorder to violence—the fact that the traditional holding is that there is not much of a relationship, except if the mentally disordered person was violent before, but that more recent research suggests somewhat higher rates of violence in both mentally disordered and intellectually handicapped clients.

Be prepared to discuss the issue of "least restrictive alternative" as a variable in commitment, and some alternatives that might be used, e.g., community-based treatment centers, electronic monitoring, random drug screens, and open access to treatment records to third parties such as probation officers.

Problems in Predicting Dangerousness

Be able to discuss how to deal with problems in predicting violence, balanced against the constant requests from various agents of society, e.g., judges, to predict violence. For example, professional opinions in this area should be rendered in some type of probability statement that clarifies any qualifiers. (Examples of this type of statement could include *usually low probability behavior, there is a low base rate issue, the time frame used is important, many incidents are situationally generated, alcohol and drugs are often motives and catalysts, access to means is critical to short-term predictions, issue of ideation vs. behavior— whether or not ideation about violence or suicide increases or decreases the related behaviors.*)

Such opinions should also include statements regarding the anticipated level of aggression, e.g., verbal versus an assault rifle, and the possible level of damage to the victim, such as hurt feelings, setback in therapy, probable death. Finally, the distinction between state and trait factors might be underscored. The inability to correctly predict violence is often more associated with the state variables, i.e., how the environment impinges upon the person, such as losing one's job or the death of a relative or friend. Such factors are nearly impossible to predict. An interactionist model of violence prediction is most accurate, albeit the most frustrating model to apply.

Other Cases

Schloendorf v. Society of New York Hospital (1914)   provided the first clear statement that informed consent requires that a client be apprised of the potential benefits and major risks of any proposed treatments, as well as the available alternative treatments. A tough question is how detailed one must be in giving informed consent. The modern trend is the "details ad nauseam" model.

Miranda v. Arizona (1966)   the Supreme Court basis for most Fifth Amendment issues relating to informed self-disclosure.

Canterbury v. Spence (1972)   using the "patient criterion," i.e., "what the typical patient would want to know," this case defined the elements of modern informed consent, and the need for full disclosure of the possible effects of a therapeutic procedure. In this case, surgery on a 19-year-old patient with a ruptured disc resulted in paralysis and other side effects. The case also articulated the concept, then developed in subsequent cases, that the treater must attempt to get the permission of a relative if possible, even in an emergency.

Rouse v. Cameron (1966)   considered whether those committed could be confined only for the purpose of custodial care, and concluded that there was a constitutional right to treatment. Confinement alone did not serve the purpose of civil commitment; there must be a *bona fide* effort at treatment" (it is not necessary that it be successful). This case also held that "habeas corpus" can be used if constitutional rights are not observed in a mental hospital.

Lake v. Cameron (1966)   a federal appeals court case that first clearly outlined the concept of "least restrictive alternative."

Wyatt v. Stickney (1971)   this case was occasioned by conditions at Bryce Hospital, in Alabama, and the hospital was put in receivership pending satisfaction of the court. This was the most significant effort to define the right to treatment, even to the point of spelling out very specific and concrete requirements, and influenced standards of inpatient care in many sectors. Minimal standard of care was defined in terms of patient-to-staff ratios, hours of active treatment per week, existence of continuing therapeutic programs, and the utilization of individualized treatment planning.

O'Connor v. Donaldson (1974) Kenneth Donaldson, 48 years old, divorced, and unemployed, went to visit his parents in Florida in 1957. An unusual character in many respects, he alarmed his family when he began to claim that someone was poisoning him. They contacted the authorities, and he was subsequently committed to the Chattahoochee State Hospital.

Staff at the hospital suggested that Donaldson take medication (neuroleptic drugs had been widely available for about two years). He steadfastly refused on two grounds: first, that he did not see himself as mentally ill; second, that he was a Christian Scientist and viewed medical treatment as a violation of his religious beliefs. The only other treatment offered during his confinement was "milieu therapy," which in this case consisted of sitting in dayrooms filled with other persons who were deemed mentally ill.

If Kenneth Donaldson had no purpose in life prior to his hospitalization in Florida, he certainly had one after it. He became driven by two objectives: getting out of the hospital (but only on his own terms), and establishing his right to reject medical treatment. He filed a lawsuit to gain his release and eventually accomplished both of his goals, but at considerable cost to himself. He was released in 1971 at the age of 62. The Supreme Court finally reviewed his case in 1975, and upheld a monetary judgment against the physicians who had kept him confined for 14 years.

Baxtrom v. Herold (1966) in the 1960s, New York state maintained a significant population of "criminally insane" patients in the Matteawan and Dannemora hospitals. These were completely separate from the public mental hospitals and served primarily to warehouse convicted offenders believed too dangerous and mentally disordered to be released. Johnnie Baxtrom had been convicted of a crime, found mentally ill, and then detained in one of these security hospitals throughout the maximum length of his sentence and beyond. In *Baxtrom*, the Supreme Court found this system unconstitutional and found there was a denial of equal protection to a person who was civilly committed at the expiration of a prison sentence if there is no jury review and if a jury review is available to all others who are civilly committed. The court ordered that Mr. Baxtrom be released or processed through state civil commitment procedures, as any other citizen would be, and he and nearly a thousand other criminally insane individuals were either transferred to public hospitals or released.

Subsequent research on the *Baxtrom* patients revealed that the frightening predictions of their potential for violence in the less restrictive hospital and community settings were exaggerated. Only about 20% (although some commentators have argued this is an underestimate based on design flaws) engaged in assaultive acts during the next four years (though this is a significantly higher percentage than one would expect in normals).

Foucha v. Louisiana (1992) the Supreme Court held that the Louisiana statute permitting an insanity acquitee, i.e., Terry Foucha (who no longer manifests mental illness), to be indefinitely committed to a mental institution until he proves he is no longer dangerous is in violation of the Fourteenth Amendment's due process clause. They could continue the commitment if he were *both* mentally ill and dangerous.

Rennie v. Klein (1976) this was the first significant case to recognize that those who are civilly committed have a right to refuse medications, though it was also held that this right can be overridden by due process. Mr. Rennie, who had been hospitalized on 12 previous occasions, refused to take medication ordered by his psychiatrist. A federal district Court held that involuntary mental patients may have the right to refuse medication or other treatments in the absence of an emergency, founded on the constitutional right to privacy. Further, in the absence of an emergency, some type of due process protection is required prior to forcing medication. To overrule the patient's refusal, four factors should be considered by an independent party: 1) the patient's capacity to decide on his particular treatment; 2) the patient's physical threat to other patients and staff; 3) whether any less restrictive treatment exists; and 4) the risk of permanent side effects from the proposed treatment.

Although the Supreme Court later considered *Rennie*, it did not establish an absolute constitutional right to refuse, as the district court had, but remanded the case for further attention at the state level. Incidentally, though the district court established the basis for a right to refuse treatment, in subsequent action it determined that, based on these four considerations, Mr. Rennie's refusal was properly overridden by the hospital. The court's reasoning in *Rennie* has been very influential in other jurisdictions, such as the following.

Rivers v. Katz (1986) New York, elaborating on *Rennie*, unanimously found there was a state constitutional right to refuse treatment, a right that the state can invade only if the patient is dangerous or incompetent.

It was also held that for forced nonemergency treatment purposes, a) incompetency to make the treatment decision must be determined in a judicial hearing and b) the proposed medication regimen must be shown to meet the treatment needs of the individual. This is an important case because of the clarity of the decision and the unanimity of the New York court.

Rogers v. Okin (1979)   held that: a) committed patients are generally competent to make treatment decisions; b) committed patients may be forcibly medicated in an emergency if not doing so results in dangerousness; c) a voluntary patient has the same rights as an involuntary patient to refuse medications in nonemergency situations; and d) use of seclusion may violate a mental patient's rights.

Kaimowitz v. State of Michigan (1972)   Louis Smith, a "sexual psychopath," agreed to psychosurgery, an agreement that would be a factor in his disposition. Due process appeared to be optimal, as informed consent was scrutinized through one screening committee of physicians and another composed of a law professor, a clergyman, and a layperson. However, before the surgery took place, Smith was released and, not surprisingly, rescinded his agreement. The court in Michigan considered the case anyway and concluded that institutionalization made this process "inherently coercive"—so it would have intruded on the right to privacy, allegedly derived from the First Amendment.

Knecht v. Gilman (1973)   inmates claimed that those with behavior problems were given aversive therapy, consisting of an injection of apomorphine, which caused vomiting lasting from 15 minutes to an hour. A federal court held that this treatment could be considered cruel and unusual punishment if administered without truly informed and voluntary consent.

U.S. v. Charters (1988)   allowed forcible administration of psychotropic medication to restore competency to stand trial. Also supported the concept in *Youngberg v. Romeo* (1982) that courts should ordinarily defer to the decisions of trained professionals if operating in accord with professional standards.

Washington v. Harper (1990)   the Supreme Court, though asserting that Harper, a manic-depressive, had the "right to be free" from the arbitrary administration of antipsychotic medication, held that prisoners may be forced to take antipsychotic drugs—with only an in-house institutional-based due process review, if they (1) suffer from "mental illness," and (2) are dangerous to self, or others, *or* are "gravely disabled." The Court saw three factors as critical: a) a rational connection between the prison regulation and a legitimate government interest; b) the impact the accommodation of the asserted constitutional right would have on staff and inmates; and c) the existence of ready alternatives.

Riggins v. Nevada (1992) approaching this case as a fair trial (and due process) case, whereas *Washington v. Harper* was a prison security case, the Supreme Court holds that not allowing the discontinuance of antipsychotic medication (in this case, a high dosage of Mellaril) to David Riggins during his murder trial, in the absence of findings by the district court as to the need for a particular course of treatment and the medical appropriateness of the drug administered, as required by *Washington v. Harper*, created an unacceptably high due process risk that the defendant's constitutionally protected trial rights were violated. The Court did hold that such forced continuance of medication would have been allowed if deemed medically appropriate, is the least intrusive means of maintaining the individual's competence to stand trial, and is essential to Riggins's safety or the safety of others by the trial court.

Parham v. J. R. (1979) the Supreme Court held that juveniles may be civilly committed, upon consent of parents, without a judicial hearing but with an independent review at the hospital to which they are committed.

Youngberg v. Romeo (1982) the Supreme Court holds that the state has an obligation to provide the institutionalized mentally retarded "minimal habilitation" along with at least "minimal services" that permit 1) the least restraint possible and 2) basic safety. Also supports the concept that courts should normally defer to decisions made by trained professionals, if made in accord with professional standards.

United States v. Salerno (1987) this Supreme Court decision indicates that at least some forms of preventive detention will be found constitutional. The case involved denial of bail to a suspected organized crime boss subjected to federal prosecution. Language in this decision indicates that detention may be justified if it serves a compelling interest, such as promoting "the safety of any other person and the community." The court found that denial of bail could be construed as "permissible regulation" and was not punitive because that had not been Congress's intent in the Bail Reform Act of 1984. Paradoxically, this type of pretrial detention may become a kind of civil commitment (due to the dangerousness issue) for those who are charged with a dangerous crime and who are not really mentally disordered.

Voluntary commitments now outnumber involuntary commitments, though the reverse was true prior to 1970. Unfortunately, it is impossible to know how many people have "voluntarily" entered mental hospitals under threat of civil commitment from family members, mental health professionals, or police officers. There are numerous cases where a defect in cognitive or emotional competency appears to render it impossible for the person to understand the admission process or the related forms with sufficient accuracy to be considered a truly voluntary admission.

Zinermon v. Burch (1990)   in this case, Darrell Burch was found on a roadside, disheveled and bruised. He was obviously hallucinating and confused, and was taken to a community mental health center shelter. He was diagnosed as a paranoid schizophrenic, placed on antipsychotic medication, and three days later was transferred to a state hospital. While supervised by clerical staff, he signed a voluntary admission form. Chart notes from the day after admission indicated he was still very confused. Because the patient was technically a voluntary admission, he was kept at the hospital for five months without any legal review. After his eventual discharge, he filed a federal civil rights action against the hospital and various individuals. The Supreme Court held that Burch could sue personnel at the Florida State Hospital because of such a problematic voluntary admission, as it is clear that Burch was incompetent to make the relevant decisions.

For more detailed information, see the 1993 article, "Coercion in Mental Health Case," *Behavioral Science and the Law, 11*(3).

CRIMINAL RESPONSIBILITY

Note that the concept of free will is the linchpin of the legal system, as are the related concepts of "actus reus" (the act itself) and "mens rea" (some form of intent). Major issues that might be discussed include: informed consent in such proceedings; the problems of evaluation at time of trial while the alleged criminal behavior may have occurred years ago; the related issues of mental retardation and criminal responsibility in many cases; critical wordings in various statutes, such as "understand" versus "appreciate," "conform" versus "control," "criminality" versus "wrongfulness."

Early History of Insanity Defense

The first insanity defense to attract widespread attention in America was the 1800 case of James Hadfield. The case was actually tried in Britain but was widely publicized in the United States. A jury found Mr. Hadfield not guilty, as he was found insane at the time the act was committed. American satirist Mark Twain (Samuel Clemens) helped crystalize a short-lived backlash against the finding through his essay *A New Crime: Legislation Needed*, which alleged that numerous criminals were encouraged to act out with the assumption that they could fake insanity and win acquittal for their crimes. Mr. Hadfield himself faded from public view, largely because he was locked away in an asylum until his death 40 years later.

The M'Naughten Rule

A delusional misfit aims to assassinate a popular political figure, but the intended target survives and continues as a nation's leader. In a dramatic and highly publicized trial, the would-be assassin is found insane and acquitted of the charges against him. A storm of protest follows as the outraged public, the press, and other political leaders push for restriction of the "insanity defense." While this is a synopsis of John Hinckley's attempt on the life of Ronald Reagan, it is also a brief account of events in 1843.

> In re M'Naughten (1843) this first and certainly most influential formal legal test of insanity used in this country is derived from English law. As early as the 1500s, common law had recognized that "lunatics and idiots" whose mentality approached that of a "wild beast" could not be held responsible for otherwise illegal conduct. Still, these issues were largely ignored until the trial of one Daniel M'Naughten, a paranoid schizophrenic woodworker from Glasgow, who held the delusional belief that Britain's Tory party was responsible for his difficult lot in life. He saw Sir Robert Peel, Prime Minister and the head of the party, as his chief persecutor and resolved to kill him. M'Naughten shot and fatally wounded Edward Drummond, one of the Prime Minister's secretaries, as Drummond left his brother's banking house. M'Naughten was apprehended by a policeman as he tried to fire a second shot into Drummond's back. It is now unclear whether he was actually trying to kill Peel or if the attack was an outburst of his disorder without so clear a focus. In any case, the judge at M'Naughten's trial instructed the jury that he should be acquitted if they believed that he was insane at the time of the crime, and he was so acquitted.
>
> On the day after M'Naughten's acquittal, the *London Times* published the following little ditty on its editorial page:

Ye people of England exult and be glad
For ye're now at the mercy of the merciless mad.

The reaction from Queen Victoria and the House of Lords, who feared politically motivated violence, was almost as swift, though the Queen did comment that, "We do not believe that anyone could be insane who wanted to murder a Conservative Prime Minister." The judges of England's highest court were convened and directed to determine a strict rule defining when an insanity acquittal would be justified. They settled on the following test:

> *That the jurors ought to be told in all cases that every man is to be presumed to be sane, and to possess a sufficient degree of reason to be responsible for his crimes, until the contrary be proved to their satisfaction; and that to establish a defense on the ground of insanity, it must be clearly proved that, at the time of the committing of the act, the party accused was laboring under such a defect of reason, from disease of the mind, as to not know the nature and quality of the act he was doing; or if he did know it that he did not know he was doing what was wrong.* (Daniel M'Naughten's Case, 1843)

Although the actual instructions to the jury in the M'Naughten trial were somewhat less restrictive, the test given above is generally associated with his name. This rule was adopted by American courts and was the basic legal test of insanity in this country until the 1950s. It continues to be used today in many state jurisdictions, and forms a basis for the most recently enacted rule for federal courts described in more detail below.

The M'Naughten test, along with its heirs, has been widely criticized for a variety of reasons, e.g., its narrow focus on "knowing," apparently confining the database for insanity decisions to cognitive functions. Recognition of the rule's limitations prompted one scholar to observe that it made it "impossible to convey to the judge and jury the full range of information material to an assessment of defendant's responsibility" (*United States v. Brawner*, 1972).

Modern History of Insanity Defense

Durham v. United States (1954) in an attempt to open up the lines of communication between experts and the courts, Judge David Bazelon of the District of Columbia Circuit Court of Appeals formulated this "Durham rule."

> *Unless* [the jury believes] *beyond a reasonable doubt either that* [the accused] *was not suffering from a disease or defective mental condition, or that the act was not the product of such abnormality, you must find the accused not guilty by reason of insanity.... He would still be responsible if there was* [sic] *no causal connection between such mental abnormality and the act.*

This test requires the jury to determine if a criminal act was causally connected to a mental disease or defect. It was originally viewed as a significant advance because it would allow experts to testify in their own terms. However, courts still found it difficult to interpret the expert's data, and attorneys often introduced an extremely broad (and often irrelevant) range of information in an attempt to explain criminal acts as the result of mental illness. In practice, it produced such free-wheeling testimony that juries were frequently confused and overwhelmed, and the D.C. Circuit (wherein it was originally adopted) dropped it in 1972. The *Durham* rule is not currently used in the United States, and offers more historic than precedent value.

In 1962 the American Law Institute (ALI) concluded an extensive study of criminal responsibility by proposing a Model Penal Code complete with a rule that combined concepts from the existing tests of insanity and that was somewhat more flexible than M'Naughten. This ALI rule is as follows:

> A person is not responsible from criminal conduct if at the time of such conduct, as a result of mental disease or defect, he lacks substantial capacity either to appreciate the criminality [wrongfulness] of his conduct or to conform his conduct to the requirements of the law. (American Law Institute, 1962)

The ALI standard provides a number of improvements over earlier tests. It embraces issues related both to cognition and to volition, essentially bridging the traditional gap between M'Naughten and irresistible impulse. Also, the traditional and narrow "know" is replaced by the term "appreciate."

In recognition of the difficulty that may arise with the volitional prong of the test, namely, deciding which acts could not be resisted versus those that were simply not resisted, the ALI standard typically carries a caveat:

> The terms "mental disease or defect" do not include an abnormality manifested only by repeated criminal or otherwise antisocial conduct.

This exception appears to make the defense inaccessible to the psychopath, sociopath, or antisocial personality. Though chronic antisocial conduct may lead to a formal DSM-IV diagnosis, the ALI standard would view this as a description of bad character rather than a discrete impairment compromising the conduct of an otherwise law-abiding individual.

U.S. v. Brawner (1972) the above standard, the ALI rule, was embraced
by the D.C. Circuit court 10 years later as a replacement for its *Durham*
rule; it was subsequently adopted by several states and the majority of
federal jurisdictions.

Other courts gradually began adopting the ALI rule or a similar combined cognitive and volitional test. Federal jurisdictions, in particular, embraced this standard over more traditional language, that is, until 1984 and the insanity acquittal of John Hinckley. One potentially disruptive factor in all this was the Supreme Court's refusal on March 28, 1994, to review Montana's abolishment of the insanity defense. Idaho and Utah also had already abolished the insanity defense and other states, and Congress, may follow.

Insanity Defense Reform Act of 1984: The Hinckley Rule or M'Naughten II?

John Hinckley's attempt to assassinate President Ronald Reagan, which gravely wounded four people including the President, riveted public attention on the insanity defense. Videotapes of the attack were replayed countless times by the television networks, allowing people around the world to witness the offense in slow motion. Mr. Hinckley's extensive history of maladjustment served more to aggravate public outrage than to mitigate his responsibility, possibly because it was known that the insanity defense was his only real option.

The trial that followed, a news event itself, featured conflicting testimony from a wide variety of experts. Data presented to the jury ranged from notes taken by Hinckley's ex-therapist, through documentation of an extensive inpatient evaluation at a federal forensic hospital, to CAT scans of his brain. Confronted with this mass of data, the jury concluded that Hinckley was not responsible under the ALI rule, and he was acquitted.

The outrage that originally focused on Hinckley himself was soon directed at "liberals soft on crime and corrupt experts." Against this background, the Congress eventually passed a statute that established a "reformed" test for insanity in all federal jurisdictions (a quasi-ALI rule, without the conformity clause; see Table 2B):

> It is an affirmative defense to a prosecution under any federal statute
> that, at the time of the commission of the acts constituting the offense,
> the defendant, as a result of a severe mental disease or defect, was un-
> able to appreciate the nature and quality or the wrongfulness of his acts.
> Mental disease or defect does not otherwise constitute a defense. (United
> States Code, 1984)

This test has been used in federal courts since 1984, and has been influential in redefining many state statutes. Under this federal rule, the burden of proof (traditionally on the prosecution) is now on the defendant to demonstrate insanity by clear and convincing evidence indicating that the jury is to have a strong presumption of sanity. The similarity of this rule to the M'Naughten standard is clear, as there is little or no consideration given to volitional factors, although the more expansive "appreciate" terminology has been retained from the ALI standard. As an affirmative defense, the insanity issue must be raised in the initial pleading of the case, at hearings well before the trial proper.

Henry Steadman and his colleagues (1993) studied 49 counties in a cross-section of eight states (though no southwestern states were included) between 1976 and 1987. He found that out of approximately 9,000 felony cases, only 1% included an insanity defense. Of this 1%, about 25% were acquitted, and only 7% of those acquittals were by a jury. Also, looking at the median length of confinement on a murder charge, he found it to be 1,828 days (about 5 years) when found guilty, 1,737 days (4.7 years) when found not guilty by reason of insanity.

Know that the Standard of Proof in criminal responsibility cases is "beyond a reasonable doubt," and that the standard that you will be expected to testify to as an expert witness is "reasonable (medical/psychological) certainty." It is not clear that juries understand some of these terms, even what "beyond a reasonable doubt" actually means, and judges may not provide percentage estimates of what this term means. And in *Victor v. Nebraska* (1994) and *Sandoval v. California* (1994), the Supreme Court joined these cases to deliver the opinion that when various instructions still convey the concept of reasonable doubt, and when there is no evidence of a reasonable likelihood that the jury understood the instructions in such a way as to allow convictions based on proof insufficient to meet the *in re Winship* (1970) standard—i.e., that the government must prove beyond a reasonable doubt every element of a charged offense—the instructions will be allowed. For example, in *Sandoval*, reasonable doubt was defined as, among other things, "not a mere possible doubt" but one "depending on moral evidence," such that the jurors could not say they felt an abiding conviction "to a moral certainty" of the truth of the charge. Ideally, one should look at all the available information, but that is not always possible. Yet sometimes a single piece of information is critical. In one criminal responsibility case, my opinion differed from three other experts, all of whom I respect. My opinion, which was validated by later data, was swayed by my talking to the alleged perpetrator's roommate and to detectives who had long periods of contact with the defendant just after the alleged crime, data the other experts did not have.

There are several related criminal responsibility concepts that are worth knowing, e.g., *Diminished Capacity*, which focuses on the inability to form a specific intent—i.e., to have "mens rea." This is used to reduce the sentence, but the individual has still been found guilty.

A related concept is *Guilty But Mentally Ill (GBMI)*. This at first seemed to be a promising concept, but it soon became clear that there were problems with it. In those states that adopted the GBMI, there were even fewer NGRI (Not Guilty by Reason of Insanity) pleas, not that there were many to start with (it can on occasion be a way for a jury to simply avoid a difficult decision; in that sense, it makes it easier for a jury to convict in the "gray" area between sanity and insanity. Also, being found GBMI taints the processing within the corrections system, e.g., less chance to go to a camp or a negative bias when the person comes up for parole.

You may be asked to discuss how compelling is the presence of either severe mental illness or horrific event details to a decision of insanity. As Dr. Laszlo Kreizler, the forensic psychologist in Caleb Carr's 1994 novel *The Alienist* states, "'They'll want him to be mad, of course,' Laszlo mused, not hearing me. 'The doctors here, the newspapers, the judges; they'd like to think that only a madman would shoot a five-year-old girl in the head. It creates certain...difficulties, if we are forced to accept that our society can produce sane men who commit such acts'" (p. 33).

Know that if the NGRI examinee is unwilling to cooperate, you may proceed under court order, but you should know the limits of what you can evaluate and comment upon. You should inform the client that you will proceed and will inform the court of the situation.

If relevant to your subdiscipline, know the related research on the MMPI-2, e.g.: 1) that there is no clear NGRI profile; 2) the revised Megargee typology of offenders based on MMPI-2 profiles; and 3) the changes in MMPI-2 (know why the changes were made—clearer language; more up-to-date, more diverse, and

TABLE 2B
Comparison of Insanity Defenses

Test	Legal Standard	Final Burden of Proof	Who Bears Burden of Proof
M'Naughten	"Didn't know what he or she was doing or didn't know it was wrong"	Varies from proof by a balance of probabilities on the defense to proof beyond a reasonable doubt on the prosecutor	
Irresistible impulse	"Could not control conduct"		
Durham	"Criminal act was caused by mental illness"	Beyond reasonable doubt	Prosecutor
A.L.I.-Brawner	"Lacks substantial capacity to appreciate the wrongfulness of the conduct or to control it"	Beyond reasonable doubt	Prosecutor
Present federal law	"Lacks capacity to appreciate the wrongfulness of his or her conduct"	Clear and convincing evidence	Defense

Adapted in part from "Insanity Defense" by Norval Morris, *National Institute of Justice Crime File Study Guide*, 1986. Washington, DC: U.S. Department of Justice, National Institute of Justice/Criminal Justice Reference Service.

more appropriate norms; eliminating odd, religious, and sexist items). Some changes that are important are that a 65T score is the accepted cutoff, rather than 70 T as in MMPI-1 and that there is equivalence on the basic scales in T scores, i.e., a T score of 60 on 4(Pd) means the same in normative population scores as a T score of 60 on 6(Pa). This was not the case in MMPI-1.

Be able to discuss the issue of the pros and cons of computer-generated reports—for the MMPI-2, or for other tests. For example, John Graham talks about a suit where it was held that the on-site practitioner is held responsible for the quality of any computer-generated report, which is consistent with the newly proposed ethics code. So there are advantages (cost not being one of those advantages) to using the standard service, i.e., National Computer Systems (NCS), which owns the scoring copyright—but not the interpretation rights. Also, if you use a computer-generated report, you need to make that known in your report. Please note that such reports tend to lock you into the computer-generated interpretive statements. Some of these may be inaccurate, yet in a courtroom they look like they are set in stone when they appear in the computer printout.

Know your state's statute on insanity, and also be aware how substance abuse relates to it, usually through a diminished capacity defense. Lastly, be aware that you don't give an ultimate answer, i.e., that you provide data or an opinion for the ultimate trier of fact, the jury.

CHILD CUSTODY

Basic concepts that you should be prepared to talk about include *parens patriae*, tender years doctrine, best interests of the child, joint custody (physical? legal? equal split?), and psychological parent.

Two major trends have reshaped the law of child custody, particularly in the last decade: a) the destigmatization of divorce, including the abandonment of fault-finding; and b) increased attention to gender-fair property division and custody. Historically, ancient Roman law dictated that the father had absolute power over his offspring and was always awarded custody. Children were viewed as "chattel," and under the doctrine of *parens potestas* only men could hold legal title to their offspring. Since the developmental and emotional needs of children were not considered significant, custody was treated strictly as a matter of title over property. This orientation carried over into English common law and persisted into the nineteenth century, by which time it was also firmly established in America.

The doctrine of *parens patriae* then gained influence in the latter half of the nineteenth century and eventually led to greater recognition of the state as the guardian of helpless and needy individuals. These themes were adapted to child custody matters via judicial efforts to structure custody decisions according to the welfare and interests of children rather than the "property rights" of parents.

Perhaps due to social and political realities, the legal view of "welfare and interests" remained strictly paternalistic. Custody decisions still overwhelmingly favored fathers because they had the financial resources to provide for a child's material needs. Thus, the status quo was preserved, albeit under new theories.

Finlay v. Finlay (1925) first clearly articulates the view that custody decisions should reflect the "best interests of the child," yet this is seldom actually applied at this point in time. Gradually, courts in the United States began to pay greater attention to the emotional and developmental needs of children, rather than focusing on financial support alone. This change in emphasis led courts to completely reverse the gender bias.

Tuter v. Tuter (1938) clearly articulates the emerging "tender years doctrine" claiming that "there is but a twilight zone between a mother's love and the atmosphere of heaven."

Courts commonly acted on the "tender years doctrine," which led to a favoritism toward mothers in custody decisions. During the twentieth century, fully 90% of all divorce decrees involving minor children gave the mother primary legal custody, most without contest by the father. However, within the last two decades there has been an increasing effort to truly consider the best interests of the child as verbalized in *Finlay v. Finlay*.

The Uniform Marriage and Divorce Act (National Conference of Commissioners for Uniform State Laws, 1971), which has influenced legislation in many states, generated five general factors to be considered in custody decisions:

(1) The wishes of the child's parent or parents.
(2) The wishes of the child.
(3) The interaction and interrelationship of the child with his or her parents, his siblings, and any other person who may significantly affect the child's best interest.
(4) The child's adjustment to his home, school, and community.
(5) The mental and physical health of all individuals involved.

Even when both divorcing parents are relatively poor custodians, one or both will almost invariably retain custody, which makes it evident that the "best interests of the child" is seldom literally applied. This bias is articulated in the "reversion doctrine," which states that under a variety of conditions a child's custody will revert to a biological parent over others.

Joint custody is the newest major development in child custody. Taken together, a number of studies of the pros and cons of joint custody suggest consistent themes: a) parents in general are satisfied with joint custody; b) children are generally more satisfied with the amount of contact with each parent; c) problems arise from home-switching, disruption of school functioning and peer relationships, and confusion over family relationships, values, and identity. Based on available information, several factors positively predict joint custody as a viable alternative for a given family:

(1) General parental agreement on child-rearing practices and the issues for shared parenting (usually longer-term, "policy" matters); acceptance of some divergence in parenting styles and goals.
(2) Acceptance and respect between parents; a sense of equality.
(3) Recognition and appreciation of benefits of coparenting.
(4) Parental ability to make joint decisions without escalating hostilities, or at least without allowing conflict to affect or be communicated through children.
(5) Compatibility of children's needs and developmental tasks with shared parenting.
(6) Parents' present status and future commitment to living in close proximity.
(7) Family recognition of child's legitimate needs for continuing relationship with both parents; parental ability to show empathy with each other's sense of loss after divorce.
(8) Availability of psychological, financial, or other resources that promote flexibility in accommodating the logistical demands of joint custody.

Contraindications to joint custody include the following:

(1) Different values in child-rearing which cannot be resolved or accepted (e.g., religious orientation), especially if these contributed to the divorce.
(2) Intense and/or unremitting hostility that spills over to using children as weapons, conduits, or targets.
(3) Lack of respect or tolerance between parents, or marked differences in power.
(4) Joint custody as court ordered rather than the product of voluntary negotiation.
(5) Preschool or adolescent children or children of widely divergent ages.
(6) History of family violence.
(7) Major emotional disturbance in one or more family members, including drug or alcohol abuse.
(8) Inability of one parent to accept the reality of the divorce or to incorporate failure of marriage into self-image.

Related Child Custody Cases

Painter v. Bannister (1966) though an odd set of circumstances, this Iowa case helped to establish the concept of "psychological parent." The court allowed the grandparents to keep custody of the child over the claims of the natural father, who, though apparently at least an adequate parent by any standard, was seen as having a "Bohemian lifestyle." (By modern standards he'd probably be termed a "straight.")

| Santosky v. Kramer (1982) | this Supreme Court case overturned the use of a "fair preponderance" standard, and established "clear and convincing" as the standard of proof required to terminate parental rights.

Issues that are often a focus of questions and discussion are the following:

(1) What if there are allegations of child abuse? Know the relevant statute in your state. Does it use terminology like "suspect," and what does that mean to you? Realize that you will probably need to state any allegations, denials, etc., in your report, and consider how this can be handled.

(2) Who is your client? It is best if you do the evaluation as a friend of the court, and it's important to be able to observe the central characters in different conditions, and in different combinations.

(3) How to deal with confidentiality in related cases—for marital or family therapy, e.g., use appropriately signed releases. One individual censured by a State Board had come over at the call of an attorney and testified, without checking with one of the parties, and without waiting for a legal subpoena. (See also *Cheatham v. Rogers, 1992.*)

(4) Most courts accept that the older the child, the more his or her desires will be considered. Be prepared to discuss that concept, and how and when to evaluate and weigh the child's input. Discuss how this discussion should go in light of a) the child may not be aware a divorce is imminent, and how this can be handled, or b) how the child may be "whipsawed" between the wishes of each parent.

(5) Discuss how to deal with "moral fitness" issues: know any relevant statutes, discuss the issue of community standards, and specifically, the issue of gay parents.

(6) Understand that you are not the ultimate decision maker. Be prepared to discuss how you would respond to a request to answer the ultimate issue, as the expert will often be pressed to render a decision rather than an opinion.

(7) Be prepared to comment on what you should do if the noncustodial parent asks you to evaluate the situation. For example, you might a) advise that person to seek a court order to have you do the evaluation; b) understand that this is a gray area, and in those cases where you believe the noncustodial parent may need a "foot in the door," comment how you would proceed, and with what cautions. Remember that in this situation the expert must be very careful to not become an advocate.

(8) Discuss whether or not you can be therapist for any participant in such a case, before or after the disposition of the case.

Be able to discuss what procedure you should use. The following procedures are generally useful in conducting custody evaluations:

(a) Observation, interview, and assessment of children, individually and collectively.
(b) Collection of information from relatives, relevant physicians, teachers, daycare facilities, neighbors, and others.
(c) Psychological testing, and specifically designed rating scales. Be able to discuss related issues of reliability and validity.
(d) Interview and assessment of parents individually.
(e) Observation and assessment of each parent with children.
(f) Interview of each parent with relevant significant others.

JUVENILE LAW

Juvenile court evolved out of the *parens patriae* model into a rehabilitative model, and now more closely to the adversarial model. The first juvenile code was formulated in 1899 in Illinois. Prior to that, and similar to most other states, juveniles had come under the criminal code, with age as reducing variable. The shift to a juvenile code resulted in a number of specific changes: a) petitions were taken out—not charges made; b) there were no findings of guilt—only allegations supported as true; c) there was no sentencing—only recommendations for disposition.

Also, there are other changes: a) juvenile court records are not public—they are treated as "sealed"; b) juveniles are separated from adults while incarcerated—at least, that's the ideal, if not always met in practice; c) informal proceedings are used; d) theoretically, it is a nonadversarial model that is designed to come up with the plan that's best for the child; e) there is a new category of "status offense" (based on a behavior that was not illegal for adults), as opposed to a criminal offense.

Over time, there was an increasing consensus that the system was not working as it was intended, i.e., that juveniles were not being rehabilitated as hoped, and yet they were not being afforded the legal rights or due process accorded to adults. This consensus emerged in the following cases. For some additional, specific information on law, psychology, and children, the reader is referred to the February 1993 issue of *Law and Human Behavior, 17*(1).

Kent v. U.S. (1966)   the first Supreme Court case to formally require due process in juvenile proceedings. The opinion was written by Judge Fortas shortly before he was forced off the Supreme Court.

In re Gault (1967)   Gerald Gault, 15 years of age, was committed as a juvenile delinquent to a state institution at the end of what he and his mother thought was a simple hearing. He was charged with making obscene telephone calls. No witnesses appeared and the only evidence was hearsay. The Supreme Court reversed and remanded, placing the due process requirement for juveniles from *Kent* within the Fourteenth Amendment. The *Gault* decision established: a) a requirement of notice of charges, b) a right to an attorney, c) a right to cross-examine and confront witnesses, d) a right to avoid self-incrimination. So, the process was becoming more adversarial again, though this evolution to an adultlike process was mitigated by cases such as:

McKeiver v. Pennsylvania (1970) the Supreme Court holds that a juvenile has *no* right to a trial by jury even though the states do retain the right to require a trial by jury for juveniles if they so choose.

In a similar vein, a primary legal issue in dealing with many childhood disorders is the right of a minor to refuse treatment. Should minors, by law or through ethical principle, have the power to object to their treatment when their parents have already consented? Generally, a minor's ability to refuse treatment has not been recognized by law. Problems can quickly arise, however, in determining how much review should be given to a parent's or guardian's consent to hospitalization and treatment.

Kremens v. Bartley (1977) a Supreme Court case concerning five mentally disordered youths, age 13 to 18, who challenged the constitutionality of a 1966 Pennsylvania law governing commitment and voluntary admissions to state mental health institutions. It can be broadly interpreted as allowing those 14 years and older to be treated as adults in such proceedings.

Parham v. J. R. (1979) in this Supreme Court case, a minor alleged that he had been deprived of his liberty without procedural due process by laws permitting parents to voluntarily admit minors to mental hospitals. The Court's majority opinion held that parents should be allowed to maintain a substantial, if not dominant, role in making the decision, absent a finding of neglect or abuse and without evidence to contradict the traditional presumption that the parents acted in the best interest of their child. It was further noted that the child's rights and the nature of the commitment decision are such that parent's consent does not always carry absolute and unreviewable discretion over whether to have a child institutionalized. But the Court did say that the review need not be held by judicial or administrative boards, but could be held as an internal hospital matter. Also, children are granted access to emergency medical or psychological treatment without parental consent.

There are a few other cases that further the adversarial mode:

In re Winship (1970)   the Supreme Court establishes that just as in adult criminal cases, "reasonable doubt" is the standard of proof where there is a formal adjudication, and all elements of a charged offense must be proved beyond a reasonable doubt.

Breed v. Jones (1975) the Supreme Court holds that if you adjudicate a juvenile in a juvenile court proceeding, it is then double jeopardy to try him as an adult.

On the other hand,

Schall v. Martin (1984)   the Supreme Court held that juveniles may be denied bail for their own protection, or to protect the community.

New Jersey v. T. L. O. (1985)   while upholding a student's right to be free from unreasonable search and seizure (Fourth Amendment), the Supreme Court puts limits on these rights by holding that teachers could search a student's locker without a warrant, even if this was not for a suspected criminal offense, but only for a suspected violation of school rules.

U.S. v. R. L. C. (1992)   this case involved a 16-year-old Chippewa Indian boy who was convicted of involuntary manslaughter and received a longer sentence in juvenile court than he would have under the federal guidelines. He had drunk heavily one night in 1989 and stole a car on the Red Lake Reservation in Minnesota. He drove it into another car, killing a two-year-old passenger. He was held to have committed an act of juvenile delinquency equivalent to involuntary manslaughter. Under the federal law that applies to the reservation, the maximum sentence for involuntary manslaughter is three years. But, under federal sentencing guidelines, an adult with his background would be sentenced to 15 to 21 months. A federal appeals court ruled that he could not be sentenced to more than that. The Supreme Court then concurred, 7–2, though from a narrow statutory position that may turn out to have limited precedent value, that federal judges cannot sentence juveniles to longer terms of detention than adults would serve if they committed the same crime.

There are other areas of ambivalence that occur in juvenile cases because of the confluence of the above trends: a) Do juveniles have a right to an insanity defense? It is generally held that they do not, as there cannot really be a "criminal act" under the juvenile code; b) Is plea bargaining available? It is not, at least formally, but of course it occurs informally in most situations; c) What is the standard of proof for waiver to adult courts? It varies by state, from "clear and convincing" to "preponderance" to "substantial evidence."

Outpatient Juvenile Treatment Issues

Regarding outpatient treatment, Grisso and Vierling (cited in Grisso, 1986) state that authorities should not burden minors with decisions they cannot make intelligently, or inadvertently deny to some the opportunity to make decisions of which they are fully competent. The results of their work suggest that:

(1) No circumstances sanction independent consent by minors under age 11, given the developmental evidence of their diminished capacities.

(2) Ages 11 to 14 appear to make up a transition period involving cognitive, developmental, and social expectations. Independent consent by these minors may be justified for limited purposes, especially when competence can be determined in individual cases.

(3) There appear to be no psychological grounds why minors age 15 and above cannot give competent consent.

(4) In some minors, diminished capacity to provide meaningful consent may sometimes present such risk to the psychological or physical welfare of the minor as to offer a compelling reason for denial of the right to consent in certain circumstances.

In re Kevin F. (1989) a related issue occurs when a juvenile threatens violence. A California appeals court concluded that evidence Kevin gave to his therapist was properly admissible under Section 1024 of the state's Evidence Code, which provides: "There is no privilege under this article if the psychotherapist has reasonable cause to believe that the patient is in such mental or emotional condition as to be dangerous to himself or to the person or property of another and that disclosure of the communication is necessary to prevent the threatened danger." In so ruling, the court rejected Kevin's argument that *Tarasoff* precedents restricted the statutory exception to circumstances in which there was a threat of harm to a readily identifiable victim. The court also ruled that Kevin was not entitled to *Miranda* warnings before talking to the therapist, because there was no evidence that he was subjected to interrogation.

Juvenile Death Penalty Cases

Thompson v. Oklahoma (1988) the Supreme Court held that states may not execute children who were under 16 at the time of the crime.

Stanford v. Kentucky (1989) the Supreme Court held that states may execute children who were over 16 (i.e., in the disputed 16–18-year range) when they committed the crime. The justices cite the fact that juveniles as young as 14 years of age were executed with reasonable regularity at the time of the signing of the Constitution, arguing that it is at least not unusual, though it might be cruel—the Eighth Amendment does say "cruel *and* unusual."

In a related case, relevant to the issue of mental retardation:

Penry v. Lynaugh (1989) the Supreme Court held in a 5–4 verdict that an IQ of 50–55 did not preclude John Penry from being executed. He was convicted in 1980 of the stabbing murder of a woman he had raped in her home. A significant part of the majority's rationale is that he had already been found competent to stand trial.

For more on this subject, see the section on school psychology later in this chapter.

CHILD ABUSE

People v. Jackson (1971) the first clear affirmation of the "battered child syndrome" in the legal arena, asserting it had become an accepted medical diagnosis. The battered child syndrome was first articulated in 1962 by Kempe and his colleagues. The "child sexual abuse accommodation syndrome," coined by Summit in 1983, is more controversial, as it emphasizes that the victim's retraction of the accusation is evidence that the abuse actually occurred.

Landeros v. Flood (1976) this case clearly established the basis for liability for a failure to report child abuse.

Consider this potential examination question. "A 70-year-old man is in therapy with you. He eventually confides that 45 years ago, when his daughter was about two years old, he regularly fondled her over a period of six months. It never happened again, no one ever knew about it, she has adjusted well, and is now happily married with children of her own. He says he just wanted to get if off his conscience after all these years. What do you do?" This highlights the issue of a "statute of limitations" for child abuse reporting laws, which apparently do not consistently exist across jurisdictions, and forces discussion of prior informed consent about the need to report abuse, how to deal with a need to report and the effects on therapy, and considerations for others, in this case the daughter. (See also *Riley v. Presnell*, 1991.)

All states now mandate psychotherapists to report cases of abuse, and many states require anyone aware of abuse to report it. Most states also require the reporting of any cases of "suspected" abuse. In most states, failure to report constitutes a misdemeanor, usually involving a fine and/or short jail term. Failure to report would also open the psychotherapist to civil liabilities. Of course, such reporting breaks confidentiality, but state laws typically provide protection from civil suits when one breaks either any ethical principles of confidentiality or any legal statutes regarding privileged communication. However, there is no way to guarantee protection of the therapy relationship once the reporting occurs. An excellent review of the issue of mandated reporting of child abuse is found in Kalichman (1993).

Within this context, be prepared to discuss the thorny issue of "recovered memories of abuse," first from the perspective of how to respond therapeutically and legally to the apparent arousal of such memories in a client. In addition, consider how those cases that are false memories (whatever percentage that is) may have arisen, or cases where therapists are being held liable for implanting or facilitating such memories. (See the upcoming case of *State v. Huss*, 1993.)

The probability of abuse in a specific instance is increased by the following "individual" factors in the perpetrator:

(a) History of experiencing abuse as a child, as a victim or witness
(b) Low emotional stability and/or self-esteem
(c) Low ability to tolerate frustration and inhibit anger
(d) Ligh impulsivity
(e) Lack of parenting skills
(f) High emotional and interpersonal isolation
(g) Problems in handling dependency needs of self or others
(h) Low ability to express physical affection
(i) Unrealistic expectancies for child's performance
(j) Acceptance of corporal punishment as a primary child-rearing technique
(k) Presence of drug or alcohol abuse

A false accusation of abuse is more likely in:

(a) the midst of a bitterly contested divorce case
(b) subsequent to a difficult divorce case when upset flares over visitation issues
(c) in reports by younger children, especially age four and younger
(d) when the reaction of the adult first reporting the abuse is "I knew it…" rather than disbelief or perplexity
(e) when the child's report is sparse, fanciful, and/or inconsistent
(f) when the professionals involved quickly jump from the analytic assessor role to that of advocate/accuser

Pennsylvania v. Ritchie (1987)   the depth of societal feeling regarding child sexual abuse is clear from this case that held that people accused of sexually abusing children have no right to see confidential state records that might help in the preparation of their defense unless a judge determines it is material and important to the defense. Ritchie was convicted in 1979 of rape, incest, and corrupting the morals of a minor. He had sexually abused his daughter over a four-year period, beginning when she was nine. State appeals courts set aside the conviction because the state's Children and Youth Services had withheld records from Ritchie. The Supreme Court, citing the "vulnerability and guilt" of young victims of sexual abuse, then ruled 5 to 4 that the Pennsylvania Supreme Court was wrong in ordering child welfare officials to make confidential records available to Ritchie.

DeShaney v. Winnebago County (1989)   the Supreme Court held that there was no liability on a state for the failure of its child protective service agencies to protect a child and to prevent the child's death at the hands of its parents, even when the abuse had been repeatedly reported. Reinforced in *Suter v. Artist M.* (1992).

State v. Huss (1993)   the Supreme Court of Minnesota overturned a father's conviction for criminal sexual assault, stating that the child's sex abuse allegations against her father were "improperly influenced" by "a highly suggestive book on sexual abuse," *Sometimes It's OK to Tell Secrets*.

Not long after divorcing her husband, Nancy Huss observed some behaviors in their three-year-old daughter that would at least warrant some initial concern, i.e., increased rebellious and destructive behavior, trying to urinate standing up, using nicknames for body parts, and kissing on the lips. Ms. Huss also observed that the daughter came back from nonovernight visits wearing different clothes, and that the child's vaginal area was "bright red." No medical corroboration of abuse could be found, but Ms. Huss contacted a therapist. The therapist used play therapy, as well as several books on sex abuse. The book noted above included a tape, which referred to abuse events as "yucky secrets." Ms. Huss checked the book out of the library and played the tape for her daughter numerous times, after which the child told her that she had a "yucky secret," that her father, Robert Huss, had put his fingers into her vagina and her butt." Ms. Huss told her she was proud of her and that she had been very brave.

A week later, the child made a similar statement to the therapist, and several weeks later the therapist reported this to the authorities and the father was arrested. At trial, the child's testimony was summarized by the court as follows:

> *The child was on the stand for almost an hour before she made any accusation of abuse, and then she said both her mother and her father had touched her in a bad way. When she was asked repeatedly on direct examination whether she had any "yucky secrets," she answered in the negative. ... She also called a hug and a touch to her hair "bad touches." Although the child had not seen her father for approximately a year before trial, she testified that she had taken a shower at his house on the day she gave her testimony. The child was not able to identify [her father] in the courtroom.*

Testifying for the defense were a family physician and two clinical psychologists. The physician testified that he had never seen any physical evidence of sexual abuse in his examinations of the child. The first psychologist testified that the child had made no disclosures of abuse to him. The second psychologist testified to the suggestive nature of the book and tape and to his belief that the therapist's notes revealed the use of "suggestive and repetitive techniques." He also testified that "the book might cause a child to make false statements about being abused."

Nevertheless, Mr. Huss was convicted, and the Minnesota Court of Appeals affirmed, basing their decision on the fact that the victim and other witnesses had testified that sexual abuse had occurred.

However, this decision was appealed, and on October 1, 1993, the Minnesota Supreme Court reversed the decision, found the book in question "a highly suggestive book and ... its repeated use by the child's mother and therapist, combined with the mother's belief that abuse had occurred, may have improperly influenced the child's report of events."

Emphasizing that such use of this book was the key to its decision, the court concluded: "In sum, the child's testimony was contradictory as to whether any abuse occurred at all, and was inconsistent with her prior statements and other verifiable facts. However, even given this contradictory testimony, we might not have been persuaded to reverse [the conviction] absent the repeated use of a highly suggestive book on sexual abuse."

In a somewhat related issue, be prepared to discuss the issue of anatomical dolls, e.g., lack of uniform stimulus values, little data on normative responses, issues of setting, other potential conditions of suggestibility, and levels of training and competence of examiner. For more specific information, see Everson and Boat (1994).

THE CHILD AS EYEWITNESS

As far back as 1687, in *R. v. Love* (see H. Lilles, *Canadian Journal of Family Law*, 5, 237–251), it was held that a child had to be 14 years old to testify in a court of law, and that a child under 14 could not testify regardless of intelligence or religious instruction. This was predicated on the belief the child did not know truth from lie and did not understand the moral obligation to tell the truth. In a relatively progressive decision, *Young v. Slaughterford* (1709) allowed the testimony of a child under 12 provided that he or she knew the danger of violating the oath. *R. v. Travers* (1726) then replaced the lower boundary, stating that there was an automatic disqualification of witnesses under age nine, but allowed for the admission of unsworn testimony from younger children. Following this decision, an investigative panel of 12 judges ruled unanimously that an infant under seven years could be sworn to oath in criminal proceedings, given that they possess sufficient knowledge of the nature and consequences of the oath. This decision was supported by *Wheeler v. United States* (1895), when the court stated that a child could not be disqualified as a witness by reason of age alone.

Understand that this issue includes the separate concepts of both competency to testify and credibility to testify. Consider that the issues of competency and credibility center around: a) the degree that suggestibility affects the judgment; b) quality of memory; c) level of intelligence and its effect on such judgments; and d) level of moral development, e.g., as it relates to the child's ability to tell the truth and to know what the consequences are of not telling the truth.

In such cases, it is important to consider: 1) the child's ability to appreciate the difference between a truth and a falsehood; 2) the child's ability to understand there is a duty to be truthful; and 3) the child's ability to understand there are consequences if he or she is not truthful, including the nature and probability of those consequences. For more detailed information see John Myers, The competence of young children to testify in legal proceedings (*Behavioral Science and the Law*, 1993, *11*, 121–133).

| Kentucky v. Stincer (1987) | the Supreme Court held that the defendant need not be present at a *preliminary* hearing to determine if a child witness victim was competent to testify.

Coy v. Iowa (1988) the defendant could dimly see and hear the victim through a screen, but the victim could not see the defendant. The Supreme Court found this to violate the Sixth Amendment–based right to confront one's accuser "face-to-face."

Maryland v. Craig (1990) the interrogation and cross-examination over closed circuit television (with defense attorney present in the room with the alleged victim, and in phone contact with the defendant) of the alleged child victim was held by the Supreme Court to not violate the Sixth Amendment. The finding was based on the concept that the state's interest in protecting children from emotional trauma overcomes the Sixth Amendment right.

White v. Illinois (1992) Randall White was convicted of sexually molesting a young girl and sentenced to 10 years in prison. The victim had described the attack to her baby-sitter, her mother, an investigating officer, an emergency room nurse, and a doctor who examined her. Ultimately, she was excused from testifying by the trial judge. White appealed, saying his constitutional rights were violated because he could not confront his accuser in court. A unanimous Supreme Court ruled that defendants charged with molesting children have no absolute right to confront their young accusers at trial, thus admitting "hearsay" evidence. The justices said statements made by an alleged victim outside court could be presented to a jury, even when the child was available to testify.

Thus, despite the Sixth Amendment's guarantee that criminal defendants can face their accusers, the court said states can grant exceptions and allow limited "hearsay" evidence in order to shield child victims from harm.

CREDIBILITY OF TESTIMONY

Know something about the eyewitness identification literature, e.g., the pioneering efforts of Robert Buckhout, that the researcher who has contributed most extensively to this literature is Elizabeth Loftus, and that the opposing point of view on this issue was first significantly articulated by McCloskey and Egeth *(American Psychologist,* 1983, *38,* 550–558; for an updated version of this view, see the article by Gary Wells in the May 1993 issue of *American Psychologist),* who argued that the data in this area were not yet of sufficient validity, so that the prejudicial effects of testimony would outweigh the probative value of such testimony.

Neil v. Biggers (1972) the usual, current perspective from the legal community with respect to the accuracy of eyewitness identification is derived from this case. The Supreme Court listed the following five factors to be considered in determining accuracy: 1) the opportunity of the witness to view the criminal at the time of the crime, 2) the witness's degree of attention, 3) the accuracy of the witness's prior description of the criminal, 4) the level of certainty demonstrated by the witness at the time of confrontation, and 5) the length of time between the crime and the confrontation. Since 1972, numerous lower courts have been influenced by the *Biggers* standards.

HYPNOSIS

Hypnosis has typically been scrutinized in the legal arena for the following issues: a) is it a fraudulent procedure per se; b) is it being used by unauthorized practitioners, e.g., lay hypnotists, police interrogators; c) is it a procedure by which the hypnotist could take advantage of the client-subject, e.g., signing over money, sexually, etc.; d) is it a procedure by which the hypnotist could intentionally produce later (post-hypnotic) problematic behaviors in the client-subject, e.g., criminal actions; e) is it a procedure that will inherently although inadvertently increase the risk of problematic side effects or problematic behaviors in the client-subject. For those who have a specific interest here, see the excellent book by Laurence and Perry (1988), especially as regards the historical evolution of these issues. For a discussion of the modern legal context of these issues, see Chapter 17 of Meyer (1992). Let us focus here on the most controversial issue in the present day, whether or not the subsequent (or all) testimony of a witness is tainted by hypnosis. Regarding the specific subissue on the use of hypnosis in uncovering memories of sexual abuse, see Peter Bloom's article on this topic in the *International Journal of Clinical and Experimental Hypnosis*, 1994, *42*, 173–178.

State v. Hurd (1981) the New Jersey Supreme Court, recognizing the hazards of hypnotically influenced testimony, and influenced by noted hypnosis researcher Martin Orne, adopts a highly influential set of six procedural safeguards (known as the "*Hurd* Rules" or "*Orne* Rules"): 1) the session should be conducted by a licensed psychologist or psychiatrist; 2) the hypnotist should be independent of, and not responsible to, the prosecutor or the defense; 3) any prior information provided to the hypnotist should be in writing; 4) before inducing hypnosis, the facts the subject has should be obtained and recorded; 5) the session should be recorded (videotaping is desirable, not mandatory); 6) only the hypnotist and subject should be present at pre-hypnosis meetings, the session itself, and any debriefing.

State v. Mack (1980) the Minnesota Supreme Court, applying the *Frye* test (see the earlier section on professional-legal issues), holds that hypnotically refreshed testimony is inadmissible.

People v. Shirley (1982) the California Supreme Court, without reference to *Frye*, at least until appeal, rejects the *Hurd* rules as "pretense," and applies a sweeping rule of inadmissibility to hypnotically influenced (or tainted, from this perspective) testimony.

Rock v. Arkansas (1987) Vickie Rock was charged with shooting her husband. She had a partial amnesia for the details of the shooting. She was hypnotized to enhance her memory, and after hypnosis she remembered that the gun had misfired because it was defective. The trial court refused to permit this testimony because it had resulted from hypnosis, and was therefore considered unreliable.

The Supreme Court held that it was a violation of one's constitutional right to testify in one's own defense to arbitrarily prevent the defendant from testifying concerning the memory recalled under hypnosis. It was the absolute rule in a *criminal* trial prohibiting the *defendant* from presenting hypnotically enhanced testimony that the Court found objectionable, stating, "In applying its evidentiary rules a State must evaluate whether the interests served by a rule justify the limitation imposed on the defendant's constitutional right to testify." So states could prohibit such testimony by other witnesses in criminal trials, or by anyone in civil trials.

Justice Blackmun noted that a number of courts had imposed limitations on the use of hypnotically enhanced testimony and that "the most common response to hypnosis, however, appears to be an increase in both correct and incorrect recollections." The Court felt this difficulty with hypnosis could be cured by a good cross-examination or by rules regulating hypnotically enhanced testimony, without prohibiting it altogether. Presumably, a state could enforce such rules as procedural safeguards to help reduce hypnosis-caused bias. Note, however, that this decision still leaves it up to the states to decide the admissibility of hypnotically enhanced testimony in civil cases.

PERSONAL INJURY

Personal injury law has evolved within the overall tort law, i.e., a subdivision of civil law. "Tort," probably derived from the Norman word for "wrong," generally refers to intentional or negligent wrongs to another person for which the offender may be liable. Rather than implying some sort of moral judgment, tort law is intended to distribute the results of frequently occurring risks in accordance with social policy. A wide range of civil wrongs can be conceptualized as torts, including false imprisonment, invasion of privacy, sexual harassment, malpractice, product liability, defamation that results in personal injury of some sort, and intentional or negligent infliction of emotional trauma (but not breach of contract).

To prove the *intentional* infliction of emotional injuries, permitted as an independent tort in most jurisdictions (i.e., sustained independently of, or in the absence of, any additional recognizable tort), the four required elements are: 1) an intention to inflict injury or "substantial certainty" that the injury would result; 2) defendant's conduct is "extreme and outrageous"; 3) conduct directly or proximately causes the injury; and 4) the emotional injury is severe. In practice, less severity is accepted to the degree the causal behavior is outrageous.

To prove the *negligent* infliction of emotional injuries, claims must first meet the four elements for *physical* injury claims: 1) legal duty to conform to a standard of conduct, 2) breach of that duty, 3) breach proximately causes harm, and 4) harm is legally compensable by an award of damages. Common additional requirements, depending on the jurisdiction, are such elements as physical impact, concomitant physical damage, physical damage causes emotional injury, "zone of danger," and foreseeability.

> Victorian Railways Commission v. Voultas (1888) this English case probably best summarizes the reasons why nineteenth-century courts were loathe to recognize emotional damages, citing (1) a lack of legal precedent, (2) the possibility of fictitious lawsuits, (3) the difficulties of tying emotional distress to a physical event, and (4) the danger of a huge flood of litigation if precedents were overturned and emotional damage were recognized. Courts still warn of many of these problems, and with good reason in some instances.

> Lynch v. Knight (1861) the prevailing legal view up and into the nineteenth century was that emotional suffering or psychogenic pain from a personal injury incident (PII) was not appropriate for remedy, probably most clearly articulated here, in which this court stated, "Mental pain or anxiety the law cannot value, and does not pretend to redress, when the unlawful act complained of causes that alone." So, the basic concept at that time was that, in order to allow redress for emotional trauma, that trauma had to be directly related to evident physical disorder that was in turn a direct result of the "impact" in the PII, i.e., the "impact rule."

> Bell v. Great Northern Railway Co. (1890) interestingly enough, while English courts rather quickly abandoned the "impact rule," two years later, American courts in this case embraced the impact rule.

Ewing v. Pittsburgh Railroad Co. (1892) this impact rule is further supported as a liability-limiting concept in this court's statement: "If mere fright, unaccompanied with bodily injury is a cause of action, the scope of what are known as accident cases will be greatly enlarged." They were certainly correct in this prophecy. Although there were continuing exceptions to the impact rule, it became the dominant legal concept for many years.

Jones v. Brooklyn Heights Railroad (1897) the absurdity of the impact rule was probably best demonstrated in this case. The defendant alleged that a miscarriage occurred because she was in an automobile wreck with a train. Even though there was no true physical injury from the accident, the plaintiff was eventually allowed to recover simply on the basis of what could be termed an "impact fiction," i.e., that a small light bulb had fallen from the roof of the defendant's automobile when hit by the train and hit the plaintiff on the head.

Christy Bros. Circus v. Turnage (1928) a Georgia case involving a young girl at a circus. Horseshit fell into her lap (so there was an impact), and the court allowed damages even though there was no *physical* damage.

The "Zone of Danger" Rule

Until the last decade or so, the usual concept under which a litigant was permitted to recover damages for psychological harm was the fear experienced by the person in the "zone of danger" that was generated by the defendant's negligence or malice. Under this and related concepts, a person could recover damages as a witness to a trauma involving a close relative. The victim actually had to be within a range where he or she could have also been injured.

Palsgraf v. Long Island Rail Road (1928) though not a clear precedent case to the "zone of danger" rule, the judge herein articulated a related "orbit of danger" idea. This case does establish the basis of "proximate cause."

Waube v. Warrington (1935) the prototypical bystander recovery case for the next 30 years. A woman dies soon after seeing her daughter struck by an auto driven by a negligent driver. Her husband is denied recovery by Wisconsin Supreme Court saying it is unreasonable "to include an obligation to render them liable to harm through nervous shock caused by the apprehension of damages to third persons."

Dillon v. Legg (1968) this is the critical case in the development of the "zone of danger" rule. The plaintiff witnessed her daughter being struck and killed by a car as the daughter crossed at an intersection. Interestingly enough, the dead girl's sister was with the mother, but a few yards closer to the actual point of impact. Following traditional "zone of danger" precedents, a lower court in California permitted the surviving daughter to recover for damages, asserting she was in the "zone of danger," while dismissing the mother's claim. The clear set of facts in *Dillon* then allowed the California Supreme Court, when reinstating the mother's claim, an opportunity to point to the rather absurd artificiality of the "zone of danger" rule by stating:

> *We can hardly justify relief to the sister for trauma which she suffered upon apprehension of the child's death and yet deny it to the mother merely because of happenstance that the sister was some few yards closer to the accident.*

The *Dillon* court generated three criteria that helped to clarify the zone of liability (under the umbrella of a "foreseeability standard"): 1) the plaintiff must have a close relationship with the victim; 2) the plaintiff must be in close proximity to the scene of the accident; and 3) the emotional shock has to be the "sensory and contemporaneous result" of the incident.

There have been many and varied interpretations springing from *Dillon*. A major question that continues is: What is a "close relationship"? Certainly mother-child or brother-sister would qualify. But what about stepfather-stepdaughter, good friends, tennis partners, or a stepgrandmother, as supported by one court. Most states, however, would not find some of these relationships to be compelling ones. Note that some states do not even accept the "zone of danger" concept.

Since the 1960s, the trend is toward recognizing that there can be emotional harm without necessarily either an actual physical injury or a direct observation of the event, especially if the harm is "foreseeable."

Molien v. Kaiser Foundation Hospital (1980) a husband successfully sued a physician who had negligently misdiagnosed his wife's condition as syphilis, leading to marital upset and eventual divorce. While there was no physical harm to anyone involved and while there was no direct observation of the relevant situation as it occurred, the California Supreme Court recognized a right to gain compensation because of psychological distress.

TXO Products Corp. v. Alliance Resources (1993)   the Supreme Court gave great latitude to states in permitting the award of very large punitive damages as long as there are basic guidelines to juries concerning the award of such damages. It upheld punitive damages of $10 million in a case in which the plaintiff received $19,000 in compensatory damages. The Court was badly split on the reasons for its decision, but it gave no indication that it is about to begin carefully reviewing large punitive damage awards made in state courts. No single opinion represented a majority view, although six members of the Court upheld the sizable verdict.

Overall, the standard of proof in such civil cases is preponderance of evidence. Findings speak to "general" damages, e.g., pain and suffering, and "specific" damages, e.g., wage loss, psychological treatment. An important concept is the "eggshell skull doctrine," which means you take a person as he or she exists at time of injury, broadened by the findings of some courts to what I would term the "eggshell psyche" doctrine. To assess in the area of personal injury, use: 1) interviews, observations, records; 2) baseline behavior and trait-state assessment; 3) malingering and response-set assessment.

In order to recover damages for intentional emotional distress, a plaintiff generally needs to prove four elements: 1) defendant's behavior was intentional, or at least in reckless disregard of plaintiff's "repose"; 2) the behavior was outrageous; 3) defendant's behavior and plaintiff's distress are causally connected; 4) the distress is severe. (For further discussion, and an excellent review of PTSD and the law, see Alan Stone's article in the (*Bulletin of the American Academy of Psychiatry and the Law 1993, 21*(1), 23–26.)

Molzof v. United States (1992)   the Supreme Court rules that separate damages for loss of enjoyment of life are legitimate and recoverable if allowed under applicable state law. In effect, it approves *Thompson v. National Railroad Passenger Corp.* (1980) in which five types of damages were recognized: 1) expenses incurred, 2) pain and suffering and fright, 3) permanent injury (disability), 4) impaired earning capacity, and 5) impaired enjoyment of life. Loss of enjoyment of life was therein defined in terms of "the limitations on the person's life created by the injury," thus setting forth the distinctiveness of the loss of enjoyment of life for collecting damages.

WORKERS' COMPENSATION

This is not a true tort concept, as it is basically a "no fault" system designed to protect earning ability. Thus, the issue is not one of negligence or liability, but the injury must 1) arise out of work, and 2) be accidental. Originally, this was a German concept, and was designed to reduce tort liability for employers. Yet, it did not really replace tort actions in the United States until the twentieth century. The focus is on actual rather than proximate cause, and it comes under the doctrine of strict liability.

An important concept is the "but for" test (i.e., "but for" the incident, there would have been no injury), to determine if there is a causal connection. However, the injury need not be sole cause of an impairment, though it should be an *actual and significant* cause. Under Workers' Compensation, one may compensate 1) cumulative injury, 2) psychological disorders, 3) even where there is a preexisting condition. Each state has its own laws, which usually cover loss of wages, medical costs, reimbursement for loss of body member or function, etc. One may seek both Workers' Compensation and tort liability at the same time when there is 1) third-party liability, e.g., product liability; or 2) intentional tort by an employer.

Workers' Comp costs have often been enormous. For example, in California 10 billion dollars were required to provide coverage in 1992, compared to 3.6 billion in 1982. Out of every dollar spent in 1992, 28.2 cents went to insurance carriers; 42.3 cents went to attorneys, expert witnesses, and allied services; and 29.5 cents went to the employees.

Possible ways to reduce costs: a) increase communication among staff, pursue any fraudulent claims, and work to make fraudulent claims a felony for all who carry it out (it is a felony in some states); b) designate one person as responsible for the care of any employee, and document how this was done; c) conduct exit interviews where an issue appears, documenting lack of, or possible emergence of, problems; d) encourage insurance carriers to pay off promptly and to cooperate with investigators; e) push safety programs, e.g., with bonuses.

OTHER CIVIL LAW CASES

Griggs v. Duke Power (1971)   the Supreme Court held that a violation of the Civil Rights act does not require there be any intent to discriminate. It also said that tests that have the effect of discriminating are illegal if they are not directly relevant to a measurement of job capability, and that if there are disparate effects on a minority, the employer must demonstrate the relationship of the employment tests to the job.

Wards Cove v. Atonio (1989) overturned legal standards evolved from *Griggs*, e.g., the burden no longer shifts to defendant, but remains with the plaintiff in challenging an employer's articulated justification for an employment practice, and in other related issues. Also, the causation standard is tightened, such that to establish a prima facie case, plaintiffs must "pinpoint" the specific practice that generated the disparate impact. The Civil Rights Act of 1991 then appeared to restore this area of law to its status before Wards Cove, but controversy continues to reign.

Psychologists who work in this area would be well advised to consult Schwartz and Goodman (1992) as a starting point for an in-depth study of the legal issues in this area.

Larry P. v. Riles (1972) although there were many aspects to this case, the use of IQ tests to place children in educably mentally retarded (EMR) classes was at the center of the decision. The plaintiffs claimed that the IQ tests that were used resulted in the placement of a disproportionately large number of minority students in EMR classes, which worked to their disadvantage. Considerable testimony was presented both in favor of and opposed to IQ testing. This court found that the tests violated federal law and the Constitution, and permanently enjoined their use. It further required that any intelligence tests given for educational placement or selection must yield the same pattern of scores for different groups of students, yield approximately equal means for all standardization sample subgroups, and yield scores that were correlated with relevant criterion measures. Essentially, the court found that the tests were racially or culturally biased and that the differences between interracial group means on the tests had not been explained.

PASE v. Hannon (1980) this somewhat similar suit reached a contrary conclusion to *Larry P. v. Riles* when a different court determined that standardized intelligence tests (used with other criteria) were not racially biased against minorities in the placement of students in special classes. In that case the judge personally reviewed each question on standard intelligence tests and "determined" himself that very few of them were racially or culturally biased.

In the *Larry P.* case, the court essentially required that IQ tests produce the same overall result for different racial groups, evidencing blatant misunderstanding about the purpose of tests. In the *PASE* case, the judge intuitively decided whether specific test items were racially or culturally biased, a highly unreliable form of decision making. Both cases illustrate a serious lack of judicial sophistication. The question should not be whether they really measure some innate ability, but rather whether they adequately measure whatever they are being used to determine (e.g., classroom placement).

In the civil area, tests like the MMPI-2 can pose a risk to the evaluator. In July 1993, Target Stores agreed in an out-of-court settlement to pay $1.3 million, to be distributed to up to 2,500 prospective security guards who took the Rodgers Condensed CPI-MMPI, or "psychscreen," in California between 1987 and 1991. An additional $60,000 will be awarded to four plaintiffs named in the lawsuit. Improvements in MMPI-2, including elimination of a number of offensive-invasive items, at least reduces the possibility of such actions in the future.

Detroit Edison v. NLRB (1979) this case found that the privacy interests of test takers were sufficient to bar a union's requested access to scores. But, the Supreme Court ignored the argument that access to test scores would ruin the validity of tests, thus leading to later "truth in testing" legislation.

Meritor Savings Bank v. Vinson (1986) the Supreme Court found sexual harassment to be a violation of the victim's civil rights under Title VII of the Civil Rights Act. (See also *Harris v. Forklift Systems*, 1993.)

Farmer v. Brennan (1994) supported the potential liability of prison officials for "deliberate indifference" in denying humane conditions by failing to take reasonable measures to protect a transsexual inmate who was raped by fellow prisoners.

In a series of cases, starting with *Batson v. Kentucky* (1987), through *Holland v. Illinois* (1990), *Powers v. Ohio* (1991), *Edmonson v. Leesville Concrete Co.* (1991), and *Georgia v. McCollum* (1992), the Supreme Court precludes either side using race, and extended to gender in *J. E. B. v. T. B.* (1994), as the basis for exercising peremptory challenges, in both criminal and civil trials.

SCHOOL PSYCHOLOGY

Most experts view school psychology as having emerged as an identifiable profession in the 1950s, especially stimulated by the Thayer conference, organized by APA in 1954. The profession has developed under the guidance of both the American Psychological Association and the National Association of School Psychologists (NASP). NASP governs the National School Psychology Certification System. Those school psychologists who come from a training program that meets NASP standards, and who also pass NASP's national exam and meet continuing education requirements, may use NASP's term, "Nationally Accredited School Psychologist" or N.A.S.P. A major difference between the standards of APA and NASP is APA's emphasis on the doctorate as the standard for licensure-certification.

Numerous cases discussed elsewhere in this book (e.g., *Larry P. v. Riles, PASE v. Hannon*, etc., and see the section on juvenile law) are directly related to the practice of school psychology. The following are some other cases with specific relevance to school psychology.

San Antonio Independent School District v. State Board of Education (1973) citizens have no direct, fundamental right to an education under the U.S. Constitution. However, under the Tenth Amendment (powers retained by states and the people), state governments have assumed the duties to educate, to tax for it, and to compel attendance. It is given by the state as a property right.

Brown v. Board of Education (1954) each state must provide equal educational opportunity to all its citizens regardless of race. It is seldom noted, but the Supreme Court allowed separate but equal facilities in theory, but said it was apparently impossible in practice, thus disallowing it.

Pennsylvania Association for Retarded Children v. Commonwealth of Pennsylvania (1971, 1977) the eventual consent decree that settled this case redefined "education" in the legal context, in this specific instance broadening it beyond the "three R's" to include training toward self-sufficiency for handicapped children. Pennsylvania was required to provide notice to parents before placing their children in special education classes and, in general, to provide a "free program of education and training appropriate to a child's capacity" for all school-age children.

Tinker v. Des Moines Independent School District (1969) a school's policy of banning the silent wearing of black arm bands in protest of the Vietnam conflict was seen by the Supreme Court as unduly infringing on a student's freedom of expression under the First Amendment. In subsequent decisions, freedom of expression and assembly have been disallowed if they significantly interfered with the school's functioning.

Goss v. Lopez (1975) responding to a suspension without a hearing, the Supreme Court holds that due process (from the Fourteenth Amendment) must include notice and the opportunity to be heard, but procedures need not be lengthy, elaborate, or complex. The need for more elaborate procedures for the suspension of handicapped students for more than 10 days emanates from state law.

Ingraham v. Wright (1977) the Supreme Court held that corporal punishment administered to maintain discipline does not come under the "cruel and unusual punishment" component of the Eighth Amendment because that amendment was written to protect those convicted of crimes. They found corporal punishment was not *per se* unconstitutional, but later decisions held against excessive punishment.

Merriken v. Cressman (1973) a federal district court rules that parents have a right to be free from invasion of family privacy by their child's school, in this case where a private consultant administered questionnaires designed to gain information to identify eighth graders at risk for drug abuse. Such a right adheres to the parent, not to the child.

Such rights were strengthened by the Buckley Amendment or "FERPA" (Family Educational Rights and Privacy Act of 1974, a part of P.L. 93-380), under which schools would lose federal funding if they did not adhere to the pupil record-keeping procedures dictated by law. In 1978, this thrust was continued by the Hatch Amendment (part of P.L. 95-561), which amends the Elementary and Secondary Education Act of 1965. Under the Hatch Amendment, a student may not be required to submit to psychological or psychiatric examination, testing, or treatment as part of any federally funded program unless there is informed parental consent. Collecting certain types of information is expressly forbidden, e.g., embarrassing psychological data, criminal or sexual history, family income, political (affiliation) without such consent.

John K. and Mary K. v. Board of Education for School District #65, Cook County (1987) though somewhat limited in precedent value, a judge held that under FERPA (see above) "raw test data," in this case Rorschach test responses, were part of "educational records," thus allowing access to the parents.

A related issue is test reliability and validity. Jacob and Hartshorne (1991) argue that within school psychology practice, reliability coefficients of 60–65 or above are adequate for group performance measures, 80–85 or above suffice for screening instruments, and 90 or above are desirable where the instrument is a key factor in educational decisions about individual students. Though "construct" and "content" validity is important, most emphasis is usually placed on "criterion" validity, both concurrent and predictive criterion validity.

Debra P. v. Turlington (1984) the critical case supporting the right of a state to require a student to pass a competency test in order to receive a diploma.

Kelson v. the City of Springfield (1985) the primary case that suggests (i.e., it is at the circuit level rather than the Supreme Court) that schools have some staff who have had training in suicide prevention. Jacob and Hartshorne (1991) read the consensus of the professional literature as saying that: 1) each school must orient staff and have a planned response to suicidal students; 2) the designated-trained staff member should be brought in when suicide potential emerges; 3) the student's parents should be informed, and the school should be prepared to appropriately refer the student; 4) the school should be prepared to transport the student to the referral if a parent is uncooperative or unavailable.

Pesce v. J. Sterling Morton High School District #201, Cook County (1987) Pesce, a school counselor, had heard, among other things that a male student, J. D., possibly had some sexual contact with a male teacher. Later that same day, J. D. told Pesce no sex acts had occurred, but that the teacher had shown him some pictures. After considering all the issues, Pesce concluded that it was in J. D.'s best interest for Pesce to keep their confidential relationship intact. The courts ultimately held that the requirement of prompt reporting of suspected child abuse does not unconstitutionally infringe on any federal rights of confidentiality. This trend became universal, and all school psychologists are required to report all cases of suspected child abuse.

Zobrest v. Catalina Foothills School District (1993) the Supreme Court upheld a public school district's payment of a sign language interpreter for a deaf student in a parochial school. This was permitted even though it was clear that the religious aspects of the school were thoroughly mixed with the educational program of the school. In earlier cases, the Court rejected public payment of parochial schools' teachers or guidance counselors. Justice White, now off the Court, provided the majority vote on this issue, so it is unclear how far this principle may be carried in future cases.

NEUROPSYCHOLOGY

Neuropsychology is the specialty area of psychology devoted to the study of brain-behavior relationships. Neuropsychology is one of the fastest growing specialty areas in psychology. Since it commonly deals with trauma and other medical issues, it is not uncommon for neuropsychologists to find themselves in the legal arena. Hence, much of the material in this section and in the next chapter is relevant to their everyday functioning.

Since neuropsychologists often appear in court, but are not physicians (i.e., not "real doctors" in lawyer lingo), their qualifications for testifying are often scrutinized. Indeed, there is little definitive case law here, though the flexible standards of the *Federal Rules of Evidence* (1992) should certainly allow their testimony. Case law has not yet been made at higher levels, such as the Supreme Court and most U.S. Circuits. So, it will depend on state precedents; in many instances, no definitive precedent is available.

People v. Wright (1982) the Supreme Court of Colorado holds "en banc" that testimony by a neuropsychologist regarding test evidence of minimal brain dysfunction can be properly allowed into evidence, in this case in support of the defendant's successful insanity defense.

GIW Southern Valve Co. v. Smith (1986) the Florida Court of Appeals reverses a lower court ruling that allowed neuropsychological testimony. On the basis that psychologists are not medical doctors, it holds that they are not qualified to render an opinion about the presence of brain damage.

Horne v. Goodson Logging Co. (1987) in a more relevant North Carolina case, the plaintiff, Mr. Horne, was injured when a 1,000-pound log fell 14 feet and struck him on the head. As a result, he suffered compression fractures and disc injuries in his back, the loss of his teeth, and multiple lacerations to his face. These injuries were compensated by the Industrial Commission. However, Mr. Horne also suffered a complete personality change, transforming from a gregarious, family-centered, and secure person into a paranoid, depressive recluse who had auditory and visual hallucinations and could not control his temper.

Horne's estimated 60% permanent brain disability was documented in a psychologist's 17-page report based on an exhaustive neuropsychological examination and extensive interviews with him and members of his family. However, the deputy commissioner who served as the hearing officer in this case refused to consider this evidence, and his refusal was affirmed on appeal by the full commission. The commissioners chose, instead, to believe the conclusion of a neurosurgeon who had examined Mr. Horne for 15 minutes almost one year after the accident and had concluded, without any medical history of the case but based on a negative X-ray and CAT scan, that Horne had suffered no permanent brain injury.

The North Carolina Appeals Court agreed that it had been an error for the Industrial Commission to conclude that the testimony of the neuropsychologist was "incompetent." However, a two-judge majority of the appeals panel ruled that because the Industrial Commission is the sole judge of the believability of all witnesses, the case should be remanded to the commission for consideration of the neuropsychologist's credibility. The majority also found that, since the neurosurgeon in this case qualified as an expert witness and testified that plaintiff had suffered no permanent brain disability, it would not reverse the lower decision as a matter of law, but would rely on the commission's reconsideration.

The dissenting judge on the appeals panel agreed that the case should be remanded, but he would have gone much further. This judge would have remanded the case with explicit instructions to consider the evidence presented by the neuropsychologist" (*APA Monitor*, *11*(1), 1987, 6–7).

Sanchez v. Derby (1989)   the Supreme Court of Nebraska validated the testimony of a neuropsychologist who offered the possible diagnoses of a) post-traumatic stress disorder and reaction to chronic pain in a previously marginal personality, or b) organic affective disorder secondary to mild subcortical brain injury. It is also noteworthy that he was also allowed to testify to the uncertainty between these disorders as a reflection of the real world. Thus, this opinion provides a "safe haven" for situations where there is pressure to require absolute commitment to a single diagnosis.

Morris v. Chandler Exterminators (1991)   as noted elsewhere, a Georgia Appeals Court supported the ability of psychologists, specifically neuropsychologists, to testify about the physical causes of nervous disorders. Unfortunately, this holding was then unanimously overturned by the Georgia Supreme Court on May 21, 1992. This is a difficult precedent for neuropsychology.

Some of the legal controversy may derive from the typical neuropsychological exam where the issues are complex, the damage is diffuse, and the number of tests administered is often large. Given the latter factor, it's not hard to find some performance deficit in most examinees.

In preparing for a board or licensing exam where some attention will be directed toward neuropsychology, it is recommended the examinee be familiar with H. Doerr and A. Carlin's (Eds.), *Forensic Neuropsychology* (New York: Guilford, 1991), and *Brain Damage Claims: Coping with Neuropsychological Evidence* (and subsequent updates) by D. Faust, J. Ziskin, and J. Hiers (Los Angeles: Law and

Psychology Press, 1991), and Martell (1992), as well as books that focus more directly on content.

The following schemata is offered as a guideline for discussing, and providing, neuropsychological assessment.

Neuropsychological Assessment Process

(1) Behavior During Interview(s); Physical Appearance
(2) Presenting Problem
    A. Symptoms
        1. Self-report
        2. Observation
        3. Corollary reports
    B. Dimensions of Problem
        1. Duration
        2. Pervasiveness
        3. Severity
        4. Frequency
(3) Background
    A. Historical Setting
        1. Onset of symptoms (acute? gradual?)
        2. Circumstances surrounding onset
        3. Evidence of data re premorbid functioning
        4. Attributions of present and past disorder
    B. Identifying Baseline Data
        1. Age
        2. Sex
        3. Educational background, military record
        4. Socioeconomic status
        5. Occupational history and status, responsibilities
    C. Current Physical/Physiological Condition
        1. Medication: types and dosages, and compliance
        2. Medical complications (e.g., metastasis)
        3. Other factors not directly related to presenting problem
    D. Mitigating Variables
        1. History of alcohol, illegal drug, and prescribed drug use and abuse
        2. History of legal involvement: prior arrest and/or criminal record; prior civil litigation
        3. History of medical and/or psychological treatment
    E. Consequences and Implications of Presenting Problem
        1. Functional aspects of impairment regarding
            a) Job

        b) Family
        c) School
        d) Social milieu

    2. Legal status (e.g., pending litigation)
    3. Necessary changes in habits, roles (especially if acute)
    4. Adoption of coping skills, defense mechanisms, both healthy and unhealthy

(4) Evaluation of Current Performance Capabilities Based on Results of Comprehensive Assessment Procedure

  A. Content of comprehensive assessment battery

    1. Analysis of current intellectual functioning, using global instrument (e.g., WISC-R, WAIS)
    2. Assessment of language skills
        a) Reading
        b) Writing
        c) Comprehension
        d) Speech and articulation
    3. Evaluation of reasoning and problem solving, both verbal and nonverbal
    4. Evaluation of motor speed and coordination, both unilaterally and bilaterally
    5. Evaluation of somatoperceptual sensitivity, both unilaterally and bilaterally
    6. Assessment of memory functions
        a) immediate
        b) short-term
        c) long-term
    7. Evaluation of ability to concentrate and attend reliably to instructions and tasks
    8. Evaluation of visuo-spatial, visuo-constructional skills
    9. Rough screening for evidence of primary sensory impairment
    10. Evaluation of emotional functioning; history and relation to present status.

Application of Data Obtained from Neuropsychological Evaluation

(1) Detailed description of strengths/weaknesses based on an analysis of formal test data

  A. Identify current level of overall functioning
  B. Indicate consistency of current performance
  C. Estimate quality of present functioning vis-à-vis premorbid characteristics
  D. Estimate stability of current results

(2) Evaluation of patient's current attitudes toward his/her situation:
   A. Expectancies regarding recovery, compliance, and outcome of litigation
   B. Attitude toward disease
   C. Motivation for treatment
   D. Understanding of status/condition
   E. Coping skills, responses to stress and crisis
(3) Identification of targets for modification, intervention
(4) Priority of treatment recommendations (including reevaluation and follow-up), based on available resources
(5) Judgment regarding prognosis, based on
   A. Age at time of onset
   B. Phase of illness or disease
   C. Known morbidity rates
   D. Severity of affliction
   E. Accessibility of family, other social support systems
   F. Test results
   G. Patient's attitude
(6) Arrangement for follow-up and continued monitoring

SECTION II:

Special Topics

Chapter 3

PROFESSIONAL CASE PREPARATION AND PRESENTATION: FOR OFFICE OR COURTROOM

This chapter presents suggestions for discussing and preparing cases, whether they are expected to remain as in-office cases or have (and possibly later fulfill) the potential for moving into the legal arenas. By following these guidelines, the psychologist will not only function more ethically and efficiently, but will as a result significantly lessen the probability of being accused of malpractice. After discussing malpractice in general, the first set of guidelines is concerned with case preparation in general, followed by guidelines for entering into a case as an expert witness, preparing for a deposition, and preparing for the courtroom appearance, if actually required. The chapter concludes with an examination of some of the major role conflicts a clinician often encounters in the legal arenas.

MALPRACTICE

Malpractice considerations have been increasing for all mental health professionals. Claims are much higher against psychiatrists, in large part because they prescribe medication and use a number of intrusive techniques, such as ECT and psychosurgery. However, claims are increasing in every mental health sector. For example, during the first 10 years (1961–71) of the malpractice insurance program of the American Psychological Association, only a few malpractice claims were made, and none were paid. During the 1976–80 period, however, 122 claims were processed, with estimated payments totaling $435,642; as indicated in Chapter 2, both claims and payouts have continued to markedly increase since then.

While some malpractice claims have been based on intentional torts (e.g., battery, false imprisonment, or intentional infliction of mental distress), most are based on the torts of negligence and/or contract liability, i.e., out of the mnemonic *D*ereliction of *D*uty *D*irectly causing *D*amage. A *duty* is *breached* (standard of care) *causing* an *injury*. Overall, claims commonly arise from concepts such as unfair advantage (e.g., sexual improprieties), incorrect or inadequate treatment or diagnosis, failure to obtain informed consent, breach of confidentiality, wrongful involuntary commitment, failure to prevent suicide, nonfulfillment of contract (implicit or explicit), defamation, or failure to refer and/or to avoid practicing in a specific area where competence is lacking. As regards actual claims, sexual-impropriety claims and payouts are the most common for mental health practitioners in general.

Dual Relationships

Dual relationships, especially involving sexual intimacies, can occur with any client. They are the primary malpractice risk issues for mental health practitioners as a whole. You should be extra alert if the client: a) reports a history of sexual abuse; b) reports "problems" with a prior therapist; c) has a history of being litigious, even if "in the right"; d) specifically sought treatment because of your "reputation" or particular treatment approach; e) reports sexual affairs, especially if with authority figures; f) seeks out physical contact of some sort or reports particular pleasure in coming to therapy; g) brings you gifts or sends cards; h) dresses or behaves in a seductive manner; i) attempts to control time or place for therapy, becoming upset if you do not meet these demands.

The following related suggestions can be useful:

(1) Be cautious in handling client requests for special considerations (meeting times, payment arrangements, etc.), which, if granted, could be interpreted as signals of more than professional caring. The Chinese proverb "The journey of a thousand miles begins with a single step" is very appropriate here.

(2) Be especially attentive if your attraction to or fantasy about a client causes you to adjust your routine, especially if you find yourself allowing appointment times and places that could facilitate developing a liaison, or if you have increased the frequency of contacts without clear case indicators for same.

(3) Be sensitive to your own vulnerabilities, e.g., the quality of your own intimate relationships. Do you feel alone and need someone to feel close to? If so, is this a resurfacing of a past personality flaw? Would you have any special vulnerabilities that would make this more problematic, e.g., an alcohol problem?

(4) Be sensitive to any fantasies of being a rescuer, hero, or sexual savior to your client, or to becoming excessively absorbed in a client's case, or fantasizing about a client.

(5) Be sensitive to the potential interactions of each client's psychological style with any therapist behavior such as hugging or praising that could possibly be perceived as inappropriate.

(6) Be careful of "role trading" wherein the therapist either too casually or for personal reasons shares life experiences to the point of shifting the dependency balance.

(7) Avoid any bartering of services to cover fees. This can be considered an unethical nonsexual dual relationship, and it can break down professional role behaviors that help inhibit sexual involvement.

(8) Avoid, to the degree feasible, therapy with high-risk clients, especially those with a history of litigation or complaints against therapists. Be at least cautious with those who show dissociative, psychopathic, histrionic, borderline, narcissistic, or dependency characteristics.

(9) Discuss limits of ethical therapist behavior with all clients during initial meetings. A handout that reviews ethical and legal issues and limitations will be informative and even helpful to your client, and may be invaluable to you, should litigation ultimately arise.

(10) If a client seems to be "testing the waters" or is even subtly provocative, seek advice from another professional and make clear plans for confronting this behavior in a sensitive fashion.

(11) If a client does express a desire for a romantic or sexual relationship, do not respond in an offensive way. Express appreciation for the embedded compliment and reframe the client's feelings with an appropriate commitment to the uniqueness and integrity of the therapy relationship. Be clear in indicating that a sexual liaison is not in the client's interests, is not acceptable professionally, and will therefore definitely not take place.

If you do sense a problem developing in this regard, consider the following actions, as adapted from Boyer (1990):

(1) Obtain permission from the client to consult regularly with a colleague, preferably one with hospital privileges. Document the results. If the client needs hospitalization during the course of treatment, collaborate on the case. A team approach can help to keep the client from overwhelming any single psychologist.

(2) Use a treatment plan that is rather traditional. Set clear limits on therapy sessions and phone calls, especially with respect to place and time.

(3) Avoid the appearance of a friendship by not giving cards or gifts to the patient. If small gifts or cards are given to you by the client, clarify that this is not expected. Record any such events in progress notes. Do not accept large gifts.

(4) Avoid touching or behaving toward the client in any way that could be interpreted as sexual. Do not meet the client in places or times that could be misconstrued.

(5) Place responsibility with the client for the solving of reality problems. Avoid interceding on the patient's behalf with her or his employers, attorneys, friends, or family.

(6) As always, clearly document the relationship or transference issues in the client's record. Records of any consultations on the client should also be included in the record.

(7) As a rule of thumb, assume that any set of client records may be viewed by a jury as reflecting the degree of competency, ethical treatment, professionalism, etc., that was afforded to your client. If records are minimal, sloppy, cavalier, etc., then a jury may be prone to view your treatment of the client in a similar fashion. Remember that even though records are generated to help you help the client, they may also be scrutinized by any number of other individuals, e.g., jurors, judges, plaintiff's attorney(s), other expert witnesses, etc.

(8) Refer the client to a colleague if you believe you may be vulnerable to dual relationship pressures. Sometimes even a competent psychologist can fall into some form of dual relationship with such clients.

(9) If, after all of the above precautions, the client complains about your actions to some authorized body, pay attention to the considerations noted subsequently in this chapter.

Avoiding Malpractice

As noted above, the guidelines that are discussed throughout this chapter will help avoid the specter of malpractice, in addition to promoting their primary purpose: effective and efficient professional functioning. In addition, several specific steps may be taken to lessen malpractice probabilities:

(1) Think of records as eventual legal documents, i.e., a complete file record for at least three years (three years beyond the age of majority for a juvenile); critical records or a summary for an additional 12 years (*American Psychologist, 48*(9), 984–986).

(2) Remember that courts can be very concrete in the assumption that "if it wasn't written down, it didn't happen."

(3) Get written releases.

(4) As noted, unless necessary, avoid touching clients, especially those of the opposite sex.

(5) Avoid dual relationships to the degree possible—especially avoid business relationships that involve clients; these easily lead to later lawsuits.

(6) Clarify billing issues up front, i.e., the amount of the fee, rules and costs

concerning missed sessions, when fees are due, duration of sessions, what happens if the client does not or cannot pay the bill.

(7) Don't collect overdue bills from clients whom you could reasonably expect to be litigious and/or who expressed disappointment with their treatment.

(8) Avoid, to the degree feasible, high-risk clients, e.g., paranoid, borderline, or narcissistic clients; chronic legal offenders; sexual problems in a fragmenting marriage; the seriously depressed and/or suicidals.

(9) If you are supervising students or other psychologists, make sure communication and insurance-liability issues are covered and clear.

(10) Remember that courts judge the "standard of care" from hindsight, and from the expert testimony of your colleagues; maintain and document colleague counsel and supervision where necessary (or better, whenever there is a controversial client or issue, or better still, as a consistent part of your practice, e.g., if you feel a client is attracted to you and/or vice versa.

(11) Use any other professional or community resources whenever indicated, and be aware of the confounding and/or exacerbating effects of any psychotropic medications the client is taking.

(12) If you were a supervisor, you should have a) supervised only what you know, b) clarified responsibilities and boundaries, c) been supervised in supervision; d) have had adequate knowledge of the clients, e) documented your supervision.

(13) Make an effective termination with any problematic client: a) discuss it fully as regards issues of why, when, transition, finances, and referral; b) if you feel further intervention is indicated, make that clear, provide some referral options, offer to do whatever would facilitate referral, and clearly state the possible consequences if the client does not seek further intervention; c) send a termination letter to the client, with the relevant details as noted above, in a form that requires a return receipt.

If you become aware that a malpractice, ethics, or licensing complaint has become active, take the following actions, as suggested by professional activity groups in the various relevant professional organizations:

(1) Consider the merits of the complaint. If the complaint is of minor nuisance value, it is possible (though I don't recommend it) that you will not need legal assistance in responding to it. If the complaint seems at all serious, you should most certainly seek the advice of an attorney in responding to it.

(2) Cooperate with the ethics committee or licensing board in their investigation of the complaint. Become familiar with their rules and procedures. Provide the ethics committee/licensing board with the documentation they request. Contact the chair of the ethics committee or licensing board if you have any questions regarding their investigation.

(3) Gather all relevant documents and records, but do not show them to anyone except the ethics committee or licensing board and your attorney.

(4) Do not alter or destroy any documents.

(5) Prepare additional documents, such as chronicles of events to refresh your memory.

(6) Remember that professional case consultation with colleagues is not generally considered privileged information.

(7) Be familiar with all the issues in your case.

(8) Do not attempt to resolve or settle the case yourself.

(9) Provide copies of your files, calendars, notes, etc., as advised by your attorney. Keep the originals.

(10) Avoid any public comments and do not make self-incriminating statements. Remember, most professional liability policies do not cover ethics committee or licensing board complaints, since malpractice coverage is usually restricted to lawsuits. Consider consulting with an attorney before responding to an ethics committee or licensing board complaint.

PROFESSIONAL LIABILITY SUITS

If a psychologist becomes aware of the possibility that a suit may be filed against him or her, the proper procedure is to gather together all available information on the matter, meticulously follow all of the relevant steps noted above, and additionally take the following steps:

(1) Contact your insurance carrier.

(2) Do not attempt to resolve or settle the case yourself or with the plaintiff's attorney while not working with your own attorney.

(3) Provide the insurance carrier with all the written information you have regarding the allegations.

(4) Contact the attorney assigned to handle your case by the insurance company. Follow his or her advice. Remember, though, that you may additionally retain your own attorney on certain issues, if you wish.

(5) Do not panic or discuss the situation with anyone not directly representing your interests except for privileged conversations with your attorney. Avoid any incriminating statements, i.e., don't rehabilitate yourself in public.

(6) Prepare any additional documents that could be useful in refreshing your memory.

(7) Do not distribute any documents without your attorney's approval and refer all communications from the plaintiff or plaintiff's attorney to your attorney.

Response to Public or Media Inquiries

These and similar issues often bring inquiries from the public and/or media. A good rule of thumb is to say "No comment" and to keep in mind the words of the British dramatist Oscar Wilde (spoken in the late 1800s, so think of what he would say now), "In old days men had the rack. Now they have the press." If you fear that one or two of your comments will be taken out of context, and at the same time you do not want to be portrayed as avoiding making a comment, state that you would be willing to comment as long as it is stipulated that the interview as a whole will be broadcast or published. You could then challenge, in whatever fashion seemed appropriate, a published statement suggesting or stating that you were unwilling to make any comment. But, if you do speak out (on this, or just in response to inquiries in general from the media), observe the following guidelines to minimize complications:

(1) Try to make sure the reporter and the news organization are reputable.
(2) Ask that quotes be read back to you as a condition of talking, if possible.
(3) When reporters call, tell them you want to think over their questions and you will call them back.
(4) Think about the context of your comments within the article and how controversial the topic is. Will your comments hurt anyone?
(5) Ask the reporter what assurances can be given that he or she won't draw conclusions you are not making. And then, if you wholeheartedly believe those assurances, ask yourself if you are losing your sanity.
(6) Ask yourself if you are violating anyone's confidentiality in speaking to the media, and if you need a signed waiver.

In any case, using the specific steps noted earlier, as well as the following guidelines, should help you practice more effectively and avoid malpractice.

Response to a Request for Records

You may be asked how you should respond to a request for a release of records.

If the request is from a third party, you need to do the following: a) clarify the identity-validity of the person making the request; b) verify the basis for the request, i.e., a valid release signed by your (competent?) client or legal representative, or what condition makes it a valid issue, e.g., imminent dangerousness of the client, a valid subpoena; c) consider who "owns" the file, e.g., the client's true records versus your "work product"; whether other individuals have some ownership, i.e., if you are employed by someone or are in a joint practice, and also, in the client's world, was it group, family, or marital therapy; d) attempt to make contact with your client to clarify the issues further and, if at all feasible, obtain a more detailed (written) request, with parameters about what should be released; e) consider reasons why you may want to resist the request, i.e., consent is ambiguous, the information requested is not relevant to the request, the release of information would be harmful to the client; f) consider any relevant state laws, practice guidelines, ethical principles, etc.; g) obtain some colleague and/or legal counsel, especially the latter if you decide to resist a subpoena.

If the request is from your client, you will need to consider many of the above issues as well, especially if you decide to resist that request. But, along the way, you should try to clarify (orally and, if possible, in writing) why the client wishes to see the record, what portions he or she desires to see or copy, and why. You certainly need to consider if some of the information may be harmful to the client or to someone else, e.g., if it was marital, family, or group therapy. Consider an offer to your client to counsel him or her, without fee, about the issues that have led to the request, to more clearly assess his or her status or motivation. Be clear in your communication to the client about your response to the request, and record any of the above relevant information for the record. This will be useful if the issue later moves to a court setting.

Another related issue that is murky is what happens to the records after the death of the client or of the mental health professional. Psychologists are ethically bound to dispose of records "in accordance with law and in a manner that permits compliance with the requirements" of their ethics code. Clinical psychologists are given further direction by their specialty guidelines to provide for the disposition of client records after the clinician's death. The most efficient way is to provide instructions for disposition in a will. Other alternatives include specific instructions delivered to one's spouse, or executor, or by taking advantage of a prearranged disposition with a colleague or professional organization.

Most professional groups, including APA, consider confidentiality to survive the death of the client. This issue is highlighted in the case of Dr. Martin Orne (see the section in Chapter 2 on hypnosis). With the consent of a client's daughter, also the executor of the estate, Dr. Orne released audiotapes of his sessions during the 1950s with Anne Sexton, the Pulitzer Prize-winning poet. They were provided to Diane Middlebrook, who wrote a 1991 book that chronicled Sexton's life. Also, Orne wrote a foreword for the book.

Sexton had ultimately committed suicide, in 1974. Orne reports that she had earlier given an oral release to use the tapes "as I saw fit to help others, though she retained a few for herself." Orne is a good example of how someone of even the highest ability and deserved professional and ethical repute can apparently err, especially as he expressed opinions about Sexton and an affair with her subsequent therapist, and other matters. The consensus is that confidentiality survives death, no matter what the family or an executor says.

GENERAL PRINCIPLES FOR CASE PREPARATION

Psychologists can take a number of measures to ensure that their procedures are ethical, appropriate, and expert. This first set of suggestions concerns general issues with which most professionals in these areas would concern themselves; later, we will discuss the preparations for depositions and the active courtroom appearance. The general suggestions for case preparation are as follows:

(1) Don't take on a client in an area in which you do not have a reasonable degree of expertise. For example, there are numerous examples of mental health professionals taking on cases in which they have only a passing awareness of the issues or the requirements of practice. If you are trying to branch into a new area, make sure that you receive appropriate background education and supervision. After all, even the best and most experienced psychologists continue to use colleague consultation throughout their careers; indeed such psychologists are more likely to be the best. It is also appropriate to inform the client, in a nonthreatening fashion, if this is a new area for you and to tell the client what the limits are that can be expected from your participation.

(2) Establish a clear contract with your client. At the very least, make a thorough oral presentation in a contractual manner of what the client can expect from you and also of what you will expect from the client. It is usually advisable to put this in writing. The contract should clearly cover the issues of confidentiality (especially when you are seeing a child or adolescent) and compensation.

(3) Keep meticulous notes on your encounter with the client and on related events, especially in diagnostic cases, because these often will have implications in the legal arena or in other decision-making agreements. Make sure that when you return after a lengthy period of absence from the case that you will be able to clearly reconstruct what occurred between you and the client and that you can report clearly what the client told you. Additionally, it is worthwhile to record your overall impressions at the time when you first summarized the data in your own mind.

(4) Observe relevant guidelines in keeping records. The following are modeled on federal guidelines, and are the guidelines put forth by the Board of Professional Affairs of the American Psychological Association (*American Psychologist, 48*(9), 984–986). A record should contain, at a minimum, identifying data, dates of services, and types of services. Where appropriate, it may include a record of significant actions taken. Providers make all reasonable efforts to record essential information within a reasonable time of their completion. If treatment is involved, a treatment plan must be included. The guidelines for retention of records are governed by state, federal, and professional regulations. From a conservative perspective, the full record should be maintained intact for three (3) years after the completion of planned services or after the date of last contact with the user, whichever is later. A full record or a summary of the record should be maintained for an additional 12 years; the record should be disposed of no earlier than 15 years after the completion of planned services or after the date of last contact, whichever is later. If those records

are subsequently submitted to another professional or an agency, the records should be accompanied by an indication of whether or not the psychologist considers the information (especially assessment data) to be obsolete.

(5) Make sure your relevant history is a thorough one. Many cases have related issues that occur in the history of the client. The relevance of these issues may not be apparent at the time. Make sure that you have looked at all of the potential issues that are possibly relevant.

(6) Use standard procedures, tests, and interventions. Your results will then be more acceptable to other professionals and to the courts. This does not preclude using some unusual techniques, but do so in a context of commonly accepted practices.

EXPERT WITNESS CASE PREPARATION

While these suggestions and principles are important for virtually any professional psychologist, there are several other suggestions that are important if you eventually become directly involved in the judicial process in a client's case:

(1) Take some time to observe courtroom procedures in general and try to observe various mental health professionals in the role of an expert witness. This will allow you to become familiar and comfortable with courtroom process.

(2) Even though experts who are called by one party should be an advocate for their opinions and not for the party, they still must operate within the adversary legal system. Therefore, you should not discuss the case with anyone other than the court or the party for whom you have conducted an evaluation without the knowledge or permission of the court or that party.

(3) Once the opinion has been formed, insist that the attorney who employs you provide the basic facts of the case, the relevant statutory and case law, and an explanation of the theory under which the case is to be pursued. An understanding of these issues is crucial to your preparation for the case, and reports and testimony should specifically address these legal issues.

(4) Prepare your case in language that will be meaningful to the court. Remember that jurors are going to be put off by jargon, or they will misunderstand and, thus, not give proper weight to your testimony.

(5) Prepare yourself to give a thorough overview of all the examination devices that you will be referring to. In the courtroom, you may be asked about the reliability and validity of these devices, about how they were derived, or about what they are purported to measure. You should be ready to answer this in a crisp and efficient fashion, in a language that people will find understandable and useful.

(6) Make sure you are current on the relevant literature.

(7) Make sure ahead of time of the role you will take in the courtroom situation and communicate this to the attorney who has brought you into the case. It is especially helpful if you can get the attorney to role-play all of the questions he expects to ask you, with your answers, so that you both know what to expect. It is also helpful if he will role-play the questions he expects the opposing attorney to ask. Ask him to be a true "devil's advocate" in this process.

(8) When you are close to actually presenting the case in deposition or in court, make sure you can be comfortable with your knowledge of the client. This may entail bringing the client in for visits shortly before the court testimony. In many court cases, the professional may do the evaluation years before actually going into court. In such a case, you really ought to see the client again, if at all possible, to check on prior data that had been collected and to update your impressions and inferences.

Deposition Preparation and Presentation

In virtually every case that takes on a legal dimension, there is a strong likelihood that the psychologist will be deposed. Indeed, in many cases there may be no courtroom appearance after a deposition, either because the case is settled out of court or the material that came to light in the deposition eliminated the need or desire to have the psychologist testify in person.

Many of the suggestions already mentioned as critical in general and in expert-witness case presentation—or that will be mentioned shortly as important in preparing for a courtroom presentation—are relevant to the deposition as well. However, the following are more specific to preparation for a deposition:

(1) Organize and review all materials pertinent to the case and request a predeposition conference with the attorney.

(2) Bring to the deposition only those records, notes, etc., that you are willing for all involved parties to be aware of or, in many cases, to gain access to.

(3) Be aware that there are two types of subpoenas. The first, the *subpoena ad testicandum*, is what most people assume it is, a summons to appear at court at a specified date and time. The second, the *subpoena duces tecum*, requires the professional to bring specific materials to the court.

(4) Remember that just because a particular set of records has been requested, or even subpoenaed, does not mean they must be released. If in doubt, the professional should a) insist that the attorney requesting the information provide a valid authorization from the affected person; b) request a court order before releasing the information (in some jurisdictions, even a court order is not sufficient); and c) remember that it may be in the best inter-

ests of your client or yourself to further resist a subpoena. If you feel this is the case, consult your attorney on how to proceed.

(5) Bring an extra copy of your curriculum vitae, as it is likely it will be incorporated into the record at this time.

(6) Be courteous and speak in a voice that is audible to everyone, especially the stenographic reporter.

(7) Be honest in all responses, but do not provide information that is not requested. Avoid any elaboration.

(8) Think before you respond. You can take as much time as you wish to think out your response since, if your testimony is only recorded in writing (this piece of advice does not apply if it is videotaped for later use in the courtroom), there is no issue of conveying a confused or tentative image to the jury, as there may be in the courtroom.

(9) If an attorney objects, stop talking. It is best to let the attorneys deal with the point in question.

(10) Remember that the opposing attorney will be evaluating you as a witness and may try many things in deposition that won't be used in trial.

(11) Thoroughly read and check the deposition when a copy is sent to you for your signature; do not waive your right to sign it. Correct any errors in it as your attorney instructs. Keep a copy of the deposition with your other records pertaining to that case.

(12) Prior to going to court, review your copy of the deposition and take it with you to the witness stand.

Courtroom Presentation

While all cases in which a psychologist is deposed do not result in a court appearance, many do. The following suggestions are useful when it actually comes to presenting testimony in the courtroom:

(1) First and foremost, be honest in all of your testimony. If you do not know the answer, say so, and offer to give related information that may clarify the question. But do not try to answer questions when you really do not know the answer. Aside from the ethical issues involved, it is very likely that you will be tripped up later in the cross-examination.

(2) Don't be overly reluctant to admit limitations in your expertise or in the data that you have available. If the cross-examining counsel presents a relevant and accurate piece of data, acknowledge this in a firm and clear fashion and do not put yourself into a defensive position.

(3) Acknowledge, by eye contact, the person who has requested your statement, be it the judge or one of the attorneys. But at the same time, as much as possible, maintain eye contact with the jury.

(4) Be aware of the classic errors of the expert witness: becoming a) too technical, b) too complex in discussion, c) too simplistic, d) too talkative

and/or overdramatic, or e) condescending and/or hostile. Any of these approaches is likely to lose the attention of the jurors and may also turn them against you and the content of your testimony.

(5) Avoid long, repetitive explanations of your points. If at all possible, keep your responses to two or three statements, but occasionally vary the format of your presentation so that you do not come across as some sort of automaton. If you feel more is needed, try to point out that you cannot fully answer the question without elaborating.

(6) Never answer questions that you do not really understand. If you are uncomfortable with the wording of the question, ask to have it restated and, if need be, describe your problems with the question as originally posed.

(7) Similarly, listen carefully to what is asked in each question before you answer. If there is a tricky component to the question, acknowledge that and then try to deal with it in a concise fashion. Try to avoid "Yes, but…" answers. If the attorney has made an innuendo that is negative to the case or to you, respond, if you feel it is appropriate, without becoming adversarial. Keep your response unemotional. This *may* be a good time to bring in a bit of humor. However, the use of humor requires *great* caution, as it can easily communicate hostility, which is usually counterproductive.

(8) If you feel the attorney has misstated what you have just said, when he or she asks a follow-up question, take the time to unemotionally clarify what you actually did say, and then go on and answer the next question.

(9) Speak clearly, fluently, and somewhat louder than you would normally speak. Make sure the jury hears you. Speak when spoken to, and avoid smoking or chewing. Avoid weak or insipid speech patterns, commonly marked by: a) hesitation forms, such as "Uh," "You know," "Well"; b) formal grammar; c) hedges, such as "sort of," "I guess," "I think"; d) overly polite speech; e) the use of a questioning form of sentence structure rather than straightforward sentences. Communicate a confident, straightforward attitude.

(10) Avoid using any graphs, tables, or exhibits that are not easily visible, readable, and comprehensible by the average juror.

(11) Be prepared for questions about journal articles, books, etc., relevant to issues in this particular case. This is more important now than it was at the deposition stage. You can't check up on all of the relevant literature, but by familiarizing yourself with some key recent articles, you can more easily blunt an attack.

(12) Be prepared to be questioned about the issue of fees. Attorneys who know they can't impeach you any other way, and fear the truth value of your testimony, especially like to use this ploy, often ad nauseam. Attorneys may ask questions like, "How much are you being paid to testify for this client?" You need to correct that and state that you were asked to do an evaluation, then give your full and honest opinion to the best of your knowledge, and that it was then up to the attorney to decide whether he or

she wanted to go ahead and use you in the courtroom. Also, make sure that you state that you are not being paid for your testimony, but that you are being paid for the time that you put into this trial, no matter what testimony would emerge from that time spent. Attorneys are more likely to attack you for charging a flat fee for a case than by the hour, probably because most of them charge by the hour, a point they would like the jury to forget, especially when it's obvious to everyone they are repeating points, using redundant witnesses, or using delay tactics. If you feel there is any residual implication that you are being biased by the fee, confront that directly.

(13) Be professional in both your dress and demeanor. Informal dress is seldom appropriate in a courtroom. Reasonably conservative attire makes a more positive impression on the jury. Similarly, your demeanor should be professional, and you should avoid becoming involved in any kind of tirade or acrimony.

(14) Never personalize your interactions with an attorney who is attempting to disrupt you. At times, you may find it useful to call the attorney by name, but avoid any type of condescension. If you become emotional and make any kind of personal attack, you will likely taint the value of your testimony. There may be times when you do need to express some emotion in giving an opinion in order to emphasize that opinion. But make sure the emotion is properly placed on the opinion and not as a defensive or attacking response toward the court, jury, or a cross-examining attorney.

(15) Be prepared to go beyond a simple, linear presentation of data. Jurors look for a "gestalt," a scenario that integrates and explains the data. Develop the scenario in your own mind, ahead of time, that makes your data meaningful, one that fits with the other facts of the case.

Just as the psychologist is organizing to make an effective presentation to the court, the attorneys are preparing to devalue any or all parts of the professional's testimony. The well-prepared psychologist reminds himself or herself of the strategies that he or she is likely to encounter.

Anticipating the Cross-Examination

Cross-examination is designed to challenge or discredit those data and opinions that have been presented by the psychologist that are inconsistent with that attorney's case. Severity of the attorney's cross-examination, including the use of techniques mentioned throughout this section, is often motivated by the quality of that attorney's case. The weaker the case, the more likely the cross-examining attorney is to resort to such ploys, as they may help distract the jury from the content of the case. There are a variety of ways in which the cross-examining attorney will attempt to challenge this testimony. Some approaches are straightforward. However, many attorneys are not out to get at the truth, but will resort to whatever means they can (means that are often considered unethical in other professions) to distract or confuse the jury. Among these are:

(1) A primary target for examination is the expert's qualifications. Two kinds of questions concerning qualifications are: (a) whether a witness is sufficiently qualified to be permitted (by the judge) to testify as an expert, and (b) the "weight" that should be given (by the judge or jury) to the expert's opinion. Presumably, the more highly qualified the expert, the greater the weight should be given that professional's opinion. The expert's experience in the area and the level of relevant education are common targets. More often, the critique is directed toward the specialization that is important in this particular case. For example, an expert clinical psychologist may have had little involvement in the area of neuropsychology, and yet the critical point in the case may involve a neuropsychological issue. This, of course, would appropriately reduce the credibility of the expert.

(2) If you have strong credentials, ask the attorney who brought you into court to avoid the "stipulation" ploy by the opposing attorney, quickly stipulating that the expert is qualified, in order to avoid having the jury hear the relevant information about expertise and credentials.

(3) Some attorneys like to use the "original source," "historic martyr," or "stupid experts" gambits. In the "original source" ploy, the expert is asked if he or she did the original work relevant to the issue, or if he or she ever did any research in this area. Conversely, in the "historic martyr" gambit, the witness is asked about those experts who went unrecognized in their own time for their brilliant findings in order to set a basis for criticizing your testimony. In the "stupid experts" approach, studies are brought forth that purport to show that experts are quite often wrong or do no better than laypersons. Be prepared to handle these issues in a direct, straightforward manner.

(4) Another common way to challenge the expert witness is through contradictory testimony from other experts in the field. These experts may testify in the trial, or the challenge may be in the form of a book or article submitted as written authority. A favorite approach is to attempt to lead the witness down the garden path by asking if such-and-such a source is authoritative, etc., and then presenting the contradictory testimony from that source. So, when an expert is asked if this book or person is authoritative, it is often appropriate to say that, "Dr. ——— does write in this field. Other experts might agree with some of the things he says, but he's not my authority [or the only authority]."

If you are pushed to accept the results of an article, you can also appropriately reply to the effect that "There are many articles in this area; this is but one, and it would be inappropriate for me to comment on the findings you mention without looking at them in the context of the whole article. If the court wishes to grant a recess to allow me to do that, I'll be happy to comment on it." The court never likes to grant extra recesses.

(5) Cross-examining attorneys often try to attack the procedures that are used by the expert witness. A classic instance is the discovery that the expert spent a very short period of time with the client. An expert who so cavalierly comes to such an important decision would be vulnerable in the cross-examination.

The particular tests used in an evaluation are also important. For this reason, most expert psychologist witnesses prefer to use a variety of objective psychological tests in their examination. It is debatable whether having the tests computer-scored and interpreted adds something to the testimony. It can be argued that this adds a validation by an "apparently objective other." At the same time, sending off a test for scoring or interpretation can be construed, through the presentation of the cross-examining attorney, as dependency on outside opinions because of a lack of expertise. Also, one is prone to be "locked into" all of the statements made in the computer-generated report. Some may clearly not fit this individual case, and the psychologist may disagree with a number of the statements.

In appropriate cases, data from projective tests can, of course, be used in court, but they are much more vulnerable to cross-examination. A sophisticated attorney is likely here to pull out an ink blot and ask for the expert's response, or a typical response, and then try to get a statement from the expert as to what is the appropriate idea here or what can be made of a response the client made. This is one of those times when it is very critical for the expert witness to communicate that the opinions and inferences have been based on a variety of data and not from any individual piece of datum.

(6) Another area in which the psychologist can be impeached is through bias, for example, by attacking the expert witness as a "hired gun" and asking a variety of questions about how the individual has been paid. The expert should be prepared to note that it was his or her evaluation that was paid for, not any outcome or particular slant to the testimony, and that it was stated up front, "I will make my evaluation and give you my honest opinion."

(7) Another possibility here is to attack the expert as a "professional witness," one who spends virtually his or her entire career going from courtroom to courtroom. People who do a lot of court work are vulnerable to this characterization, and they need to be ready to present a picture of how they become involved in court cases and why they appear frequently.

(8) Another potential point of attack is any special relationship to the client. If there is any sense in which the expert is a friend of the client, is doing the client a "favor," or in turn is receiving "favors" for the testimony, the expert's testimony is likely to have little positive impact on the jury.

(9) Expert witnesses are occasionally cross-examined on their personal vulnerabilities or deficiencies. Any general indications of instability or deviation in the history of the expert witness may be brought out if they can be discovered. Persons who have obvious vulnerabilities, possibly a history of alcoholism or hearing or vision problems (which may in some instances be relevant), should consider means of handling such an attack.

(10) Just as attorneys will try to challenge the sources of an inference, they will also try to impeach the process of deriving the inference or opinion. They may try to introduce at least apparently contradictory data or they may just simply ask, "Isn't this alternate idea *possible*?" It is important for the expert witness not to become too defensive here. There may be a reasonable admission that other interpretations are possible. The expert witness needs to define that we are in a world of probabilities, possibly stating something to the effect that "Yes, almost anything is possible, for example, it's possible it will snow tomorrow but it's really very improbable (this has more impact if you are testifying in Florida in summer than in Minnesota in winter). But I do want to emphasize that in my opinion the bulk of evidence supports the opinion I have rendered."

(11) An excellent way to impeach an expert witness is to disclose prior reports or transcripts of court testimony given by the same expert that are contradictory to the present testimony. The expert should be aware of this possibility, and experts who publish a great deal are even more vulnerable. They need to be able to explain this situation reasonably, e.g., that opinions do change over time and that they may have made a statement some time before in a book with which they do not wholly agree now (it may even be an out-of-date earlier edition), or they need to point out why the earlier comments do not exactly apply here. Again, defensiveness is a bad strategy here. Openness can be the best method of handling this type of attack.

It is important to remember that at its root cross-examination is a process of searching for the truth by challenging the ideas and conclusions of the expert. In this sense, it compresses into a short time the long process of challenge to publication and research. Cross-examination is not a perfect process of truth-finding. The presentation of information to a lay jury may, in a few instances, cause obfuscation through cross-examination. Some attorneys unfairly attack or even badger witnesses. The fact that some attorneys try these tactics, however, does not mean that they have succeeded; such tactics often backfire. Juries probably resent trickery used against credible experts. If an expert has drawn reasonable conclusions based on full examination and has avoided exaggerated statements and emotional responses to cross-examination, the expert will have succeeded in making his or her point to the jury. A dry run, a practice cross-examination, can be especially helpful, particularly for the expert who has not testified before. It may also be instructional to review Ziskin and Faust (1984) or similar materials so that the approaches any sophisticated attorney may take in a cross-examination can be anticipated.

THE PSYCHOLOGIST'S ROLE IN COURT

As an increasing number of psychologists enter the forensic arenas, they encounter ethical situations and practical problems that are seldom found in other areas of practice. One of the most frequent dilemmas concerns being asked to take, in the same case, more than one of the following three roles: expert witness, consultant, advocate. Each has a different ultimate client focus: expert witness—court; consultant—client/attorney; and advocate—cause. Any one of these roles can be proper for a psychologist, but accepting more than one role in the same case, or even blurring the roles' boundaries, is inappropriate (Smith & Meyer, 1987).

Pressure to take more than one role in a single case may come either from within the expert or from the attorney. Pressure from within the expert often comes when there is a late call for help with the case. Demand characteristics of the situation, i.e., the "pull to affiliate," can readily couple with personal needs to put the expert in the classical role of "rescuer." In the extreme, the unsuspecting psychologist may soon be agreeing to testify as an expert witness, to suggest theories of defense, to offer advice on how to make the client more presentable to a jury, and to help select a jury.

A closer look at the three roles will make clear the reasons why the roles should not be combined or blurred. The expert is present to assist the jury with questions that it does not have the required special knowledge to address by itself. In that sense, the "client" is the court. The designation "expert witness" refers not only to the qualifications and expertise of the person in the role, but especially to the rules that will govern the person's testimony. Unlike other witnesses, the expert witness may render an opinion. Further, the expert witness may incorporate "hearsay evidence" that other witnesses may not use, and opinions may be based on this evidence. As Shapiro (1984) notes:

> Whenever one testifies in court,…one should not consider oneself an advocate for the patient, for the defense, or for the government. One is an advocate only for one's own opinion. When the expert witness allows himself or herself to be drawn into a particular position, because of a feeling that the patient needs treatment, that the patient should be incarcerated, or that society needs to be protected, the credibility and validity of one's testimony invariably suffers.

The role of consultant in forensic cases is also one that psychologists are occasionally called upon to take. The "client," in this case, is the side that retained the consultant. Preparation of relevant research data, jury selection, preparation of direct- and cross-examination questions, review of treatment records, procurement of appropriate expert witnesses, recommendations for packaging and sequencing of evidence, courtroom jury monitoring, and other consultant functions may be performed. However, the consultant must maintain some distance from the advocacy role taken by the attorneys.

Thus, as an expert witness, the psychologist will find a primary allegiance to the opinion rendered to the court; as a consultant, to the best information rendered to the client; and as an advocate, to service to a cause or point of view. Again, though each role can be appropriate, each has limits and one should neither take more than one role per case nor blur the role boundaries. In difficult cases of this sort, colleague consultation can be especially helpful. But if doubt still persists, the old adage "If in doubt, don't" is the wisest course.

Chapter 4

SPECIAL CHALLENGES AND CONDITIONS

Several subpopulations of the mentally disordered provide special problems for the psychologist, e.g., substance abusers, the various psychotics, the dangerous (to self or others), the child abusers, psychopaths, malingerers, etc. These are the subject of this chapter. However, before turning to these specific populations, let us first consider the overall issues of comparisons of research methods, the DSM-IV, and the incidence rates of specific mental disorders.

RESEARCH METHOD COMPARISONS

Since there has been less emphasis on the "scientific model" in at least some psychology graduate programs in recent years, licensing and certification boards have given more attention to this issue, even in oral exams. Table 4A provides an overview of the positive and negative aspects of the standard research methods and concepts. You could discuss the evolution of scientific knowledge within the following sequence: a) general ideas and insights, b) observations, c) hypotheses, d) operational definitions, e) experiments, f) models or paradigms, g) new hypotheses, h) further experiments, i) new models or paradigms.

You may be asked about Type I and Type II errors. If so, you may feel like the old sea captain who, on each and every morning when out at sea would arise, have a cup of coffee, open a small drawer in his desk to which only he had a key, peruse a piece of paper, and then take the helm. This went on for over 40 years. Then, one day, he gracefully died at the wheel. The other ship's officers all rushed to his room and forced open the drawer only to find a piece of paper on which was written "starboard is to the right, port to the left." In any case, a Type I error, or false positive, tells you something works when it doesn't; or in judicial terms, there is a conviction of an innocent person. A Type II, or false negative, says it doesn't work when it does; in judicial lingo, a guilty person is found not guilty.

Issues about the validity of various research studies are common in most fields, certainly including psychology. You may be asked how one might go about obtaining more valid research. Some possible points are:

Replication—A major fault in many fields is the acceptance of findings from unreplicated studies, especially when the original finding was obtained by someone with a vested interest in that finding and/or a related theory. Science makes much of its progress in a plodding fashion, not just by new insights and innovative research.

The Use of Adequate Control Groups—Indeed, some research has only an assumed control group. Often, more than one type of control group is needed but is often not included.

Adequate Sample Size—If sample size is not adequate, a few extreme responses can distort the data so as to make it appear there is a group effect of some significance, even if most of the group changed only minimally.

TABLE 4A
Positive and Negative Aspects of Each Research Method

Method	Positive Aspects	Negative Aspects
Case study	a. Generates new theories b. Records rare situations c. Inexpensive and easy to carry out	a. Highly subject to selective and observer bias b. Can't generalize the results c. Can't determine any true cause
Natural event observation	a. Allows study of major event and overall cause b. Is not artificial	a. May introduce observer bias and/or disturb a natural event b. Can't repeat the event; difficult to generalize any results
Correlation	a. Allows quantification and replication b. Need not be artificial, though often is	a. Cannot define the specific cause
Experiment	a. May control, isolate, and define specific causes b. Allows manipulation of variables, repetition, and generalization	a. May become too focused, thus become artificial and miss the overall reality of the issue b. The control that is available is subject to unethical methods and abuse of subject rights
Model or paradigm	a. Provides new insights and hypotheses, and coherence between specific issues	a. Attachment to model may blind one to data that is contradictory

Representative Samples—Using Psychology 101 students is defensible in many stages of research. But, samples that represent society as a whole need to be considered before any significant generalizations can be attempted.

"Blind" Participants—One of the biggest problems in psychological research is the relative lack of experimenters who are blind to the purpose of the study. This lack may be acceptable at the initial stages of a research program, but it should be controlled for in later stages. To the degree feasible, and within the constraints of reasonable informed consent, subjects should also be blind to the purposes of the study.

Reasonable Levels of Significance—Recognize that the .01 and .05 levels of significance were not set in stone by some god of research, but are accepted as a result of consensus decision rules. As such, they may not always work well. For example, in an exploratory study using a small N, reaching a significance level of only .15 may be valuable, as it can be used to refine the research to a point where a higher significance level may be appropriate.

Clinical Versus Statistical Significance—Be able to discuss the difference between "statistical" significance and "clinical" significance. For example, a relaxation technique may produce an average decrease of two points of blood pressure, hardly of clinical significance. But, if sample size is huge, this will attain "statistical" significance, and may confer some undeserved validity on the relaxation technique.

For those needing more specific information regarding research in psychotherapy, consult the excellent article on statistics and psychotherapy research by Dar, Serlin, and Omer (1994). They view the three major problems as: 1) inappropriate uses of null hypothesis tests and p values, 2) neglect of effect size (a variant of the immediately prior point), and 3) inflation of Type I error rate.

DSM-IV

The DSM-IV (American Psychiatric Association, 1994), the fourth edition of the *Diagnostic and Statistical Manual of Mental Disorders*, was preceded by DSM-III in 1980 (DSM-III-R in 1987), DSM-II in 1968, and DSM-I in 1952. One important format shift from DSM-III through DSM-III-R to DSM-IV is from a "monothetic" to a "polythetic" model for qualifying a diagnosis. In the monothetic model, criteria A, B, and C, for example, are specified, and *all* are required to make the diagnosis. In the polythetic model, a certain number within an array of possible diagnostic indicators (for example, five of nine) are required to make the diagnosis. In some instances, the symptoms are ranked by discriminating power, as determined by research. The polythetic model is favored because, overall, it attains greater reliability, yet has more flexibility and more effectively lends itself to empirical validation.

Even though its various editions have been criticized for a number of reasons, the DSM-IV is the official document of the American Psychiatric Association, it has received approval from the American Psychological Association, and it has received wide international acceptance through its coordination with ICD-10 (International Classification of Diseases). For several reasons, the DSM-IV has even more influence than its predecessors. It has a more thorough and extensive description of categories and criteria for diagnosis (there is an increasing demand of third-party payers for a full diagnosis), and it is the dominant influence on all types of health service providers. Another major reason is that there is simply no alternative system that has reached even a minimal level of usage and acceptability.

A major change in the DSM-III—continued into the DSM-IV—is the use of a multiaxial diagnostic system, which allows the clinician to provide several different types of information. You may be asked to discuss these axes, as well as changes from DSM-III-R to DSM-IV. There were numerous changes. Indeed, the simple listing of changes took up 28 pages in the DSM-IV book. A concise list of some of the more important changes are as follows: only the personality disorders and mental retardation remain on Axis II; Rett's disorder, childhood disintegrative disorder, and Asperger's disorder have been added as childhood disorders; there is no separate category of attention-deficit disorder (it is subsumed under attention-deficit hyperactivity disorder); there is now a separate overall category of eating disorders; there are now two separate bipolar disorders, with bipolar disorder II referring to the traditional, severe form, where both recurrent manic and depressive patterns are observed; the phrase "outside of the range of normal human experience" has been deleted as a criteria for post-traumatic stress disorder, and the related category of acute stress disorder has been added; the term multiple personality disorder has been changed to dissociative identity disorder; passive-aggressive personality disorder has been deleted as an Axis II personality disorder but has been retained in revised form as a "criteria set...for further study"; two new patterns in "other conditions that may be a focus of clinical attention" are "religious or spiritual problem" and "acculturation problem." You should be especially aware of any changes relevant to your areas of specialty or strength.

MENTAL DISORDER INCIDENCE RATES

Over the last several decades, there have been many efforts to assess the overall incidence of mental disorder. Previous endeavors in this area provide some useful data, but these efforts pale in comparison with the landmark 1984 study developed by the National Institute of Mental Health (NIMH). This study was initially reported in a series of six articles in the October 1984 issue of *Archives of General Psychiatry*, as well as in numerous follow-up articles, and was then summarized by Robins and Regier (1990).

The sheer scope of the NIMH study is unprecedented. A sample of more than 17,000 representative community residents (virtually a fivefold increase over the most exhaustive previous studies) were studied at five locations (Baltimore, New Haven, rural North Carolina, St. Louis, and Los Angeles). Participants were given a thorough and standardized structured interview, which was followed up a year later with a reinterview. Unlike many previous investigations, this study was not restricted to reporting only on hospitalized mentally disordered persons, or only on prevalence of treatment, or only on current symptoms or level of impairment.

The researchers first measured these groups from the perspective of six-month prevalence rates—that is, how many people showed a particular disorder at some time in the six months during which the population was assessed (Robins & Regier, 1990). They found that about 19% of adults over age 18 suffered from at least one mental disorder during a given six-month period. Somewhat different results were obtained by taking the perspective of lifetime prevalence rates—that is, how often a disorder occurs percentagewise in the population. The lifetime prevalence of any mental disorder in the general population is about 33%, but only 22% if alcoholism and substance abuse are excluded. More common disorders, based on lifetime prevalence in the general population, are anxiety disorders (15%; particularly phobias, 13%); alcoholic disorders (13%); affective disorders (8%, particularly major depressive episodes, 6%); and drug disorders other than alcoholism (6%, particularly marijuana dependence or abuse, 4%). Some disorders were much more common than previously thought. These include dysthymia (3%); obsessive-compulsive disorder (2%); and post-traumatic stress disorder (1%, with a 15% prevalence in Vietnam vets). For schizophrenia, the lifetime prevalence rate in these studies was 1.0 to 1.5%, and for the antisocial personality disorder, it was 2.5%.

The NIMH study also looked at differences in incidence of mental disorders among those who lived in urban central city areas, in suburbs, and in small towns and rural areas. For schizophrenia, organic brain disorder, alcoholism, drug abuse, and the antisocial personality, the rates were highest in the central city, at the middle level for suburban areas, and lowest in the rural and small town populations. Incidence was relatively even throughout these three areas for major depressions and phobias, though somatization disorders, panic disorders, and some affective disorders were a bit higher in rural and small town areas than in the other groups. The only disorder that was found to be higher in the suburbs was the obsessive-compulsive disorder—not surprising, given that many of the characteristics of this disorder have functional value in a competitive society.

Overall median age of onset is less than 25 years of age. There has been an increasing prevalence in persons born after World War II, especially for affective disorders. Also, it is estimated that about 20–30% of those diagnosable as mentally ill never receive any treatment. And only about 20% of these receive care from mental health specialists; most receive it from medical practitioners other than psychiatrists.

Let us now turn to a consideration of those populations that provide specific problems for virtually all service-oriented psychologists.

SUBSTANCE USE DISORDERS

Before proceeding further in this area, let us clarify several traditional terms that are common in the substance abuse literature.

- *Synergy*. A compounded effect resulting from using a drug combination. The effect is *antagonistic* if the effects of one or more of the drugs are reduced or canceled out; *additive* when the effect is a sum of the effects of the separate drugs; or *supra-additive* when the effect of the combination is greater than a sum of the separate drugs. A good example of supra-additive synergy is the lethal potential that results when relatively small amounts of alcohol and barbiturates are taken together.
- *Physiological dependence*. This state occurs when a drug that has been used for some time alters the user's physiological functions in such a way as to necessitate continued use of the drug in order to prevent withdrawal symptoms, such as happens with heroin, nicotine, and even caffeine.
- *Habituation*. Dependence on a drug because of a strong desire to replicate the psychological state produced by the drug and/or from indirect reinforcement of psychological needs, such as oral needs and relief of depression.
- *Tolerance*. The need to ingest increasing amounts of a drug to gain its effect and/or the capacity to absorb large or continuous doses of it without the usual desired or adverse effects.
- *Withdrawal*. The production of a characteristic pattern of physical symptoms upon reduction or cessation of use.

The DSM-IV offers various options for diagnosis, depending upon the characteristics of the substance being used, e.g., intoxication, withdrawal, delirium. However, the two major diagnostic categories, used for all potential substances (except nicotine-only dependence and caffeine dependence or abuse), are substance dependence and substance abuse. The diagnosis of substance abuse requires one or more of the following in the same 12-month period: 1) recurrent use causing failure to meet major role obligations; 2) recurrent use causing physical hazard, e.g., driving while drinking; 3) recurrent use-generated legal problems; or 4) recurrent use despite related social or interpersonal problems, and never having met the criteria for a substance dependence diagnosis.

Substance dependence requires a maladaptive pattern, with significant impairment or distress, with at least three of the following in the same 12-month period: 1) tolerance; 2) withdrawal; 3) increased (over what is intended) amount or duration of usage; 4) persistent desire, or inability to control usage; 5) much time devoted to obtaining or using the substance, or recovering from it; 6) giving up important activities because of use; 7) continued use despite knowledge of having consequent physical or psychological problems.

Modern society provides an increasing number of substances that are abused, and accurate evaluation is difficult. A critical component of the process of evaluation is to sort out the validity of the client's various self-reports. The following schemata may help in this process:

Conditions Conducive to Invalid Self-Report	*Conditions Conducive to Valid Self-Report*
(1) Client shows positive blood alcohol/drug concentration, is experiencing withdrawal and/or apparent substance-related distress	(1) Client is alcohol/drug free, is not showing withdrawal symptoms or evident substance-related distress
(2) Client referral generated primarily by objective coercion, e.g., DUI, threat of job loss	(2) No objective coercion
(3) Client referral generated primarily by interpersonal distress, e.g., threat of divorce	(3) Interpersonal coercion not primary
(4) Clients doubt confidentiality of information they provide	(4) Confidentiality is assured, and apparently accepted
(5) Client keeps interpersonal distance and/or contacts are brief	(5) Adequate rapport has been established
(6) Client is unaware that self-report data will be corroborated	(6) Client understands self-report will be checked against other data
(7) Vague, unstructured interview techniques are used	(7) Structured interview techniques and psychological tests are employed
(8) Client shows psychopathic and/or antisocial personality characteristics	(8) Client is relatively low on psychopathy-antisocial dimension
(9) Client shows inadequate compliance	(9) Client shows adequate compliance
(10) Adequate attendance and/or compliance is a condition of parole, continued relationship or employment, etc.	(10) Reasons for performance compliance are minimal or do not appear to be a primary motivation

The MAC (MAC-R) Scale

An MMPI-2 content scale (49 items) that is particularly useful in diagnosing substance abuse disorders (especially with alcohol, but also with heroin, heavy marijuana use, cocaine, polydrug use, etc.) is the MacAndrew Alcoholism Scale (MAC). This scale is also useful in predicting a later abuse pattern. When MMPI-2 was developed, four religious items were dropped, but were replaced with four items that were found to differentiate alcoholics from nonalcoholics, thus producing the MAC-R. In general, the MAC-R is hard to fake unless one fakes the MMPI-2 in general, so it is usually accurate if the validity scales are within acceptable limits. A cutoff range (raw scores) at 26–28 strongly suggests past or present abuse and/or potential abusers; a score of 29–31 indicates an addiction problem of some sort is very likely; and with a score over 31, addiction is highly probable. Since minorities (especially blacks) and obese persons tend to score a bit higher on the MAC, adjusting the cutoff 1 to 2 points higher is suggested for these clients. Females tend to score slightly lower than males, so reducing the cutoff score by 2 to 3 points is recommended. From a more general perspective, persons scoring high on the MAC present themselves as self-confident and are risk-taking, assertive, exhibitionistic, extroverted, and show a history of concentration and persistence difficulties and acting-out problems, such as in school.

Other Diagnostic Patterns

Interviewers should observe for physical signs of substance abuse (needle marks, abscesses over veins, constriction of pupils) and make sure that adequate physiological screening, such as urinalysis, has been carried out. Also, refer to Table 4B.

Treatment Options for Substance Abuse

A variety of treatment techniques have been used in substance use disorders. Common to most therapeutic approaches to substance abuse are the following: 1) breaking through the denial, often massive denial, that there is a problem; 2) bolstering the often-wavering motivation; and 3) avoidance of manipulations and rationalizations. Certainly, the critical issue in treatment success in any substance abuse pattern is the client's decision to change.

Confrontation is critical with any substance abuse pattern. The following guidelines make such a confrontation more likely to succeed.

(1) The presented facts relevant to the abuse behavior should be very specific, with descriptions of concrete events or conditions.
(2) These facts should be presented in detail, and any inferences should be clearly tied to these facts.
(3) Arguments over facts or inferences should be avoided. But it should be made clear that denials or excuses (such as "I'm not an alcoholic because _____"; fill in the blank with almost any statement—they have all been tried) are not accepted.
(4) The facts should be presented by persons who are meaningful to the abuser.
(5) The confrontation should be made in a firm and clear style, but with affirmation and support. A judgmental tone should be avoided.

(6) Keep in mind that the primary goal is to help the abuser maintain an acceptance of the reality of his or her pattern, and to openly acknowledge that help in changing is needed.

(7) Once such an acknowledgment is made, available intervention options are presented, and a commitment is obtained to participate effectively in some menu of treatment options.

TABLE 4B
Physical Effects of the Commonly Abused Nonprescription Drugs

Drug	Physical Effects
Marijuana	Red eyes Dry mouth Delayed reactions to questions
Cocaine[a]	Moving faster than normal Runny nose Red or watery eyes White powder molecules in nose hairs Dilated pupils Irritable
PCP[b]	Illogical or slurred speech Difficulty standing up Unruliness and aggression Paranoid reactions
Heroin	Delayed reactions to questions Slow walking ("floating") Slow speech Sweating or scratching Dry mouth Nodding Caked white powder around corners of mouth Constricted pupils (pinhole)
LSD	Overstimulated perceptions of reality Objects appear brighter to the user Overexaggerated reactions to ordinary objects Unusual descriptions of the ordinary Users may be sad and depressed over something minor in nature Bad trips—users feel their body is actually changing or they are dying

Source: Adapted from M. Lyman, *Practical Drug Enforcement*. New York: Elsevier, 1989.

[a] When attempting to identify the cocaine user, look for horizontal nystagmus (bouncing eyes); if you move a pen slowly toward the suspect, the eyes will bounce back to look straight ahead (this differs from alcohol use, where the eyes will most likely cross).

[b] The user can be identified by horizontal nystagmus (the eyes will bounce back and forth). Vertical nystagmus may also occur, which is not common with those under the influence of alcohol. Persons dealing with them should be prepared for physical confrontations. Remember that PCP is an anesthetic, which minimizes pain in the user.

ALCOHOL ABUSE

While there are many drugs of abuse, by far the most abused drug is alcohol. While some experts argue that alcoholics should not be held responsible for either their alcoholism or for any criminal offenses that ensue from their alcoholic problems, most theorists, the general population, and the law require accountability. There are clear individual differences, moreover, in how people respond to a drink of alcohol. There is evidence that some individuals will drive "drunkenly" when they have received only a placebo they thought was alcohol. Clearly, most experts do agree that there is significant evidence that a biological predisposition for alcoholism can be inherited. Indeed, there is evidence that, like people, certain genetic strains of rats prefer alcohol virtually undiluted, some prefer it diluted (or on "the rocks"), some prefer either to water, and some totally avoid alcohol.

Stages of Dependence on Alcohol

Dependence on alcohol typically develops in stages, though the sequence below is not inevitable. For example, many so-called social drinkers never move into the second stage and become alcoholics. Nonetheless, this progression is not uncommon.

(1) *Prealcoholism.* Social drinking and an occasional weekend drink are the major symptoms. Both tolerance and frequency of drinking increase, usually slowly. Alcohol use serves primarily as an escape from anxiety, mild depression, and boredom.

(2) *Initial alcoholism.* Tolerance, frequency, solitary use, and abuse increase. More is drunk per swallow. Often there is a shift to more potent drinks. Depression increases, along with a loss of self-esteem. Occasional blackouts occur.

(3) *Chronic stage.* True loss-of-control patterns predominate, such as drinking throughout the day and using any source of alcohol. Inadequate nutrition affects functioning and physical health. Signs of impaired thinking, hallucinations, paranoid thoughts, and tremors emerge.

Treatment Approaches

In recent years, the primary treatment mode for alcoholism has been Alcoholics Anonymous (AA), which was founded in 1935 by two recovered alcoholics, Bill Wilson and a man known only as Dr. B. Four elements of AA seem particularly useful in helping people overcome alcoholism: first, the requirement that they clearly and publicly self-label themselves as alcoholics by admitting to themselves and to others that they need help; second, the quasi-group therapy structure of AA meetings; third, the availability of consistent rituals to respond to crises in their lives; and fourth, the chance for a broader and new spectrum of social contacts and networks with nondrinkers.

From a general treatment perspective, several techniques may be employed in various combinations, depending on the individual client:

- *Detoxification.* Many alcoholics who have been chronically imbibing need an initial period of detoxification to "dry out." This period of hospitalization, or other controlled living situations, also keeps them from giving in to compelling habits that would return them to drinking.
- *Antabuse.* Antabuse can be helpful in controlling the immediate impulse to drink, although the effects of the Antabuse can be bypassed in short order by simply not taking it (this bypass could be eliminated by a time-release, implanted form). Antabuse is of help to alcoholics who want to change, but it is generally accepted that the drug is of little use as the sole or predominant intervention technique.
- *Alcoholics Anonymous.* Involvement with AA or a similar group provides the advantages noted earlier.
- *Family therapy.* Because alcoholism is extremely disruptive to family life, family and/or marital therapy is necessary to repair the damaged relationships, as well as to help maintain abstinence.
- *Aversion therapy.* Aversion therapy can help control specific problem behaviors unique to the client.
- *Psychotherapy.* Alcoholics commonly experience conflicts, anxiety, and self-esteem problems. For these problems, a variety of psychotherapy techniques can be of help.

Treatment Follow-up

The treatment of alcoholism has made progress. Still, only a relative few of all alcoholics in treatment remain abstinent for as long as a year. Most resume drinking and may need to be rehospitalized. Virtually all experts advise support groups such as AA during the first year of abstinence. Many systematically teach clients about the "relapse process" and emphasize that resumption of drinking does not occur suddenly. This counters the myth that alcoholics are "suddenly taken by drink."

Unfortunately, even while in treatment, alcoholics consistently work to protect their opportunity to drink alcohol again if they choose to do so. Alcoholics assume that they will *need* alcohol at some future time. In response to this, several strategies are useful, such as having employees contract with employers that the latter are to be notified if the client/employee does not show up daily for medication and therapy.

Predictors of Treatment Success

Several factors increase the probability of success in treating alcoholics, and the most important of all is a strong decision to change. Older alcoholics and alcoholics who have a reasonably stable marriage have much higher success rates. Being female and/or being Caucasian increases the probability of success. Decreased success rates for certain ethnic minority groups are apparently primarily due to higher dropout rates. Not surprisingly, persons higher in motivation, self-respect, and self-esteem do better.

Prevention

The difficulty of successfully treating alcoholism once the pattern has been established suggests the immense value of prevention. The following steps can be included in any program of suggestions a psychologist might want to make or promote for prevention.

(1) Recognize that alcohol abuse patterns start to consolidate in the 11-to-15-year age range, much earlier than most people imagine. Recognize that genetic and modeling factors are both important.

(2) If children are to be allowed to drink alcohol at all in later life, introduce it to them relatively early and only in moderation.

(3) Associate the use of alcohol with food and initially allow its use only on special occasions; deemphasize its value in controlling feeling states.

(4) Provide a consistent model of low-to-moderate drinking; use beverages such as beer and wine that have a low alcohol content, rather than hard liquor.

(5) Make sure there is a thorough understanding of and agreement on the family rules for what is and is not allowed about drinking.

(6) Never associate drinking behavior with evidence of attainment of adulthood or other identity accomplishments.

(7) Label excess drinking behaviors as stupid and in bad taste rather than as stylish or "cool."

(8) Label help-seeking behaviors in people who have an alcohol problem as evidence of strength rather than weakness.

(9) Encourage alcoholism education in community and public health programs, and support restrictions on the use of alcohol in certain settings and age groups.

SCHIZOPHRENIA

Schizophrenia is generally defined in DSM-IV by at least two (for one month at least, out of a duration of six months) of the following: 1) delusions; 2) hallucinations; 3) disorganized speech; 4) grossly disorganized or catatonic behavior; or 5) negative symptoms, e.g., avolition, affective flattening. It potentially offers a major challenge to any provider of psychological services. It is arguably the most severe mental disorder, not only in terms of symptomatology, but also in its emotional and financial cost to family and society. The odds are that about one out of every hundred people in the United States will be diagnosed as schizophrenic at least once; this 1% rate has been consistent over the years and across cultures. A schizophrenic released after the first hospitalization has only about a 50% chance of staying out of the hospital for two years. Males are afflicted slightly more commonly than females.

Thought disorder, hallucinations, and/or delusions are the common features of schizophrenia, though each may occasionally be noted in other disorders. Other features often noted include confused thoughts, anhedonia, social withdrawal, a sense of depersonalization, or disturbed or inappropriate affect. See Chapter 5 for a discussion of methods of assessing malingered hallucinations and delusions.

Problems in Diagnosis

Confused thoughts, especially confused thoughts that are not persistent or recurring, take place in other disorders besides schizophrenia, occasionally making it difficult to distinguish among them. For example, the use of certain drugs, such as high, toxic doses of amphetamines or phencyclidine, can also result in symptoms resembling those of schizophrenia. Because many organic conditions (such as brain tumors and toxins) can cause hallucinations, delusions, or thought disorders, neurological screening is important in confirming a diagnosis of schizophrenia.

Pathological hallucinations or delusions are sometimes difficult to distinguish from culturally sanctioned experiences that are not particularly pathological in nature. These latter, culturally sanctioned experiences are usually characterized by socially appropriate, productive, and adequate coping behavior before and after the experience; a time limitation of a few hours to a few days; a reasonable degree of family and/or subgroup support; a resultant gain in social prestige or self-esteem; culturally congruent experiences in the delusions or hallucinations; and a relative absence of any other psychopathological indicators.

Causes of Schizophrenia

At this writing, most theorists agree that schizophrenia is a biologically generated disorder. Further, most agree that there is a significant genetic component in the development of schizophrenia. Regardless of the cause of schizophrenia, it is clear that general deficits in the ability to attend to and effectively use information are central to schizophrenia. There are also a number of premorbid predictors of schizophrenia that are worth assessing in a client:

- a schizophrenic parent or parents, or—less potently—the presence of other schizophrenic blood relatives;
- history of prenatal disruption, birth problems, or viral or bacterial infections, or toxic situations during the mothers's pregnancy;
- any indications—as through CAT scans, magnetic resonance imaging, and the like—of wider cortical sulci (the spaces in the foldings at the surface of the cortex) or larger ventricles in the brain (the cavities in the brain that are filled with the same fluid as in the spine);
- hyperactivity, cognitive slippage, any signs of central nervous system damage or dysfunction such as early motor coordination and attention problems (especially difficulties in attention tasks with distracting stimuli and/or eye-tracking), convulsions, significant reaction-time problems, an abnormally rapid recovery rate of the autonomic nervous system;
- low birth weight and/or low IQ relative to siblings;
- an early role as the scapegoat or odd member of the family;
- parenting marked by emotional and/or discipline inconsistency, including double messages;
- rejection by peers in childhood or adolescence, and perception by either teachers or peers of being significantly more irritable or unstable than other children; and
- rejection of peers, especially if accompanied by odd thinking processes, ambivalent emotional responses, and/or a lack of response to standard pleasure sources.

Overall, the preschizophrenic personality of individuals who later become schizophrenic can often be described as odd and isolated, mildly confused and disorganized, suspicious, and/or withdrawn.

A Proposed "Common Path" for Schizophrenia

Examining committees often like to ask the candidate to discuss the evolution of some disorder. Two favorites in this regard are schizophrenia and the psychopath-antisocial personality disorder (discussed later in this chapter). A common path or sequence for the development of schizophrenia is as follows. The first clear signs of schizophrenia usually occur in late adolescence. However, they are often preceded by evidence of incipient disorder, such as developmental lags and/or disabilities, learning and/or attentional disabilities, school and conduct problems, rejection by or distancing from peers, odd behavior patterns, etc. A family history and/or birth or prenatal disruption is common. Emerging problems in attention, affect, and information processing naturally lead to an increase in odd interpersonal and speech behaviors, a decrease in information helpful in effective coping, and greater interpersonal distancing. As these occur over time, interpersonal rejection by peers and family members increases. Concomitantly, academic and vocational performance declines.

Operating out of a restricted social and information base, the person is likely to experience feelings of depersonalization, and a loss in self-identity or, if expressed in psychodynamic terms, a weakening of ego boundaries.

At this point, if they have not yet been experienced, hallucinations or delusions are probable, signaling a breakdown in the sense of self and in the standard coping behaviors. Formal thought disorder, increased depersonalization, and more disorganized/bizarre behaviors also occur as allied patterns. The person may now be informally labeled as "mentally ill" or "crazy," through the actions of family, peers, coworkers, and the like. Any significant continuance of the symptoms usually leads to formal labeling and hospitalization.

This sequence is common, though not inflexible; hospitalization may occur earlier in the sequence, for example, and other factors later. One feature, however, remains constant: in Western cultures the label *schizophrenia* is difficult to discard even when the person manages to function normally.

Treatment Issues

No matter what intervention is used, treatment (more accurately, remission and rehabilitation) of schizophrenia is a difficult and long-term, if not lifelong, enterprise. There are several prognostic indicators that point to a positive chance of remission: 1) being married, or at least having a previous history and/or present status of stable, consistent sexual-social adjustment; 2) having a family history of affective disorder rather than schizophrenic disorder; 3) the presence of an affective pattern (either elation or depression) in the acute stage of the schizophrenic disorder; 4) abrupt onset of the disorder occurring later in adulthood; 5) an adequate premorbid school and/or vocational adjustment; 6) evidence of premorbid competence in interpersonal relationships; 7) higher socioeconomic status; 8) a short length of stay in the hospital; 9) an absence of indications of brain dysfunction and/or electroconvulsive therapy (ECT) treatment; 10) a nonparanoid subdiagnosis; 11) a family history of alcoholism; 12) psychomotor retardation; and 13) evidence of clear precipitating factors at the onset of the disturbance.

Negative symptoms (affective flattening, alogia, avolition/apathy, anhedonia/asociality, and attentional impairment) have been found to be directly correlated with a high rate of remission, slow onset, and higher probability of permanent disability for schizophrenics. Positive symptoms (hallucinations, delusions, positive formal thought disorder, and bizarre behavior) predicted future hospitalizations, but were relatively weak and unspecific as predictors of other variables. Two negative symptoms, anhedonia and affective flattening, were the strongest independent predictors of negative outcome. Patients with the poorest long-term outcome tend to show greater increases in negative symptoms during the early years of their illness. Early and progressive negative symptoms may signal a process leading to long-term disability.

PARANOID DISORDERS

The paranoid disorders are not a separate category in DSM-IV, and DSM-IV uses the term *delusional disorder* for the psychotic condition whose symptoms are dominated by various nonfragmented delusions. Unlike paranoid schizophrenia, there is not much fragmentation of thoughts nor as great an impairment in functioning. The nonpsychotic paranoid personality disorder is even less disturbed in daily functioning and has only the beginnings of thought patterns that could be considered to be delusions. See Chapter 5 for a discussion of malingered delusions.

Paranoid Disorders Compared

Paranoid schizophrenia shares some commonalities with both the paranoid disorders and the other schizophrenic disorders. As the following breakdown of most paranoid patterns indicates, it also contrasts with these disorders (see Table 4C).

Stages of Paranoid Development

The paranoid component commonly evolves in the following sequence:

(1) *General distancing*. Shaming during childhood, child abuse, or other environmental trauma creates an emotional distancing from others. The parents usually communicate messages such as "You are different from others" or "You should be very careful about making mistakes." Thus, the child accepts a basic concept that he or she is different and that others' evaluations are important and are often negative.

(2) *Distrust*. Lacking the emotional and interpersonal feedback available in normal relationships, the person develops an attitude of distrust toward others and the world in general.

(3) *Selective perception and thinking*. The distrust often brings about a more selective filtering in the initial perception of information and then in the processing of that information in thought. This adds to further distancing and distorting in the person's relationship with the world.

(4) *Anxiety and anger*. The person suppresses anxiety and uncertainty by viewing others as the source of problems. A hostile orientation toward the world easily flares into anger and suspiciousness toward others. Interpersonal patterns that keep an emotional distance develop further and, in turn, others tend to avoid the person, possibly making him or her the butt of social jokes or negative nicknames.

(5) *Distorted insight*. As distancing and hostility become more focused, the person develops a sense of "seeing it all clearly now," sometimes referred to as a "paranoid illumination." Targets for hostility become specific, and the person accepts his or her reasons for the behavior as fact.

TABLE 4C
Paranoid Disorders Compared

Paranoid Schizophrenia	*Other Paranoid Disorders*
The delusional system is poorly organized and may contain a number of delusions that change over time. Schizophrenia and the belief system disorder are both fundamental to the abnormality.	The irrational beliefs may not be so severe as to constitute a delusion, or when existent, there are fewer of them, and they don't often change. A belief system is the fundamental abnormality.
A generally bizarre appearance and attitude.	Appearance of normality.
Problems in reality contact.	Relatively good reality contact.
The delusions are wide-ranging, including persecution, jealousy, grandiosity, irrelevant thoughts.	The delusions are usually of persecution or nonreality-based jealousy.
Develops later in life.	There is a more consistent relation to early developmental patterns.
Biological factors are generally the significant contributing causes.	Psychological factors are generally the primary causes.

Just as paranoid schizophrenia can be contrasted with the other paranoid disorders, it can also be contrasted with the other schizophrenic disorders.

Paranoid Schizophrenia	*Other Schizophrenic Disorders*
Depression is not very common.	Depression or other mood disorder is more common.
Develops later in life.	First manifestations occur in adolescence or late adolescence.
More common in males.	Approximately equal incidence in males and females.
Often some reasonably normal-appearing outward behaviors.	More disoriented or withdrawn appearance.
Higher intellectual ability than other schizophrenics.	Often of lower-than-average intelligence.
Rare occurrence in many rural non-Western cultures.	Approximately equal occurrence across cultures.
Proportionately shorter hospital stays.	Tend toward long periods of hospitalization.
Tend toward mesomorphic body build (the body of the powerful athlete).	No specific body build.

(6) *Deterioration*. Specification of targets and acceptance provoke a break from reality, resulting in delusions. Some or all of the few supportive interpersonal relationships still available are lost. The paranoid is truly isolated emotionally and cognitively and becomes even more dependent on the erroneous belief systems that have been generated. From this point on, the disorder pattern becomes self-perpetuating.

Treatment of Paranoid Patterns

Treatment of paranoid disorders is especially difficult because paranoids are constantly on guard against intrusions and assaults on their vulnerability. They accurately interpret therapy as a situation that will force them to confront deficits and vulnerabilities in themselves. As a result, they seldom seek treatment.

To intervene effectively with paranoid individuals, one must accept and empathize with the delusions and yet not lose integrity by participating in the delusional system. For example, one may note correlates between one's own life and the client's, which gives the client a potential new frame of reference as well as a new model for coping with vulnerability and fear. Humor—which is notably absent in many paranoids—can be modeled, as can other positive cognitive coping systems.

MOOD (OR AFFECT) DISORDER PSYCHOSES

Mood (or affect) disorder psychoses involve the extremes of mood or feeling, such as mania, depression and bipolar disorder (manic-depressive disorder), and related patterns.

Mania

The three traditional cardinal features of mania are hyperactive motor behavior, labile euphoria or irritability, and flight of ideas. Disorders including a clear manic component account for only about 5% of psychiatric hospital admissions, whereas the diagnosis of unipolar depression (depression without mania) is common. Bipolar disorder is the DSM-IV term for a severe level of disorder (often manifesting a psychotic level of adjustment) that includes both mania and depression. The incidence of severe bipolar disorder, usually diagnosed as bipolar II disorder in DSM-IV, is 0.5%. Nearly all theorists accept the ideas that a biological disorder is most often the major contributory factor in primary mania and that the biological factor is genetic in nature.

Lithium reverses the symptoms of mania in about 70 to 80% of cases. It is most effective in cases of more severe manic patterns and in those whose last episode was a manic one rather than a depressive one. Lithium therapy is somewhat more demanding than other chemotherapy: Because the kidneys absorb lithium rapidly, it must be taken in divided dosages to avoid damage to the renal system. Educating clients about its use is most important. They must, for example, take it continuously and on schedule even though they may feel well (and manics feel quite well at times). A lack of informed consent in regard to this education leaves one liable if the manic is damaged by abuse of the medication regimen (see also Chapter 6). Divalproex sodium helps about one-third of those who can't take lithium. Both drugs improve clients' conditions about 50%.

Depression

These are the common diagnostic dilemmas that lead to the misdiagnosis of affective disorder as schizophrenia:

(1) Mistaking anhedonia and depressive depersonalization for schizophrenic emotional blunting.
(2) The superimposition of a manic or depressive psychosis on the substrate of an introverted personality.
(3) Affective psychosis in mentally retarded individuals.
(4) Incomplete interepisodic recovery.
(5) Rapid-cycling bipolar affective disorder.
(6) The predominance of irritability, hostility, and cantankerousness.
(7) Mistaking paranoid ideation for schizophrenia.
(8) The equation of other "bizarre" ideation with schizophrenia.
(9) Sleep deprivation and metabolic disturbances secondary to reduced caloric and fluid intake.
(10) The superimposition of unsuspected alcohol and drug withdrawal states.
(11) Difficulty in distinguishing formal thought disorder from flight of ideas.

Depression is classically manifested in one or more of the following primary symptoms:

- dysphoria (feeling bad) and/or apathetic mood
- a loss of usual sources of reinforcement in the environment (a stimulus void)
- chronic inability to experience pleasure (anhedonia)

Depression is often associated with a number of secondary symptoms as well:

- withdrawal from contact with others
- rumination about suicide and/or death, a sense of hopelessness, sleep disturbance, particularly early-morning awakening
- psychomotor agitation or retardation
- disruption of and/or decrease in eating behaviors
- self-blame, a sense of worthlessness, feelings of guilt with no solid reason

for them;
- lack of decisiveness, slowed thinking, lack of concentration;
- increased alcohol or drug use;
- crying for no apparent reason.

It is estimated that 20 to 40 million persons in the United States have experienced a serious depression of some type. This approximate rate of 6 to 10% has remained relatively stable for several decades. You may be asked to explain the phenomenon that depression is often estimated as being nearly twice as common in women as in men (though the distribution is about equal for bipolar disorder). A popular theory has been that women's lives are more oppressive, reflecting social roles, discrimination, etc. There is some support for this, i.e., some evidence of recent increases in depression in young men, possibly reflecting changes in social roles. Yet, it conflicts with other findings, e.g., that the rate of depression in blacks age 30–64 is lower than in a comparable white group. Some try to explain the phenomenon in women as a result of higher "stress," but if this is so, then why do women live longer if under so much more stress? Obviously, it is a complex issue.

About 80% of the psychotropic medication dispensed for depression is prescribed by nonpsychiatrists—primarily internists, gynecologists, and family practitioners. Depression is especially problematic for psychologists when there is the related issue of suicide (discussed later in this chapter).

Many causes may be primary in any one case of depression, but overall, the external and internal factors usually combine in a self-perpetuating sequence like the following:

(1) negative environmental conditions combine with a possible biological predisposition, leading to the first manifestation of depression (indeed, there are estimates that as high as 8 to 9% of children experience a major depression in the course of a year, and even those children age 8–13 who show a clear though even mild depressive episode have a much higher rate than average of showing significant depression in adult life); followed by

(2) social withdrawal combined with less effective information processing;

(3) inadequate social behaviors combined with guilt and self-blame;

(4) further self-devaluation combined with social withdrawal; and finally

(5) secondary biological changes that facilitate further depression.

POST-TRAUMATIC STRESS DISORDER (PTSD)

Post-traumatic stress disorder (PTSD) first appeared in DSM-III (1980) as a compromise between psychiatric diagnosticians and Vietnam vets groups that lobbied for a "post-Vietnam syndrome." PTSD is a separate subcategory of anxiety disorder in which a traumatic event, such as combat in war or a natural disaster, produces disabling psychological reactions; for legal purposes, a subjective condition is transformed into an objective situation. DSM-IV adds the category of acute stress disorder to help differentiate the problems of the PTSD category. (See also PTSD in Chapter 2.) Yet, unlike neurosis whose etiology is usually complex, the etiology of PTSD is straightforward and "face valid," making it easier for juries to understand and accept. While preexisting personality factors can facilitate the emergence of PTSD, the duration and severity of the stress itself are also directly related to the probability of an occurrence of PTSD, and to the following typical trauma-reaction sequence:

(1) *Shock period*. Victims are disoriented and feel helpless. Initially, victims may be emotionally numb or flat, but they soon become highly suggestible to cues and influences from others. Immediate intervention to provide a supportive structure is very important.

(2) *Denial period*. After the shock has worn off, many victims shift into a denial phase, even to the development of a spirit of quasi-celebration.

(3) *Reality phase*. When individuals eventually face the actual impact of the trauma, reality intrudes and delayed depression, anxiety, and phobic responses occur.

(4) *Recovery period*. Recovery occurs, even though in some cases post-traumatic responses surface and must be dealt with. Even people not seriously affected may have a continuing need to talk over the events.

Related PTSD Issues

PTSD is not necessarily a standard reaction to the stressor, but given the severity of the trauma, the PTSD is an understandable reaction. It is probably not as common or as specific in its correlates as plaintiff's attorneys would sometimes like us to believe. Estimates of prevalence vary, with the best estimates being about 1 to 10% in the general population, and about 15% in Vietnam veterans.

Some people do recover spontaneously from PTSD over varying time periods, while in others the propensity toward the terror response remains for decades. Early interventions, with chemotherapy and psychotherapy, reduce the suffering as well as the long-term vulnerability. The classic principles of crisis intervention (that is, immediacy, proximity, and expectancy) provide an excellent framework within which to carry out any such treatment. Immediacy refers to the early detection and treatment of the disorder, with an emphasis on returning individuals to their normal life situations as quickly as possible. Proximity emphasizes the need to treat them in their ongoing world, and to avoid hospitalization. Lastly, expectancy is the communication that while their reaction is quite normal, it does not excuse them from functioning adequately.

Flashbacks, or vivid reexperiencing of the traumatic event, are commonly reported in those cases of PTSD that make it into the legal arena. The dramatic quality of flashback symptoms is certainly impressive; the difficulty is in deciphering the veracity of such reports. The following criteria are effective in helping to substantiate true flashback:

- The flashback is sudden and unpremeditated.
- The flashback is uncharacteristic of the individual.
- There is a retrievable history of one or more intensely traumatic events that are reenacted in the flashback.
- There may be amnesia for all or part of the episode.
- The flashback lacks apparent current and specific motivation.
- The current trigger stimuli reasonably resemble the original experiences.
- The individual is at least somewhat unaware of the specific ways he or she has reenacted some of the prior traumas.
- The individual has, or has had, other believable symptoms of PTSD.

In early cases of PTSD in the legal arena, PTSD was more often presented as "sick," as a condition generating insanity or at least some mitigation of legal responsibility. In more recent times, it has been presented as a reasonable or normal response, e.g., in *Ibn-Tamas v. United States*, reflected in the changes in DSM-IV.

Since PTSD has the status of a "medical diagnosis," it allows a possible avoidance of recent legislative reforms that place limits on, or even exclude, damages for noneconomic losses such as pain, suffering, and emotional distress. As such, it is likely to be an even more popular diagnosis in such legal arenas.

MULTIPLE PERSONALITY DISORDER (MPD)

The essential feature of the multiple personality disorder (termed dissociative identity disorder in DSM-IV) is the existence of two or more distinct personalities in one individual. Most studies that attempt to document multiple personality find it to be relatively rare. Reports in recent years suggest a possibly increased rate. Several factors may be involved in such an increase, e.g., multiple personalities may have traditionally been misdiagnosed as other disorders, such as schizophrenia. Several experts have noted that several secondary gain factors (both for the client and for the therapist) may generate a perceived but inaccurately diagnosed case of MPD, or may expand the number of personalities in a true case. For example:

- Clients with hysteric conditions or certain personality disorders may be motivated by a desire to seem special, and the glamour and drama of the multiple personality may help them unconsciously produce a false appearance of multiple personality.
- Clients who are in legal troubles, like Kenneth Bianchi, the "Hillside Strangler," may produce a multiple personality facade in order to escape responsibility for their behaviors.

- Therapists are likely to find the prestige attached to treating multiple personalities alluring and thus help to produce false cases.

In 1993, in *U.S. v. Denny-Shaffer*, the Tenth Circuit reversed the conviction of Bridget Denny-Shaffer, who had kidnapped an infant in New Mexico while impersonating a medical student. The Tenth Circuit held that the lower court erred in not submitting her insanity defense to a jury, i.e., was her host MPD personality in control when the crime was committed? It is noteworthy that the experts on both sides did agree that she had a host (the one known to society) or dominant personality as well as several "alter" personalities. The issue and outcome may well have been different if there was disagreement about the validity of her MPD diagnosis, or the validity of MPD diagnosis in general.

Not surprisingly, even in legitimate cases, the new personalities often incorporate traits that are opposite from those of the original personality and that demonstrate behaviors that the person previously found difficult to express. The original personality tends to be relatively conservative and socially constricted, while flamboyant personal styles and the acting-out of sexual and aggressive behaviors may find an outlet in the newer roles.

Persons are especially susceptible to developing a multiple personality if they (1) were abused as children; (2) are under significant stress; (3) have had somewhat contradictory personality factors; (4) have experienced maternal rejection; (5) are impressionable, suggestible, and/or dependent; (6) tend toward overdramatic behaviors; and (7) have unrealistically high standards of performance.

Validation of the disorder is best done by: a) accurate history-taking with a match to clinical syndrome, b) use of family and other collateral contacts, c) ruling out of other possibilities, d) follow-up to assess stability, e) psychological test and lab studies for unique aspects.

The traditional treatment for multiple personality is hypnosis, which is used to get in touch with the dissociated subpersonalities. Hypnosis has generally been helpful in an overall treatment program. It is true that since hypnosis itself involves a dissociative experience, it may iatrogenically increase the tendency to produce multiple personalities, particularly in the short run.

SLEEPWALKING DISORDER

Sleepwalkers often present management-liability-control issues, and any psychologist who works with such problems is advised to present the client with the following recommendations, as adapted from Gilmore (1991):

(1) Use no drugs, alcohol, or caffeine, and use no psychotropic medications unless prescribed by a physician who is aware of the potential of such medications to exacerbate sleepwalking. Avoid any over-the-counter cold remedies or diet pills that contain stimulants.

(2) Remove, to the degree feasible, access to any lethal weapons.

(3) Take special precautions, such as placing locks on doors and windows, tying one ankle to the bedpost, and placing a "kiddie fence" by the bedroom door.

(4) Sleep on the ground floor.

(5) Get psychiatric help for depression and/or other concurrent emotional problems.

(6) Learn stress management skills and obtain skills and reassurance to lower anxiety, and consider marital counseling for related stress.

(7) Maintain a regular sleep-wake cycle and get adequate sleep at regular intervals.

(8) Get a complete assessment by an expert in sleep disorders who can monitor physiological measurements.

MENTAL RETARDATION

Mental retardation is an issue that often confounds the delivery of psychological services. It is defined in terms of deficits in an individual's intellectual functioning and in the capacity to achieve a satisfactory level of social adjustment. (See *Mental Retardation: Definition, Classification, and Systems of Support,* 9th ed, 1994, authored and published by the American Association of Mental Retardation, P.O. Box 1202, Washington, DC 20013.) Also see the special-section issue, "Mental Retardation and Mental Illness," *Journal of Consulting and Clinical Psychology, 62,* 1994, especially the article by Bersoff, Glass and Blain. About 1% of the population falls into this category. The number of institutionalized mentally retarded has dropped from 132,500 to approximately 90,000 at present, reflecting the policy of deinstitutionalization. The criteria for severity of mental retardation are noted in Table 4D. (See also *Penry v. Lynaugh,* 1988.)

THE ANTISOCIAL PERSONALITY DISORDER AND THE PSYCHOPATH

The antisocial personality is typically a narcissistic, amoral, and impulsive individual who chronically manifests antisocial behavior and is unable to delay gratification. There is a heightened need for stimulation and a lack of response to standard societal control procedures.

Evolution of Terms

The term *antisocial personality* is the result of an evolution through a number of terms, the most widely known of which is undoubtedly *psychopath.* In about 1800,

TABLE 4D
Criteria for Severity of Mental Retardation, by Age

Level	Preschool Age (birth to 5 years)	School Age (6 to 12 years)	Adult (over 21 years)
Mild Retardation (IQ of 50–55 to 70 by DSM-IV) (about 85% of retarded persons)	Can develop social and language skills; less retardation in sensorimotor areas. Seldom distinguished from normal until older. Referred to as educable.	Can learn academic skills to approximately sixth-grade level by late teens. Cannot learn general high school subjects. Needs special education, particularly at secondary-school levels.	Capable of social and vocational adequacy with proper education and training. Frequently needs guidance when under serious social or economic stress.
Moderate Retardation (35–40 to 50–55) (10% of retarded persons)	Can talk or learn to communicate. Poor social awareness. Fair motor development. May profit from self-help. Can be managed with moderate supervision.	Can learn functional academic skills to approximately fourth-grade level by late teens if given special education.	Capable of self-maintenance in unskilled or semi-skilled occupations. Needs supervision and guidance when under mild social or economic stress.
Severe Retardation (20–25 to 35–40) (3–4% of retarded persons)	Poor motor development. Speech is minimal. Few or no communication skills. Generally unable to profit from training in self-help.	Can talk or learn to communicate. Can be trained in elemental health habits. Cannot learn functional academic skills. Profits from systematic habit training.	Can contribute partially to self-support under complete supervision. Can develop self-protection skills to a minimally useful level in a controlled environment.
Profound Retardation (IQ of 20–25 or below) (1–2% of retarded persons)	Minimal capacity for functioning in sensorimotor areas. Needs nursing care.	Some motor development present. Cannot profit from training in self-help. Needs total care.	Some motor and speech development. Totally incapable of self-maintenance. Needs complete care and supervision.

Source: Adapted in part from J. M. Sattler, *Assessment of Children's Intelligence and Special Abilities*. Boston: Allyn & Bacon, 1982, p. 426.

Philippe Pinel coined the term *manie sans délire* to reflect the fact that these individuals manifest extremely deviant behavior but show no evidence of delusions, hallucinations, or other cognitive disorders. Late in the nineteenth century, the label *psychopathic inferiority*, introduced by Johann Koch, became the accepted term.

Expositions by a number of individuals, particularly by Cleckley, brought the term into common usage.

Despite this history of the term, early editions of the DSM used the term *socio-pathic personality* to emphasize the environmental factors that allegedly generated the disorder. The DSM-II substituted the label *antisocial personality disorder* to shift the emphasis to patterns of observable, definable behavior, and this term is retained in subsequent DSM's, including DSM-IV. Incidentally, if the individual is younger than 18, the appropriate diagnosis is "conduct disorder."

Many experts feel that there is reasonable evidence to further subdivide the anti-social personality category, with the traditional division into "primary" and "sec-ondary" psychopaths. They would reserve the term *primary psychopath* for those who show very little anxiety or avoidance learning and who are particularly un-likely to learn under standard social controls. Further, a special type of primary psychopath is the individual who shows a consistent and high level of aggression. Numerous brain-wave disorders have been noted in a number (though by no means all) of these latter individuals. Also, they seem to be language-disordered in the sense that the affective components of language are weak or missing, voiding the likelihood of empathy or remorse. Secondary psychopaths, when compared with primary psychopaths, show higher potential for a) learning, especially to profit from experience; b) response to standard social controls, such as guilt; and c) higher levels of anxiety. Also, secondary psychopaths tend toward introversion, whereas primary psychopaths are usually extroverted. Both primary and secondary psycho-paths are quite different from individuals who are antisocial primarily because they grew up in and adapted to a delinquent subculture.

Recent Research

A more recent conceptualization views psychopathy as composed of two main factors (#1 = Affective-Cognitive Instability, #2 = Behavioral-Social Deviance) (Hare, Hart, & Forth, 1992). This view has helped generate and, in turn, has been facili-tated by Hare's PCL-R (Psychopathy Checklist, Revised), a 20-item assessment technique that uses self-report and interview observation data, which are then cross-checked with collateral information. A score of 30 or higher (out of a potential 40) is considered as a good cutoff for indicating psychopathy. There is a newer 12-item version, which has less validation data, but which has an "r" of approximately .80 with the full PCL-R, and which is more applicable to nonforensic populations. A score of 18 or more (out of a possible 24) on the shorter version is considered as a good cutoff for indicating psychopathy.

The following components contribute to the Affective-Cognitive Instability fac-tor (#1): glibness, a grandiose sense of self, pathological lying, conning-manipula-tive behaviors, lack of remorse, shallow affect, callousness and lack of empathy, and failure to accept responsibility. Components of the Behavioral-Social Deviance factor (#2) are a higher need for stimulation, a parasitic lifestyle, poor behavioral controls, early behavior problems, lack of realistic goals, impulsivity, irresponsibility, having been adjudicated delinquent, and a history of violating supervision or probation. Factors #1 and #2 show an average "r" of about .50.

In general, recent research on the psychopath (much of which includes use of the PCL) indicates:

(1) While there is a dropoff in criminal activity for psychopaths at about age 40–45, this effect holds primarily for nonviolent crimes. There is only a slight dropoff for violent crimes, so "Life does not begin at 40" for psychopaths.

(2) Concomitantly, while the Behavioral-Social Deviance factor starts to drop off at age 40–45, the Affective-Cognitive Instability factor lessens only slightly with age.

(3) Similarly, while the Behavioral-Social Deviance factor (#2) is a good predictor of general criminality and recidivism, is highly correlated with criminality, and is negatively correlated with SES and, to a lesser degree, IQ, factor #1 is a better predictor of violence, but is virtually uncorrelated with SES and IQ.

(4) Factor #1 is negatively correlated with neuroticism and trait anxiety, and is positively correlated with narcissism and dominance. Conversely, Factor #2 is positively correlated with trait anxiety, psychoticism, and a higher Pa-Ma index from MMPI-2.

(5) While treatment may effect a positive change in the average criminal, it does not do so with psychopaths, especially to the degree they are strong on factor #1. Indeed, there is evidence that psychopaths who are high on factor #1 may even get worse with treatment, i.e., group and individual psychotherapy can be a "finishing school" for psychopaths. True to their nature, they seem to learn little about themselves in therapy, but learn more about others, and then more boldly use such information in a predatory or manipulative style.

(6) In general, while socioeconomic and family background variables are good predictors of general criminal behavior, they are relatively nonpredictive for psychopathy, especially where it is loaded on the Affective-Cognitive Instability factor. Although positive family and socioeconomic factors somewhat lessen the probability of violence in psychopaths, generally speaking, psychopaths are, nevertheless, good learners of violence.

Proposed "Common Path" for the Development of Psychopathy

Licensing or certification boards not uncommonly ask a candidate to describe the evolution of some disorder (see also schizophrenia). As proposed by Meyer, Deitsch, and Wolverton (1994), the following can be used as a skeletal outline to discuss the evolution of the psychopath-antisocial personality disorder.

Preexisting risk factors

(1) biological (prenatal, birth) disruption
(2) low SES
(3) family history of vocational-social-interpersonal dysfunction
(4) family history of psychopathy

From birth to school age

(1) child temperament factors
   a. child's lack of emotional responsiveness and lack of social interest fosters rejecting responses from parents;
   b. child's high activity levels may cause parental annoyance and elicit punitive responses.
(2) parental factors
   a. inconsistent parenting results in child's failing to learn behavioral contingencies;
   b. aggressive, punitive parenting results in child's modeling aggression, experiencing hostility, becoming enured to punishing consequences, and developing a repressive defensive style (emotional 'hardness').
(3) parent-child interaction
   a. unreliable parenting results in insecure attachment (i.e., interpersonally "avoidant" attachment style);
   b. child "goes it alone" rather than risk rejection and disappointment associated with unreliable and/or abusive parents.

School age to adolescence

(1) predisposing personality factors
   a. low baseline level of arousal (i.e., Eysenck's biological extraversion) contributes to impulsive, undercontrolled, and sensation-seeking behavior;
   b. a combination of distorted physiological arousal, repressive psychodynamics, and habitual "numbness" to social contingencies results in child being insensitive to and unable to "condition" to environmental events; therefore, does not learn or "profit" from experience;
   c. commonly noted attention-deficit hyperactivity disorder and/or "soft" neurological disorder may exacerbate behavior problems.
(2) personality development
   a. peer/teacher labeling may result in self-fulfilling prophecy effects;
   b. school and social failure result in sense of inferiority and increased

interpersonal hostility; child develops "moving against" interpersonal style;

   c. initial forays into antisociality (e.g., theft, fire setting, interpersonal violence) occur; evidence for diagnosis of conduct disorder mounts.

Adolescence

(1) the young psychopath hones exploitative style in order to express hostility and "rise above" feelings of inferiority; "proves superiority" by hoodwinking and humiliating teachers, parents, peers;

(2) continued antisocial behavior results in initial scrapes with the law;

(3) physiological impulsivity, inability to profit from experience (exacerbated by a perseverative cognitive-attentional style), and interpersonal hostility and antagonism combine to make repeated legal offenses highly probable;

(4) contact with other antisocials in the context of juvenile-criminal camps or prison results in "criminal education"; increased criminality results; criminal and antisocial behavior become a lifestyle at which the psychopath can "excel."

Adulthood

(1) antisocial behavior escalates through the psychopath's late 20s; increasingly frequent incarceration results in increased hostility and hardened feelings;

(2) unable to profit from experience, lacking in insight, and unable to form therapeutic bonds, the psychopath becomes a poor therapy-rehab risk and bad news for society;

(3) there is a crystallization of these underlying cognitive beliefs: a) rationalization—"My desiring something justifies whatever actions I need to take"; b) the devaluing of others—"The attitudes and needs of others don't affect me, unless responding to them will provide me an advantage, and if they are hurt by me, I need not feel responsible for what happens to them"; c) low-impact consequences—"My choices are inherently good. As such, I won't experience undesirable consequences or if they occur, they won't really matter to me"; d) entitlement—"I have to think of myself first. I'm entitled to what I want or feel I need, and if necessary, can use force or deception to obtain those goals"; e) rule avoidance—"Rules constrict me from fulfilling my needs."

(4) antisocial behavior decreases or "burns out" in an uneven fashion beginning in the early 30s (although less so with violent offenses); this may be due to lengthier incarcerations, to changes in age-related metabolic factors that formerly contributed to sensation-seeking and impulsive behavior, or per-

haps to decrements in the strength and stamina required to engage in persistent criminal endeavors.

Intervention Issues

Nearly all significant theorists and researchers suggest that psychopaths are poor therapy candidates, and there is some evidence that the more severe, Factor #1, or primary, psychopaths may get worse with psychotherapy, i.e., psychotherapy may provide a "finishing school" experience for them. The treatment problem with all the personality disorders—getting the client into therapy and meaningfully involved— is acute in the antisocial personality disorder. And, to the degree the person shows primary psychopathy, the poorer are the chances for any meaningful change, no matter what treatment is used.

Related Treatment Issues

All plans for treatment of the psychopath encounter difficulty with control. It is axiomatic that the greater the level of control, the greater the initial impact. But it is also true that the greater the level of control, the more other cognitive variables— such as degree of resentment—enter as problems. These are all confounded by the psychopath's inherent negativism toward being treated.

One important component in rehabilitating the criminal-psychopath and possibly lessening the probability of psychopathic tendencies from evolving into criminal acting-out is to provide an outlet for the high need for stimulation-seeking. It is reasonable to believe that there are numerous individuals whose high need for stimulation and potential for criminal behavior are kept within socially acceptable limits by their work or lifestyle, e.g., as ski instructors (or ski bums), as stock and commodity traders, even as politicians. Directing persons with some psychopathic tendencies into high-energy, high-risk activities such as mountain climbing, certain forms of racing, and physically aggressive/competitive sports can help.

Any inpatient treatment program should include four major components: 1) supervision, manipulation of the environment, and provision of education by the staff to facilitate change; 2) a token economic system that requires successful participation for one to receive anything beyond the basic necessities; 3) medical-psychiatric treatments to deal with ancillary psychopathology, such as neurological disorders and depression; and 4) the requirement that the person live in a system of necessary social cooperation to maximize conformity and encourage development of the group ethic. In general, they are more likely to be motivated by tangible rewards than by physical punishment; they are likely to respond to positive reinforcement if the reinforcement closely follows the behavior; they respond somewhat better to immediate verbal feedback; and they often seek constant and very high levels of stimulation.

Currently, subjecting psychopaths to the criminal justice system is the only practical way to limit or control their antisocial activity. As noted, the long-term prospects for successful treatment of most psychopaths appear to be rather bleak, at best.

Predictors of Criminal Recidivism

In addition to various psychological test-generated predictors of recidivism, the following reflect a consensus of literature about factors that predict that the individual will recidivate (return to a pattern of criminal behavior): 1) younger age; 2) male; 3) lower intelligence; 4) lower socioeconomic status; 5) lower educational level (having a high school degree at the time of incarceration as one predictor; having it at the time of release being a separate but highly related factor); 6) disadvantaged minority; 7) not being married at time of release (less so is not being married at time of arrest); 8) being younger at first arrest; 9) being older at time of release; 10) higher number of times incarcerated; 11) more time incarcerated; 12) having had a parole revocation; 13) lack of access to, and use of, job training or educational programs; 14) fewer financial resources at time of release; 15) lower job marketability; 16) crimes involving nonlethal violence; 17) crimes involving sexual assault or intrusiveness; 18) a property offense such as burglary, larceny, etc.; 19) history of sexual or physical abuse as child; 20) being raised in a dysfunctional family; 21) history of hyperactivity; 22) indices of true psychopathy; 23) indices of brain disorder and of dysfunction; 24) history of conduct disorder, peer rejection, or mental disorder as a child.

ASSESSMENTS OF DANGEROUSNESS TO SELF AND OTHERS

One of the most difficult times for a psychologist is dealing with a situation that involves a prediction of danger toward self or others. The *Tarasoff* (1976) decision and its spawn (see Chapter 2) haven't made things easier. Before proceeding into the discussions of the specific patterns, consider the following assessment-management strategy for any client in which there is a required assessment of any dangerous (to others or self) behavior.

(1) Obtain a thorough history. Keep detailed notes. Directly question the client on thoughts about past violent behavior issues, and about any present or recent thoughts of hurting oneself or others.
(2) To resolve specific uncertainties, check with collateral sources (with appropriate permissions) such as family, friends and coworkers, and review all prior relevant records. Deal with milieu issues that may encourage acting-out.
(3) If you feel uncomfortable about the client's ability to control such behav-

iors, seriously consider hospitalization, including the possibility of involuntary civil commitment.

(4) In those cases where the client would not qualify for involuntary commitment, but you are still concerned, strongly encourage a brief voluntary hospitalization.

(5) Develop a plan, in concert with a secondary monitor, e.g., a spouse, to keep guns and/or drugs away from the client. If no secondary monitor is available, contract with the client to make his guns, weapons, etc., immediately unavailable to him, at least on a temporary basis. As weapons can take on a highly symbolic/personalized value, permanent removal may not be feasible and you may need to contract with the client to temporarily give the weapon to a friend or neighbor for "safekeeping." If this is refused, ask the client to unload the gun and keep the ammunition in a second, preferably distant location. Any variation in plan is helpful as long as it delays/confounds the proclivity for impulsiveness.

(6) Communicate your limits to the client, at the same time expressing a wish to help. In this vein, urge your client to refrain from using alcohol and/or nonprescribed drugs. Consider the use of a secondary monitor if risk warrants it.

(7) Express your personal concern for and commitment to the client in a direct fashion; this may reduce feelings of violence to self or others.

(8) Help clients to recognize and label the underlying emotions (commonly anger and/or depression), and help them to make the link to acting-out. Help them to develop alternative means of catharsis, e.g., verbal, written, artistic, and athletic expression.

(9) Consider the initiation or adjustment of a medication regimen to control symptoms such as depression, anxiety, or impulsiveness.

(10) Periodically review your intervention plan and your client's mental status. Provide assurances about confidentiality, but in the context of a discussion of your special duty (under the law and/or ethics code) to design a plan that protects specific others and/or society as a whole if interventions are unsuccessful. Consider putting some or all facets of this plan in a form of contractual agreement. Have the client read and sign his or her copy as well as your copy of the contract.

Interacting with Potentially Dangerous Clients

You may be asked how you would protect yourself in a situation where you had to interview, evaluate, etc., a potentially dangerous client. Some points to make are:

(1) Don't see the client alone, or at least arrange access to immediate, sufficient help.

    (2) Consider having a prearranged code word(s) that could alert other staff that you are in a difficult situation and need someone to come to your office, or that you are in an emergency situation.

    (3) Be careful how you position yourself and others during such interactions, both to minimize threat and maximize protection. Certainly, consider leaving your door open.

    (4) Attempt to provide a calming environment, i.e., speaking in a straightforward and calm manner.

    (5) If agitation is evident, acknowledge it, e.g., "I can see that you're very upset. How can I help here?" At the same time, try to avoid appearing scared, even though you might be.

    (6) If necessary, don't be reluctant to institute adequate physical control procedures, including notifying security or police.

    (7) Meticulously and immediately record and log all that went on, including the disposition and related rationale.

    (8) When the event has passed, debrief-consult-cathart with a colleague.

AGGRESSION POTENTIAL

Given the low base rates of severe aggressive behaviors (and suicide, as well), making an accurate prediction of specific actual behavior is virtually impossible, and overprediction is common.

The Problem of Overprediction

Three factors primarily contribute to overprediction. First, predicting rare events is an inherently difficult task, and violence is something of a rare phenomenon. Any attempt at predicting a low base rate event will guarantee a significant number of false positives. A second bias toward overprediction stems from the relative costs of mistaken predictions. Mistakenly labeling an individual dangerous, i.e., a false positive, may result in continued confinement to a hospital or treatment program, with little potential for adverse consequences for the therapist. By comparison, incorrectly labeling someone safe who later commits a violent act, i.e., a false negative, exposes the predictor to public outcry and civil liability. Since the costs of false negatives are high, there is a bias to overpredict out of self-defense.

Third, "dangerousness" is not a simple trait or predisposition. People vary along many dimensions, so they may be dangerous or violent at some point, but no one is invariably and constantly dangerous. Under the right conditions, nearly any individual may become assaultive, while even very impulsive, hostile individuals are not violent most of the time. Unlike other characteristics that are viewed as highly stable, dangerousness fluctuates over time in accordance with a variety of environmental factors, maturation, changes in level of adjustment, and so forth. Violence and dangerousness may be viewed most parsimoniously as an interaction of personality and environmental factors. It is the second group, i.e., environmental factors, that greatly confounds the prediction problem due to their constant variation.

Causes and Correlates of Violence

The best known "predictor" of violence is past violence (ironically, "violence" stems from the Latin "vis," signifying "life force"). Aggression has been shown to have a high degree of behavioral consistency under many conditions, even when the predictions were made many years prior to the criterion. Thus, violence is attributable to a complex interaction of individual predispositional and situational factors. A working fivefold typology of violent offenders is as follows:

(1) Chronic antisocial-psychopathic—Habitually undercontrolled and socially maladjusted individuals who commit aggressive acts with little concern for others or for long-term consequences.
(2) Peer-stimulated—Individuals who are seldom aggressive or violent when alone, but manifest it under the influence of a crowd or gang.
(3) Psychotic episode—Persons who become overwhelmed by chronic, unbearable problems and suffer an acute loss of reality contact, often with delusional motives for aggression.
(4) Episodic and situational violence—Explosive "rage" incidents associated with alcoholism, organic impairment, or mania.
(5) Extended suicide—Severely depressed individuals who for "altruistic" reasons kill others in the process of their own suicide.

Reviews of contributing environmental factors have identified four common etiologic relationships between situational stressors and aggression. These include:

(1) Arousal—Stressors increase arousal and the propensity for active behavioral responses, including aggression.
(2) Stimulus overload—Stressful environments often lead to misperception or misinterpretation of social cues, increasing the probability of maladaptive behavior.
(3) Interference with behavior—Stressors often impede ongoing behavior or render usual behaviors ineffective. The possibility of unusual behavioral responses, such as aggression, is increased.
(4) Negative stimulation—Many stressors are irritating, annoying, frustrating, or uncomfortable. This is true of physical stressors, such as noise, or psychosocial incidents, such as marital discord.

Predicting Violence

Integrating the range of potential data relevant to dangerousness involves two major processes. In the first process, one evaluates the base rates for violent activity for a given pattern of demographics, as this should serve as a starting point or anchor for judgments of probability. Without this anchoring effect, there is little to connect clinical factors with probabilities in the "real world."

In the second or more global process, the examining therapist must integrate individual factors, situational information, and base rate information into a coherent picture. Monahan (1981) summarizes this process as answering three questions:

(1) What characteristics describe those situations in which the person tends to react violently?
(2) What characteristics describe the situations the person is likely to encounter in the future?
(3) How similar are the situations the person is likely to encounter in the future to those that have elicited violence in the past?

The above model, while theoretically sound, has a major drawback. It requires some knowledge of the situations the individual "is likely to encounter," and it is this factor that confounds the process. Who can say with certainty what environmental stresses will or will not occur? The vagaries of prediction ensure that when required to make such an assessment, the best one can do is to describe the general predisposition of an individual toward violence and those factors that will increase and decrease risks.

Specific Indicators of Aggression. Monahan (1981) has pointed to the eight most critical demographic predictor variables for aggression. It is more common if the potential perpetrator (1) is young (this variable correlates strongly up until the 30 to 35 age range, after which the correlation is close to random), (2) is male, (3) is of a lower socioeconomic class, (4) is from a disadvantaged minority, (5) is less educated, (6) has a lower intellectual level, (7) has an unstable school and/or vocational history, and (8) has a history of juvenile violence and/or alcohol and/or drug abuse.

Other demographic indicators of a potential for violence that have been noted throughout the literature are (1) a prior history of violent behaviors, (2) a prior history of suicide attempts, (3) a history of family violence, (4) soft neurological signs, (5) command hallucinations, (6) fascination with weapons, (7) histrionic personality traits, (8) a pattern of cruelty to animals as a child or adolescent, (9) a rejecting or depressed father, and (10) recent stress, especially if associated with low levels of serotonin (Bongar, 1991; Monahan, 1981).

In addition to these predictors, assaultiveness on the ward by inpatient psychiatric patients is correlated with hallucinatory behavior, emotional lability, and a high level of activity. An excellent treatment of the issues of violence in psychiatric patients is found in Hersen, Ammerman, and Sisson (1994).

There is also increasing evidence of "bio-vio" indicators, e.g., low cerebrospinal fluid 5-hydroxindoleacetic acid levels and a low blood glucose nadir in a glucose tolerance test predicted to aggressive acts, with the latter factor being the most predictive. Additionally, there are test data that can help the psychologist to make predictions at a higher level than that allowed by impressionistic data or chance.

Test Predictors. A classic and useful scale, embedded in the MMPI-2, is the Overcontrolled-Hostility (O-H) Scale, devised and refined over the years by Edwin Megargee and his colleagues. This scale is a subset of 31 MMPI-2 items and effectively identifies a subgroup of assaultive criminals who are generally overcontrolled in their response to hostility, but who sporadically are extremely assaultive. This scale can often be helpful, though it is less useful to the degree one tries to predict chronic aggression rather than sporadic aggression. It has been generally correlated with a reported lack of overt anxiety or depression, denial or repression of interpersonal conflict, and rigid control of emotional expression. Blacks and females tend to score higher on this scale, so this should be accounted for in any interpretation.

The type of individual discovered in this scale is similar to the one originally described by Davis and Sines (1971) as the "4-3" profile type. The profile peak is on scale 4, the second highest elevation is on scale 3, and there is little significant elevation elsewhere. This profile is characteristic of men who maintain an ongoing quiet adjustment, yet who are prone toward hostile, aggressive outbursts. Consistently assaultive individuals, whose overt interpersonal patterns are more consistent with this behavior, often manifest high scores on scales F, 4, and 9, with secondary elevations on 6 and 8. All five of these scales have been classically regarded as scales that suggest a lack of impulse control.

Problems in aggression control are usually correlated with present or previous difficulties in adjusting to school. Hence, within the verbal section of the WAIS-R, scores tend to be lower on information, arithmetic, and vocabulary relative to the other three scales taken as a whole. Persons who are inclined toward easy aggression seem less able to deal with their concerns by articulating them verbally; this may be reflected in the WAIS-R, since they usually obtain a verbal score that is lower than the performance score.

On the Rorschach, individuals who are prone to aggressive behavior typically show short reaction times, do not provide extensive response records, and may give quick responses to card I and the color cards. They tend to be low in the number of FC responses and high in C, CF, and popular responses. Responses associated with fighting (swords, guns, blood) or aggressive animals (crabs, tigers) are more common in those individuals who consistently act out aggressively. Overall, elevated Rorschach special and content scales of aggressive movement (Ag), explosion (Ex), and morbid responses (MOR) raise the probability of aggression. Conversely, the potential for assault is contraindicated by a high number of F+, D, and FC responses, a high amount of abstraction content, and/or a higher number of popular and original responses.

Interventions

There are numerous potential causes of violent behavior. The following gives an overview of these causes, along with consensus intervention strategies.

A. *Violence as an inherent part of human nature*: 1) individual psychotherapy to modify basic personality patterns; 2) medications to diminish anxiety and minimize inappropriate reactions; 3) psychosurgery to change or interrupt patterns of brain functioning.

B. *Violence as a consequence of social learning*: 1) family therapy to change home environment or facilitate coping in the family setting; 2) group therapy to enhance appropriate coping in social situations; 3) assertiveness training and social skills training to give concrete training in self-assertion without violence; 4) systematic desensitization (SDT) to desensitize client to the precipitating stimuli, so as to diminish inappropriate or excessive reactions; 5) token economy, time-out, social isolation to extinguish violent behavior through removal of environmental reinforcers, as well as to strengthen appropriate responses; 6) classical conditioning to extinguish violent behavior, as in aversive conditioning; 7) parent effectiveness training, Parents Anonymous to enhance adequate coping skills and provide a supportive peer group.

C. *Violence as a consequence of frustration and other situational factors*: 1) traditional psychotherapy to release frustrations and to change coping patterns; 2) family therapy—see B1; 3) group therapy—see B2; 4) assertiveness training, social skills training—see B3; 5) token economy—provide opportunities for positively reinforcing experiences while extinguishing the violent behavior; 6) parent effectiveness training, etc.—see B7.

D. *Violence as a means of communication*: 1) expressive therapies to substitute alternate means of expression of feelings underlying violent acting-out; 2) assertiveness training, etc.—see B3; 3) SDT—see B4; 4) parent effectiveness training—see B7.

E. *Violence and aggression as protection of territorial integrity and body space*: 1) SDT—see B4; 2) assertiveness training—see B3; 3) individual psychotherapy—to improve the sense of self and self-esteem.

CHILD ABUSE

The physical and sexual abuse of children has been clearly documented throughout history and across cultures. Although such abuse is frequently abhorred, few actual preventive measures were traditionally taken. It is ironic that the first formal legal intervention in a child abuse case, that of Mary Ellen in New York in 1975, had to be prosecuted through animal protection laws and with the efforts of the Society for the Prevention of Cruelty to Animals. All 50 states, partly spurred by the federal Child Abuse Prevention and Treatment Act, have now established legal routes to identify and intervene in abusive families.

Diagnostic Considerations

The DSM-IV includes three relevant categories: Physical Abuse of Child (V61.21); Sexual Abuse of Child (V61.21); and Neglect of Child (V61.21). In the vast majority of all these cases, the first diagnostic cue emanates from the child. There are a number of common *physical* signs of physical abuse, e.g., the classic "four Bs": unexplained or unusual *B*ruises, *B*urns, *B*ald spots, or *B*leeding.

Look for bruises around the head or face or in areas normally protected from accident, such as the abdomen; multiple bruises, especially if spread over the body; or bruises in the shape of an object, such as a hand or a belt. Likewise, burns of all types should cause concern, especially cigarette burns, burns with a specific shape, such as an iron, and burns that suggest that a hand has been immersed in liquid. Concern should be heightened if the child provides an explanation that does not fit the injury.

Behavioral signs of physical abuse include accident-proneness, problems with schoolwork and peers, shrinking from physical contact, and wearing clothes that seem more designed to cover the body than to keep one warm. Be especially on guard if any of these symptoms represent a change in behavior for that child. Over and above these signs, delinquency, drug abuse, dissociative experiences, anorexic patterns, and excessive avoidance of parents may reflect an abuse situation in older children and adolescents.

Along with physical abuse, there has been increasing attention to the *sexual* abuse of children. The behavioral signs noted above are also found in cases of sexual abuse. Additional signs include extreme secrecy, excessive bathing, indications of low self-worth, provocative or promiscuous sexual patterns, appearing more worldly than friends, or suddenly possessing money or merchandise that could have been used to bribe the child to keep quiet. Specific physical signs of sexual abuse are pain, rashes, itching or sores in the genital or anal areas, enuresis, frequent urinary infections, or frequent vomiting.

Various indices in the standard psychological tests have been found to be helpful in assessing child abuse victims and perpetrators (Meyer, 1995). One of the better measures specifically designed for physical child abuse assessment is the Child Abuse Potential (CAP) Inventory, developed by Joel Milner in 1991 (c/o Family Violence Research Program, Dept. of Psychology, Northern Illinois University, DeKalb, IL 60015-2892). The CAP is a 160-item, self-administered, forced-choice questionnaire with a third-grade readability level, and it includes three validity scales. It shows classification rates, based on discriminant analysis, in the mid-80% to low 90% range, and, unlike several other scales, produces more false negatives than false positives. As noted in Chapter 2, the use of anatomical dolls as an assessment device provides a number of problematic issues, e.g., see Everson and Boat (1994).

There have also been increasing reports of "Munchausen syndrome by proxy" (see Chapter 5 for a discussion of Munchausen syndrome)—e.g., where a mother has induced multiple hospitalizations in her child by administering laxatives. These mothers are preoccupied with medical terms and equipment, and may manifest borderline personality disorder components. They also often initially present themselves as cooperative and then passively subvert or resist all interventions. In an also apparently increasing number of cases, a child is injured by the parent in order that the parent might gain the related attention.

Treatment Options

A variety of treatment modalities will be needed. In addition to individual psychotherapy, there are three core approaches that are potentially useful in almost all such cases:

Family Therapy. Since the family is virtually always disrupted, family therapy is necessary. Even where the family system eventually changes, family therapy can help to mute the damage to all concerned.

Parent Training. When the abuse comes from a parent, parent training is necessary to deal not only with the problems that led to the abuse, but also with those generated by the abuse. Parent training is also important in dealing with this latter factor when the source of abuse is external to the family, e.g., neighbors, strangers, etc.

Support Systems. Abuse is often accompanied by a sense of emotional isolation, in both victim and abuser. In this vein, Parents Anonymous is a community-based counseling and support group available to abusing parents. This organization works in the same manner as Alcoholics Anonymous or Gamblers Anonymous. A similar group is Parents United. Contact with other abusers and the opportunity to share problems with sympathetic and understanding others are helpful for parents for whom abusive behaviors are triggered by psychosocial stressors and a sense of emotional isolation. Support groups are also useful for the victims, especially with older abuse victims.

Children who have been sexually abused are more likely to show negative effects, both short-term and long-term, if a) the abuse occurred over a substantial time span; b) there were many episodes of abuse during that time span; c) the child was abused by several, separate perpetrators; d) the child was physically hurt; e) the child was threatened or psychologically traumatized in or around these episodes; f) the abuse was by the natural father or mother, or by a loved parental figure, especially if that person is still loved and is separated from the child as a result of the abuse; g) the child had to go through aversive confrontations in the legal process, especially if the perpetrator is found not guilty; h) the child was old enough to experience some normal guilt, and yet continued to participate; i) the child does not have access to a loving, secure, and stable family structure; j) the child was somehow made to feel responsible for whatever family disruption did take place.

SUICIDE POTENTIAL

As with aggression, psychologists are often called on to make predictions about suicide potential, and it is an equally difficult task. The combined suicide rate in the U.S. during this century has remained at about 12 per 100,000 per year and accounts for about 1% of deaths per year. More men than women actually kill themselves (at approximately a ratio of 3:1); in psychiatric patients it is only about a

1.5:1 ratio, although more women than men attempt suicide, again at approximately a 3:1 ratio. The majority of suicides, approximately 85 to 90%, are committed by whites (in both absolute numbers and per capita rate—as opposed to blacks), and most of the data about suicide are based on whites. According to T. Marzen et al., writing in the *Duquesne Law Review* (1985, *24*, 1–241), suicide was a crime in the United States until 1972.

Clues and Correlates to Suicide

Suicidal individuals tend to give clues to those around them, and these areas should be the focus of any evaluation. In addition to being depressed, they are likely to show feelings of hopelessness and helplessness, a loss of a sense of continuity with the past and/or present, and loss of pleasure in typical interests and pursuits. The basic risk factors for suicide have been consistent over the years: older, white male, live alone, alcoholism, a loss experience, medical illness, schizophrenia, depression. In recent years, add AIDS and a diagnosis of panic attacks or borderline personality disorder. Suicidal persons are more likely to: 1) have a personal history and/or family history of depression, especially a major endogenous depression, or of psychosis; 2) have had a parent or other important identity figure who attempted or committed suicide; 3) have a history of family instability and/or parental rejection; 4) be socially isolated; 5) have a chronic physical illness; 6) show a preoccupation with death and/or make statements of a wish to die, especially statements of a wish to commit suicide; 7) manifest consistent life patterns of leaving crises rather than facing them (in relationships: "You can't walk out on me, I'm leaving you"; or in jobs: "You can't fire me, because I quit"); 8) show a personal or family history of addiction patterns; 9) live alone, or are involved (married or similarly occupied) with a loved mate who is interpersonally competitive and/or is self-absorbed; 10) show sudden cheerfulness after a long depression; 11) are noted to be putting their affairs in order, e.g., giving away favorite possessions, revising wills; 12) show some abrupt atypical behavior change, e.g., withdrawal from family or friends; 13) show a family history of self-damaging acts; 14) have a history of self-damaging acts, often previous suicide attempts (in this context, the first axiom of psychology could well be "Behavior predicts behavior," and the second axiom could be "Behavior without intervention predicts behavior"). The initiation of the suicidal event is especially apt to be triggered by a major life stress, for example, the experience of a chronic debilitating illness or the loss of an important social support, such as a confidante. Violent impulsivity with high-risk mental disorders (e.g., depression, panic) suggests high risk.

At the biological level, a blunted thyroid-stimulating hormone (TSH) response to a thyrotropin-releasing hormone (TRH) stimulation; high levels of plasma cortisol (20 mcg % or higher); low platelet MAO, low platelet serotonin, high platelet serotonin-2 receptor responsivity; a high ratio of adrenaline to noradrenaline; and depressions marked by low levels of 5-HIAA hydroxyindoleacetic acid—a metabolite of serotonin—have all been associated with an increased probability of suicide attempts. Also, suicide completers' brains show one-half to two-thirds the number of receptor, or "binding," sites for the chemical imipramine then do normal brains.

The following factors can then increase any potential and increase the probability that an attempted suicide will be completed (there is about a 10–15% probability that a *serious* attempt will be successful):

(1) A cognitive state of constriction, that is, an inability to perceive any options or a way out of a situation that is generating intense psychological suffering.

(2) The idea of death as a catalytic agent for the cessation of distress.

(3) Acute perturbation–high distress/agitation/depression.

(4) An increase in self-hatred or self-loathing.

(5) Perception of the self as a source of shame to significant others.

(6) Fantasies of death as escape, especially if there are concrete plans for one's own demise.

(7) Easy access to a lethal means, e.g., as in physicians, who show high suicide rates.

(8) Absence of an accessible support system (family and good friends).

(9) Life stresses that connote irrevocable loss (whether of status or of persons), such as the relatively recent death of a favored parent, or even something like retirement. This factor is particularly important if the person at risk is unable to overtly mourn the loss.

(10) High psychophysiologic responsiveness: cyclical moods, a propensity toward violence, and a high need for stimulation seeking in spite of suicide thoughts. Ironically, in some previously violent psychiatric patients, sadness showed a low correlation with suicide attempts, while it was more consistently correlated with attempts in previously nonviolent patients.

(11) Serious sleep disruption and/or abuse of alcohol or drugs.

(12) Lack of a therapeutic alliance and/or constructively supportive friendship alliance.

(13) Persistence of secondary depression after remission of primary disorder, and/or recent discharge from a psychiatric hospital (in the last three months).

(14) A history of panic attacks, and even more importantly, recent panic attacks.

Ironically, most people who are severely depressed and suicidal are more dangerous to themselves when they begin an upswing out of the depths of depression, as opposed to the "bottom" of the depression. Also, various factors are differentially predictive of suicide attempts, depending on whether the attempt is early (within one year) or later (one to five years). While panic attacks, alcohol abuse, loss of interest, psychic anxiety, diminished concentration, and global insomnia are more predictive of early attempts, expressed suicidal ideation, a sense of hopelessness, and prior suicide attempts are more predictive of later attempts.

Exner (1978, 1988) has provided the most elegant and effective research on the use of Rorschach in the prediction of suicide. In 1978, he offered 11 variables that together form a prediction for suicide potential. The variables he first cited as important are as follows:[*]

1. FV + VF + V + FD is greater than 2.
2. An occurrence of a color-shading blend response.
3. Zd is greater than ± 3.5.
4. 3r + (2)/R is less than 0.30.
5. Experience Potential is greater than Experience Actual.
6. CF + C is greater than FC.
7. S is greater than 3.
8. X + % is less than 0.70.
9. Pure H is less than 2.
10. P is greater than 8 or less than 3.
11. R is less than 17.

In addition to the 11 criteria used in the original constellation, two new criteria have been established (Exner, 1988). By adding an upper range for the egocentricity scale (3r+(2)/R greater than 0.45 or less than 0.30) and incorporating the morbidity index (MOR greater than 3) the accuracy of the index has significantly improved. The original criterion (eight of 11 variables) could accurately predict 75% of suicides, categorizing 20% of depressed inpatients and 12% of schizophrenics as false positive errors. Exner asserts that the new criterion (eight of 13 variables) can predict 83% of suicides accurately, classifying only 12% of depressed inpatients and 6% of schizophrenics as false positives.

There are a number of scales specifically designed to assess suicide risk, e.g., Beck's Scale for Suicide Ideation (SSI) and the Suicide Intent Scale (SIS), the Reason for Living Inventory, Suicide Probability Scale (SPS), Index of Potential Suicide, etc. All have validity problems and are primarily research and/or minimal screening tools, but as such, can be useful in certain specific situations.

Response to Suicide

You may be asked what can be done to control suicide. You may note that several steps can be taken at a societal level to reduce the incidence of suicide. Educating the public about the myths and facts of suicide is an important first step. Second, there is evidence that suicide-prevention telephone hotlines and centers can slightly decrease the suicide rate. Third, control of access to commonly used methods (such as guns and drugs) can lower the incidence of suicide. A fourth step is the placing of some restrictions on media publicity about suicides, as there is a direct correlation

---

[*] J. Exner, *The Rorschach: A Comprehensive System*, Vol. 2: *Current Research and Advanced Interpretation.* New York: Wiley, 1978, p. 204. Used with permission of the publisher.

between suicide rates and the amount of newspaper publicity given to suicides in a particular locality.

Several precautions can also be recommended for people to take at the individual level.

- Attend seriously to people who voice a desire to kill themselves or "just go to sleep and forget it all." About two-thirds of people who actually do kill themselves have talked about it beforehand in some detail with family, friends, or others.
- Take any complaint seriously. Attend especially to depressed individuals who speak of losing hope.
- To the degree possible, keep lethal means (guns and large prescriptions of sedatives) away from suicidal individuals.
- Generate personal concern toward a suicidal person; a suicide attempt is most often a cry for help. Be affirmative and supportive. Suicidal individuals need a temporary "champion" who can point them toward new resources and suggest new options, at least in a small way, that can diminish the sense of hopelessness.
- Contract with the person for communication about his or her status, and for some positive changes to be made. Try to get the person to engage in regular physical exercise, start a diary, follow a normal routine, do something in which he or she has already demonstrated competence, confide inner feelings to someone, or cry it out. Try to get the person to avoid self-medication and other people who are inclined toward depression.
- Make every effort to see that a suicidal person reaches professional help. Making an appointment is a good first step; getting the person to the appointment is the crucial step.

Chapter 5

MALINGERING

The issues of malingering (in truth, an act, not primarily a mental disorder) and distorted response sets are often a part of any psychologist's evaluation. Deception can be defined as the knowing misrepresentation of self-reported personal or factual data. When deception involves false reports or exaggeration of medical or psychiatric symptoms, it is referred to as malingering.

Malingering is possible wherever a psychological or physical disability has a payoff. It occurs more commonly in the early- to middle-adult years, is more common in males than in females, and often follows and/or includes an actual injury or illness. Problematic employment history, lower socioeconomic status, or an associated antisocial personality disorder are also common correlates of this pattern.

Several concepts or issues are worth considering: a) tests may not provide "incremental validity," i.e., one or two tests may in some situations provide optimal power, while adding more tests may even lessen it; b) the ability to fake is not a normal curve phenomenon, or even close to it; c) how one decides if a client is good at faking, and then how to use that in assessment strategy; d) the related issues of impression management, response set, malingering, etc.

DECEPTION APPREHENSION OR GUILT

Ekman and O'Sullivan (1991) point out that two major components, deception apprehension and deception guilt, can be aroused in the process of deception, and can, in turn, facilitate detection of it. *Deception apprehension* is essentially the fear of getting caught, and it is heightened when:

- the examiner has a reputation for being difficult to deceive;
- the examiner is initially suspicious;

- the deceiver has little skill at lying, and little practice or no prior success at it;
- the perceived stakes or consequences are high;
- both rewards and punishment are at stake, or punishment alone is at stake;
- the punishment for being caught in a lie is great, or the punishment for the concealed act, if revealed, would be so great that there is no incentive to confess;
- the examiner gains no benefit from the deceiver's lie.

Deception guilt, on the other hand, is guilt about the process of lying itself. It is parallel to shame, except that shame usually requires an audience. Deception guilt is increased when:

- the deceit is totally selfish, and the examiner derives no benefit from being misled and loses as much as or more than the deceiver gains;
- the deceit is unauthorized, and the situation is one in which honesty is authorized;
- the deceiver has not been practicing the deceit for a long time;
- the deceiver and the examiner share social values;
- the deceiver is personally acquainted with the examiner;
- the deceiver cannot construe the examiner as mean or gullible;
- there is no reason for the examiner to expect to be misled, and the deceiver has encouraged the examiner to be trusting.

COMMON ASSESSMENT TECHNIQUES

Three general classes of methods are commonly employed in the detection of deception: interview techniques, psychological test methods, and physiological methods. A subgroup of psychological tests, i.e., integrity tests, are pencil-and-paper tests specifically designed for personnel selection, yet they may be adapted for other settings as well. The reader is referred to Camara and Schneider (1994) for an excellent review of this area. With the passage of the federal Employee Polygraph Protection Act of 1988, interest turned more toward nonphysiological modes of assessment.

Interview data are best obtained in a controlled format, such as the Mental Status Examination, which includes assessment of: 1) physical appearance and identifying and history data; 2) motor activities; 3) speech activity and patterns; 4) mood and affect; 5) alertness and attention; 6) content and organization of thoughts; 7) perception; 8) the general areas of memory, abstract thinking, and the client's fund of knowledge; and 9) the client's attitude toward the examination and toward his or her condition.

Examples of some of the questions commonly asked in the Mental Status Examination are: What is this place? Who am I? What date is it? Who are you? Who is the president of the United States? Who was president before he was president?

What does "Don't cry over spilled milk" mean? Would you count backward from 100 by 7's?

Even though the interview in the Mental Status Examination provides structure, the examination contains a weakness common to all data obtained from interviews: there are few or no statistical or normative standards for the obtained responses on which to base a communicable inference and eventual diagnosis. Examiners are too often left to develop their own idiosyncratic notions of what a certain response means.

Psychological test data provide control for most of the errors of interview data, if the psychological test is well designed. Some tests look at specific aspects of personality; others look at broad classes of personality factors. Overall, the tests that are most helpful are well-validated tests, with features that have been developed especially to detect deception, such as the MMPI-2, the MCMI-II, the 16 PF, the BPI, and the CPI. Also, there are basically two types of psychological tests: objective and projective. In general, the objective tests have proven most useful in detecting deception. Objective tests specifically designed to assess deception are often termed "integrity tests" and they are increasingly used by employers, in part because of increasing restrictions on the use of the polygraph in such assessments.

MMPI-2

On the MMPI-2, interest is naturally centered on the standard validity scales as predictors of distorted response sets. Yet, other measures may also be useful here. For example, one helpful index, more so for faking good than faking bad, is to compare differences on those items designated as obvious and subtle.

The standard validity scales do, however, provide much valuable information in this regard. The traditional rule of thumb has been that if the F-K ratio (the Gough Dissimulation Index) is +9, such people are trying to fake bad—that is, to present a distorted picture of themselves that emphasizes pathology. If the score is 0 or less, the emphasis is on trying to look good and deny pathology. However, it is generally agreed that these axioms hold only if F and K are relatively low and, even then, there are a high number of false positives and negatives.

The most recent comprehensive data on faking bad and good on the MMPI-2 (Graham, 1991) suggests the following guidelines. Remember, this is to gain maximum discrimination power in a statistical analysis, i.e., these are very conservative. Lower scores than those suggested may still suggest malingering, especially when combined with other MMPI-2 data, or data from other sources:

    A. For discriminating those consciously faking *bad* within an essentially normal population (using *raw* scores):
        (1) Use a cutoff score of 18 on F, with higher scores suggesting a fake bad profile.

        (2) Use an F-K score of 17 for men and 12 for women, with higher scores indicating faking bad.

        (3) Use a raw score Fb (back side F) of 19 for men and 22 for women (again, higher scores indicating faking bad).

    II. For discriminating those consciously faking bad within a psychiatric population (again), using raw scores) with higher scores indicating faking bad):

        (1) Use a cutoff on F of 27 for men and 29 for women

        (2) Use an F-K of 27 for men and 25 for women

        (3) Use an Fb of 23 for men and 24 for women.

Using these scales to assess faking good has always been a somewhat more difficult discrimination. Also, those solid findings that have been obtained are confounded by the issue of whether one is more concerned with identifying faked profiles or honest ones. L proved to be the most effective scale for males. An L score of 8 correctly classifies 93% of honest profiles, but only 67% of those faking good. To correctly classify 96% of the males faking good, a cutoff of 4 on L was necessary. Scores of 8 and 5 produced similar respective discriminations in females. An L-K index of 23 was quite effective, in both directions, for females, but did not work as effectively as L alone for males. The reader is referred to the extensive data and tables in Graham (1991) for information that will be useful in discriminations using a combination of variables in an individual case.

Also, note that profiles with F scores that are in the T range above 90 are commonly associated with confused and/or disturbed individuals who may manifest hallucinations, delusions, and general confusion. This is particularly so when one is dealing with an inpatient population.

TRIN and VRIN. Two response inconsistency scales were developed for MMPI-2, TRIN (True Response Inconsistency) and VRIN (Variable Response Inconsistency). There is good evidence that they are by far the best measures of random or inconsistent responding.

TRIN is based on 20-item pairs for which a combination of two true or two false responses is semantically inconsistent, e.g., the pair "I am happy most of the time" and "Most of the time I feel blue." In three such pairs, the response of either true or false to both indicates inconsistency; in 11 pairs, inconsistency is indicated only by a true response, and in six pairs, only by a false response. By subtracting the number of inconsistent false pairs from inconsistent true pairs and then subtracting from nine (total number of inconsistent false pairs), an index score of 0 to 20 is obtained. A high score indicates indiscriminate "true" responding; a low score points to indiscriminate "false" responding.

VRIN is composed of 49 item pairs that produce one or two, out of four, possible configurations (true-true, true-false, false-true, false-false), again, where responses would be semantically inconsistent. Scores occur in a range of 0 to 49, with high scores pointing to random responding and/or confusion.

16PF

The older versions of the 16PF are rapidly being supplanted by the Fifth Edition of the 16PF, first available in 1994. It contains a good Impression Management Scale, as well as an Acquiescence Scale (Conn & Rieke, 1994). For those who use the older versions, which are obviously also still valid, faking good and bad scales are useful. On Form A, the most commonly used older form, a cutoff score of 6 was the original criterion for determining faking both good and bad. However, Krug (1978) obtained data on a much broader and more representative sample (2,579 men and 2,215 women), and he finds a major difference in the cutoff scores. On the faking-good scale, scores ranged from 0 to 15, with a mean of 6.36 and a standard deviation of 2.87 for men, while women's scores ranged from 0 to 14, with a mean of 5.71 and a standard deviation of 2.72. Thus, Krug's data suggest that the cutoff score of 6 for the faking-good scales is much too liberal. Krug presents the following rules to be used for making the profile more accurately interpretable when scores range from 6 upward:

For Faking Good: (1) If the score is 7, subtract 1 sten score point from C and add 1 point to Q_4. (2) If the score is 8, subtract 1 point from A, C, G, and Q_3 and add one point to L, O, and Q_4. (3) If the score is 9, subtract 1 point from A, C, G, and Q_3 and add 1 point to F, L, O, and Q_4. (4) If the score is 10, add 1 point to F, L, and O, add 2 points to Q_4, subtract 1 point from A, G, H, and Q_3, and subtract 2 points from C.

For Faking Bad: (1) If the score is 7, add 1 point to C. (2) If the score is 8, subtract 1 point from O and Q_4 and add 1 point to C. (3) If the score is 9, subtract 1 point from L, O, and Q_4 and add 1 point to C, H, I, and Q_3. (4) If the score is 10, subtract 1 point from L and Q_4, add 1 point to A, H, I, and Q_3, and add 2 points to C.

Individuals who randomly mark the 16PF answer sheet show a very flat profile, with a low score on scale B.

Other Standard Tests and Scales

Many of the various standard personality scales, such as the Basic Personality Inventory (BPI), Personality Assessment Inventory (PAI), Psychological Screening Inventory (PSI), etc., have scales that are useful in assessing impression management and response sets. For example, the MCMI-II contains four modifier indices, three of which are designed to assess various forms of malingering. These are the Disclosure Scale (DIS), the Desirability Gauge Scale (DES), and the Debasement Measure (DEB). The fourth modifier, the Validity Index (VI), consists of four items with an endorsement frequency of less than .01. The DIS was designed to detect the degree to which respondents are inclined to be self-revealing and frank, and is thought to be neutral to psychopathology. The DES is thought to essentially measure "faking good," the DEB measuring "faking bad." However, all three scales appear to be bidirectional indicators of dissimulation, i.e., they tap both faking bad and faking good components, hence must be used with caution. The Weight Factor, which is best used in computer scoring, represents the extent of positive or negative deviation from a midrange of total raw scores on scales 1–8. It appears to offer the most validity in the fake-bad dimension.

Since sophisticated clients have on a number of occasions been able to successfully fake on the Rorschach, it is not commonly used to assess malingering. With that in mind, it is generally agreed that malingering clients (especially if unsophisticated) will respond to the Rorschach with a reduced number of responses; expressions of perplexity or disdain; repeated questions about the test directions; critical or snide comments about the tests or specific cards; vague or poor form responses; dramatic content such as blood, sexual anatomy, fire, explosions, and bizarre or aggressive percepts; an attitude of pained compliance to the test, frequent card rejections; and inconsistencies such as failure to give easy popular responses while recognizing more difficult ones.

Such clients tend to show slow reaction times, even when they do not produce particularly well integrated or complex responses. They may take a cautious or disdainful attitude and thereby produce few responses primarily determined by color. There are often high percentages of pure F and popular responses. They easily feel distressed by the ambiguity of the stimuli and will subtly try to obtain feedback from the examiner as to the accuracy of their performance. If the F%, L, and X+% variables are in the normal range and there are a high number of texture, shading, blood, dramatic, nonhuman-movement, vista, or inappropriate-combination responses, malingering in an effort to give an untrue appearance of a mentally disordered state should be considered.

On intelligence and neuropsychological tests there is an overall tendency for malingerers to perform too poorly and inconsistently in relation to observed behavior or abilities as indicated by indirect methods or previous test data or other data. They produce abnormal scatter, give illogical, inconsistent, or "approximate" answers, produce odd or surprising "near misses," miss easy items while they pass hard ones, and also sometimes give a bizarre response where an intellectually slowed individual might give a concrete response. Remember to look for consistency between two tests that look different but that measure the same ability.

Specifically Designed Scales and Scoring

Schretlen and his colleagues (1992) have provided interesting data to support the use of a recently developed Malingering Test (MgS), and the Bender-Gestalt and MMPI-2 in the detection of faked insanity. The MgS is a 90-item, paper-and-pencil test, composed of simple questions in both open-ended and forced-choice formats, that takes about 25 minutes to complete. On the basis of earlier research, the following scoring criteria for the Bender-Gestalt were found to be effective in detecting faked psychosis (Schretlen et al., 1992, p. 78):

(a) inhibited figure size, each figure that could be completely covered by a 3.2 cm square was scored +1; (b) changed position, each easily recognized figure whose position was rotated greater than 45 degrees was scored +1; (c) distorted relationship, each easily recognized figure with correctly drawn parts that were misplaced in relationship to one another was scored +1; (d) complex additions, each easily recognized figure that contained additional complex or bizarre details was scored +1; (e) gross simplification, each figure that showed a developmental level of 6 years or less was scored +1; and (f) inconsistent form quality, each protocol that contained at least one drawing with a developmental level of 6 years or less and at least one drawing with a developmental level of 9 years or more was scored +1. Scores for the first five of these features were then summed as a composite index of faking.

A more detailed scoring manual for this use of the Bender-Gestalt, and more information on the MgS is available from Dr. David Schretlen, Dept. of Psychiatry and Behavioral Science, Johns Hopkins School of Medicine, Meyer 218, 600 N. Wolfe St., Baltimore, MD 21205.

Psychologists also need to look to other specific tests if there is any question of dishonesty. For example, scales that tap a social-desirability response set, such as the Balanced Inventory of Desirable Responding (BIDR-6) (Paulhus, 1991) and the Marlowe-Crowne Social Desirability Scale (Marlowe & Crowne, 1964), give an idea of the direction of a client's response set, and this test has shown good reliability and validity. A validated short version of the Marlowe-Crowne (Zook & Sipps, 1985) also exists. The Marlowe-Crowne Scale and other scales of a similar nature—such as the M Scale (although it tends to pick up too many false positives) of Beaber et al. (1985) and the Structured Interview of Reported Symptoms (SIRS) (Rogers, 1988) described below—are also helpful in conjunction with the other more standard detection scales built into such tests as the MMPI-2 and 16PF.

The Schedule for Affective Disorders and Schizophrenia (SADS) (Spitzer & Endicott, 1978), a semistructured interview scale, is also of potential help here. A drawback is that it takes up to four hours to complete, although its length makes it easier to trip up a malingering client on inconsistent responses. Malingering is suggested on the SADS if 1) 16 or more "severe" symptoms are subscribed to, 2) 40 or more symptoms are scored in the "clinical" range—a score of 3 or greater, or 3) four or more "rare" symptoms are subscribed to. These rare symptoms are each only found in 5% of a sample of 105 forensic patients, and only about 1% of this population showed five or more of the following rare symptoms: 1) markedly elevated mood, 2) much less sleep in the previous week, 3) significantly increased activity level in the previous week, 4) thought withdrawal—something or someone is "pulling" thoughts from them, 5) delusions of guilt, 6) marked somatic delusions, 7) evident and recent loosening of associations, 8) incoherence at some point during the previous week, 9) poverty of speech, or 10) neologisms. These rare symptoms could probably be effectively included in a short screening procedure. Overall, most malingerers, perhaps in an effort to "prove" that they are mentally disordered, report far more symptoms on the SADS than even the most mentally disordered individuals.

Another structured interview, called the Structured Interview of Reported Symptoms (SIRS), was designed by Richard Rogers, an eminent forensic psychologist, specifically for use with suspected malingerers (Rogers, 1988), and has shown consistently good validity (Kurtz et al., 1994). Like the SADS, high scores on the SIRS are suggestive of malingering. The SIRS is based on 13 strategies that provide an excellent overview of the crucial areas of interest in the detection of deception. These 13 strategies consider and assess: 1) the individual's degree of defensiveness about everyday problems, worries, and negative experiences; 2) how the individual has attempted to alleviate or solve his or her psychological problem; 3) how many of eight bona fide but rare symptoms the individual endorses; 4) whether the individual will endorse any fantastic or absurd symptoms; 5) the symptom pairs that are likely to coexist in real clinical syndromes; 6) how precisely the individual describes the symptoms since, in reality, precision is unlikely; 7) how the individual's description of the onset of symptoms compares with actual symptom onset; 8) whether the individual has a stereotypical or "Hollywood" view of psychological problems; 9) the number of symptoms the individual reports that have an extreme or unbearable quality; 10) whether the individual's endorsement of symptoms has a random quality; 11) how stable the individual's self-reports of symptoms are; and 12) the level of honesty and completeness in the individual's report. The SIRS then asks the subject (13) to report on behaviors that can be observed by the evaluator, and the report is then compared with the actual observations.

While both the SADS and the SIRS are thorough and well validated, they are both time-consuming. And while they are reliable in placing an individual into a diagnostic category and in detecting deception, their reliability decreases as the deceiver's sophistication increases.

When claims of cognitive, sensory, or memory deficits are at issue, particularly if no organic pathology is substantiated, some variation of Symptom Validity Testing may be very helpful. These techniques operate on the assumption that subjects faking a deficit will perform at a below-chance rate on multiple-trial, forced-choice tasks that apparently (i.e., to the subject) measure the alleged deficit. The task, which is presented to the subject as a measure of an ability related to the impairment, requires a large number of decisions on simple, two-alternative stimuli. Normal Ss should easily achieve close to a 100% accuracy rate, and those with an authentic, related impairment should score close to 50%. Since random responding approximates a normal binomial distribution, it is possible to determine the probability that a given score was produced by chance. The malingering client then has to approximate random responding, which is difficult over many trials even when the client realizes what is being assessed. There are many different forms available for symptom validity testing, as this is still an emerging assessment area, and also because the task may depend upon what specific deficit(s) is alleged.

BEHAVIORAL INDICATORS

Several overall patterns have been found to be characteristic of interview and test data from malingerers. These characteristic patterns depend to some degree upon the specific distorted response pattern that is being observed, i.e., whether it is the result of malingering, defensiveness, disinterest, or other factors.

First, it is important to use your experience with the various patterns of mental disorder to evaluate the validity of symptoms presented by a suspected malingerer. Also, any symptom reports should be rigorously questioned, using open-ended questions, i.e., "What are those voices saying" rather than, "Do those voices tell you to do anything."

Overall, malingerers more often endorse relatively rare symptoms, as well as a higher total number of symptoms than do honest respondents. Malingerers are also more likely to be willing to discuss their disorder, especially how the negative effects of their disorder impact on rather narrow areas of functioning. They are more likely to report a sudden onset of the disorder; to report a more sudden cessation of symptoms if that has some functional value; and to endorse the more evident, flamboyant, and disabling symptoms. They are more likely to give vague or approximate responses when confronted, to make inconsistent symptom reports, to take a longer time to complete a test or an interview response, to repeat questions, to change responses, to use qualifiers and vague responses, tő miss easy items and then score accurately on hard IQ items, and to endorse the obvious rather than the subtle symptoms usually associated with a disorder. Because of the latter, obvious-subtle item discriminations on the MMPI-2 can be helpful.

Delusions or hallucinations are commonly reported by individuals trying to malinger psychological disorder. Some techniques that are helpful in detecting malingering of hallucinations or delusions are: first, attempt to establish a good rapport; ask open-ended questions; phrase questions to avoid giving clues about true hallucinations; make a verbatim record of the account of the events; take a detailed history of prior illnesses and alleged hallucinations or delusions; confirm symptoms with past records and recorded observations; find out if the malingerer has had the opportunity to observe individuals he or she may be mimicking; prolong the interview to promote fatigue in the malingerer; push for a quick response so that there is less time to think it through; ask strange questions that the typical psychotic would probably not respond to (Resnick, 1989).

In general, actual schizophrenic hallucinations are typically intermittent rather than continuous. Though visual hallucinations are occasionally of little people, they are usually of normal sized people and are more often seen in color rather than in black and white. Olfactory hallucinations are usually of unpleasant odors. Auditory hallucinations typically are experienced as coming from outside of the person's head. They may be familiar or unfamiliar voices, but the messages are usually reasonably clear and short. Schizophrenic hallucinations tend to diminish when the schizophrenic is involved in activities. Auditory hallucinations in drug-induced psychoses are more unformed, and are often experienced as indistinct noises. More specifically, the clues that lead one to believe that the reporting of a delusion or hallucination may be malingered are (Resnick, 1989):

(1) an abrupt onset or cessation;
(2) eagerness to call attention to the delusion or hallucination, or leading the discussion to this topic;
(3) conduct not consistent with the delusion;
(4) reported bizarre content without disordered thoughts or hallucinations;
(5) a delusion or hallucination that somehow specifically reduces the relevant responsibility or culpability.

In addition, auditory hallucinations are the most common in schizophrenia. But, the examiner should be suspicious of a report of auditory hallucinations if:

(1) they are vague or if the person reports that it is hard to hear them or to understand them;
(2) they are reported as continuous rather than sporadic or intermittent;
(3) the hallucination is reported as not being associated with a delusion;
(4) stilted language is reported as the content of the hallucination;
(5) the content specifically exonerates the client from some blame or responsibility;
(6) the person reporting the voices can give no strategy to diminish the voices;
(7) the person says that he or she obeys all command hallucinations.

Several consistent behavioral cues have been noted in individuals who present a dishonest portrayal of themselves. For example, on the average, such individuals nod, grimace, and gesture more than honest interviewees do, and they have less frequent foot and leg movements. They also talk less and speak more slowly, though they make more speech errors and smile more often. In addition, the dishonest interviewees tend to take positions that are physically farther from the interviewer. High voice pitch and many face and hand movements, relative to the individual's standard behavior, are also indicative of deception.

There is no real support for the idea that people who are deceiving will necessarily avoid eye contact. There is some evidence that females will look longer into the eyes of male examiners while lying, but usually not into a female examiner's eyes. These same cross-sex results hold for males as well, but not as clearly.

Research by Michael Cody (personal communication, 1991) breaks down deceivers into those who tell "prepared lies" and those who tell "spontaneous" lies. He asserts that those who prepare ahead of time *tend* to: 1) give the answer immediately after the question is asked; 2) provide more terse answers; 3) manifest speech microtremors; 4) nod their heads at the end of the lie; 5) rub some part of their bodies; 6) lack enthusiasm and sound a bit as if they have rehearsed, which of course they have. On the other hand, people who tell spontaneous lies *tend* to: 1) show odd grammatical errors; 2) provide brief but tentative answers; 3) show speech hesitations and silent pauses or pauses filled with "Ahhs"; 4) use meaningless phrases such as "like that," "you know"; 5) employ "universal" words and phrases, e.g., "always," "never," "certainly"; 6) completely freeze or scratch their heads, or rub their hands together; 7) fail to provide important or even obvious details.

PHYSIOLOGICAL METHODS

The Polygraph

Ever since *Frye v. U.S.* (1923), there have been substantial if not virtually total barriers to the admissibility of polygraph results into court proceedings. However, Martell (1992) observes that this is changing, and there is slowly increasing precedent for allowing the introduction of polygraph results, especially by an individual whose character and/or truthfulness have been called into question. *Daubert v. Merrill Dow Pharmaceuticals* (1993) (see Chapter 2) will no doubt provide a further impetus for this direction.

The polygraph technique, often referred to as the lie detector, is the standardized measurement of physiological responses to detect deception. It is based on the observation, well known since ancient times, that lying is stressful (for most people) and is often accompanied by many of the physiological correlates of stress, such as dry mouth, accelerated heartbeat, and muscular tension. It was originally thought that measuring these correlates would make it possible to determine if an individual was lying.

The first systematic application of the polygraph was in 1875 by Cesare Lombroso, who measured blood pressure and pulse while questioning subjects. Successive versions added measures of the subjects' rate of respiration, muscular tension, and galvanic skin response (GSR). In 1927, the prototype for the modern polygraph was developed. This device provided a continuous measurement of the three physiological indicators traditionally assumed to be most sensitive to physiological arousal: GSR, respiration, and cardiovascular activity.

Of course, these physiological indicators do not themselves directly measure deception. Rather, they measure physiological and presumably emotional arousal. Thus, to maximize the effectiveness of the test, the preparation of the subject for examination is pivotal. During the preparation or pretest, examiners typically attempt to instill in the subject the sense that the polygraph is a powerful instrument and that it will detect any attempt to lie. An effective pretest often results in a confession before the subject even sees the polygraph.

Specific Polygraph Interrogation Techniques. Several different questioning techniques can be used, and they have differential validities. The Irrelevant Question Technique compares the subject's responsivity to benign, irrelevant questions (such as, "Do you live in New York City") to their responsivity to relevant questions pertaining to the investigation. It has not been supported as having any consistent validity and can easily result in inaccurate findings.

The Control Question Technique measures reactivity by comparing the subject's responses to relevant and control questions. The relevant questions are ones that have to do with the subject matter of the evaluation, such as, "Did you steal the man's watch," while the control questions are designed so that the individual is either deceptive or uncertain about the truthfulness of his or her answer, such as, "Have you ever stolen anything in your life." In other words, the subject is induced to lie, and a pattern of responsivity for lying is obtained. This pattern is compared with responsivity to case-relevant questions. If the patterns of responsivity to control and case-relevant questions are similar, deception is suggested. A major drawback of this technique is that the examiner has no way of knowing what the control questions mean to any individual. For example, if the person being evaluated stole a watch as a youth, the relevant question may show greater reactivity, even though the individual is innocent of the crime in question.

Another technique commonly used by polygraphers is the Peak of Tension Test (POTT). This test can be used only when information about a crime is available that only a guilty subject would know—for example, evidence from the crime scene that the police did not release to the press. In the POTT, questions are phrased so that the subject must answer yes or no. The subject is instructed to answer no to every question and is thus forced to lie when faced with the question about the relevant information. This relevant question is placed in the middle of a series of questions; if there is a build-up of tension (possibly to a peak) before the relevant question and a reduction after, it is suggested that the individual is guilty. This technique has been found to be effective if the relevant, critical item presented is not known to an innocent subject, if the person who committed the crime knows the detail, if the other questions appear equally plausible, and if one, and only one, of the questions is of significance to the crime.

The most sophisticated concealed information test is the Guilty Knowledge Test, originated by David Lykken (1981). It involves a multiple-question, multiple-choice format, wherein a guilty individual is presented with a question and a series of five responses of which only one response offered by the examiner is critical. Innocent subjects would have only a 0.20 probability of showing a fear-of-detection response, if indeed they made any differential response at all. The questions are analogous to those asked in the Peak of Tension Test—such as, "When Nancy was raped, something was knocked off the table next to you. Was it a glass of water? a beer bottle? an ashtray? a glass figurine? or a vase of flowers?" If six of these five-choice questions are used, the probability that an innocent subject would physiologically respond to all of the critical items in a way that might indicate guilt is 0.00065, which is much lower than the probability of a guilty subject responding in that fashion. The validity of this technique has received strong experimental support. Unfortunately, it has gone virtually unused by polygraphers, possibly because it was not developed by a polygrapher, or because there is added work required to set up this format, or because it requires more detailed information about the crime.

One problem in this regard is that the solid researchers in the area of polygraphy are small in number and have not sought political clout. On the other hand, polygraphers, who are more numerous and more aggressive politically, have a relatively low level of academic training and are scientifically unsophisticated. Yet they have gained political clout and have—possibly inadvertently—managed to impede improvements in the "lie detector," thus slowing legal acceptance and even recognition.

As more "practitioners" who are even less scientifically sophisticated drift into this arena, some even more problematic issues arise, sometimes as a result of creativity.

> Two police officers extracted a confession from a suspect by advising him the Xerox® machine was a lie detector. First they put a colander—a salad strainer—over the suspect's head and wired it to the duplicating machine. Then, under the Xerox® lid they placed a slip of paper reading "He Is Lying!" Every time the suspect answered a question an officer would press the duplicating button and out would pop a Xerox-ed® "He Is Lying!" Finally shaken, the suspect told all. His confession was thrown out by a judge who was not amused. (Jones et al., 1989, p. 47)

Voice Analyzer

It is common knowledge that stress and lying are often accompanied by an elevation of voice pitch. This is due to the tightening of the tiny muscles deep in the throat, compounded by the tightening of the musculature of the diaphragm, which controls exhalation. In 1971, the first voice analyzer, called the Psychological Stress Evaluator, was put into use. Early claims for the device were extravagant, and some people (that is, those selling it and a few unsophisticated consumers) regarded it as a foolproof truth detector. Its most common application has been in industrial settings as an aid to employee selection. Since the instrument is portable and easily hidden, it may be used covertly, without the subject's knowledge. Claims regarding the accuracy of the voice analyzer have not been validated to date.

Truth Serums

The truth serum has the reputation, no doubt perpetuated by countless spy thrillers, of being a powerful method of inducing the revelation of secret information. But, research has not been entirely supportive of the efficacy of the truth serum, especially with consciously resistant subjects (see Chapter 6).

Conclusion

The use of any single interview or any single psychological or physiological measure to detect deception may well result in a biased assessment of an individual. Each procedure has some usefulness in the detection of deception, but also some weaknesses.

PAIN AND MALINGERING

Pain is a commonly malingered symptom. It may have both conscious and unconscious components. Individuals who are more likely to use pain as a manipulator than others are people who:

- have a history of taking significant dosages of pain medicine;
- have a history of extensive medical treatment or multiple surgical procedures;
- have a history of hypochondriasis or factitious disorder;
- are highly suggestible;
- had stressful childhoods and/or are from large families;
- began working full time at an early age and/or had children at an early age;
- complain of too little pain for their injuries, as well as those who complain too much.

AMNESIA AND MALINGERING

It is unclear exactly what mechanisms underlie psychogenic amnesias and fugues. However, three main hypotheses have been proposed. The treatment response, as well as possibly the legal response, depends upon which theory one subscribes to. The first hypothesis holds that such amnesia experiences result from faulty encoding of information at initial input, i.e., the information is not even stored. The deficit is thought to occur because the extreme mood or emotional arousal that often accompanies the first appearance of such amnesias can hamper the acquisition of the information. This first hypothesis is probably best supported by the data. The second hypothesis is that the memories do exist but have been "repressed," i.e., there is "motivated (at a subconscious level) forgetting." A third hypothesis is related to the second in that the information is believed to be actually stored somewhere in memory. This third hypothesis suggests there is a primary retrieval deficit, and that the amnesiacs reflect mood-state- (or ego-state-, in psychodynamic terminology) dependent phenomena, similar to those described in depression. Thus, the experiences could be retrieved if the subject could be restored to a subjective state similar to that in which the experiences first occurred.

As noted in Chapter 2, courts have seldom accepted amnesia by itself as a primary defense supporting either incompetency to stand trial or insanity. The exceptions have usually involved incidents in which there is severe head injury. Certainly, amnesia caused by true physical trauma is seldom ever total, nor is it selective for issues pertaining only to the relevant incident. Certainly, the abuse of drugs and alcohol can distort memory; yet, again, there is little evidence that people with any significant degree of functioning during the incident have totally impaired memories because of such abuse. While hypnosis can be useful in refreshing memory in all of the above conditions, Chapter 2 points out the increasing trend in the legal system to reject any testimony that has been "enhanced" by hypnosis.

Amnesia is a commonly malingered symptom, probably because 1) it is seemingly easy to carry off, 2) acts to void responsibility, yet 3) leaves the person fully functional in his or her world. True psychogenic amnesia is typically focused on personal memory, particularly those memories directly relevant to the traumatic event. Characteristics of psychogenic amnesia that allow a differentiation from organic amnesia and faked amnesia are the more sudden onset, shorter course and sudden recovery, anterograde direction (continued ability to learn new information), some recoverability under hypnosis, and a personal focus. There are additional cues that indicate malingered rather than a true amnesia:

(1) True amnesia for a situation is seldom either total or very specific.
(2) True amnesiacs have shown lower scores on MMPI-2 scales 1, 2, and 3 than malingering amnesiacs.
(3) Malingered amnesia often results in inconsistencies between reports, as well as with usual psychogenic or organic syndromes.
(4) True amnesiacs rate themselves higher on the ability to recall information if they are told they will be given extra time or prompting; indeed, they do function better if primed. Malingerers are more likely to indicate the improbability of change in their amnesia; they then do not show much change even if prompted.
(5) Malingerers show amnesia as characterized by recall performance superior to, and recognition performance worse than, that of brain-damaged, memory-disordered subjects. In addition, malingerers' serial-position pattern resembles that of normals rather than that of amnesiacs.

It is especially worthwhile to remember that vigor and/or apparent sincerity of presentation are not indicators of true amnesia. Indeed, there seems to be no clear correlation here. It is also worthwhile to remember that there may be both true and malingered amnesia in the same case.

The Factitious Disorders

"Factitious" means "not genuine," and factitious disorder refers to symptoms that are under voluntary control, as opposed to the somatoform disorders, where voluntary control is absent. At first, this syndrome may sound like malingering. The difference is that in a factitious disorder, the goal or reinforcement sought is not obvious or inherent in the apparent facts of the situation. Rather, the motivation is understandable only within the person's individual psychology. Factitious disorders are rare, and it is one of the most difficult categories to diagnose, in part because the feigned symptoms are often accompanied by a more subtle though true physical disorder.

The factitious disorders are traditionally subcategorized into those emphasizing *psychological symptoms* and those emphasizing *physical symptoms*. The latter is often referred to in the literature as *Munchausen syndrome*, first described by Dr. Richard Asher in a 1951 article in *Lancet*, and named after Baron von Munchausen, a distinguished German politician and soldier. The baron, born in 1720, was famous for his hospitality and his skill at telling fantastic, adventure-filled tales. His stories were eventually plagiarized by Rudolph Eric Raspe in *The Amazing Travels and Adventures of Baron von Munchausen*, which became a popular children's book. Generally, these syndromes are marked by (1) the intentional production or feigning of symptoms, and (2) a psychological need to assume the sick role, with an absence of external incentives as primary, along with three other commonly associated features: an adequate-to-extensive knowledge of the medical literature on the relevant symptomatology; a history of drug abuse; and chronic pathological lying about the symptoms and associated features.

In a factitious disorder with primarily psychological symptoms, the symptoms are mental rather than physical, and as a result they are often not well defined. These people usually talk around a point or give approximate though evasive answers to direct questions (a pattern referred to as "Vorbereiten"). For example, if asked an arithmetical question such as, "How much is thirty-five minus twelve," they may respond with "Thirty" or "Thirty-five."

The essential feature of Munchausen syndrome is a plausible presentation of factitious physical symptomatology in order to elicit and sustain multiple hospitalizations. The disorder is most commonly manifested in acute abdominal, neurological, or skin symptoms. The first signs of Munchausen syndrome usually appear in adolescence and early adulthood.

The factitious disorder is more common in males. This may in part reflect a readier acceptance of verbalizations of sickness from females, so that a diagnostician would be less inclined to recognize a factitious disorder in females. Hospitalization for an actual physical disorder or a background that includes familiarity with medical issues often precedes this pathological hospitalization pattern. Many such individuals were severely abused as children, and many show a history of drug abuse. The range of symptomatology is limited only by the person's imagination and the degree of his or her sophistication about medical information. This disorder is chronic and is highly refractory to intervention, in part because the person can often find another cooperative physician or caregiver.

Attention has recently focused on "Munchausen syndrome by proxy," first clearly conceptualized and named in 1977 by Meadow, a British pediatrician. In virtually all reports, usually single-case studies, the pattern is perpetrated by the mother. False reports of allergies, hematuria, and seizures are common, as are induced vomiting and/or diarrhea. Victims are of all ages, though age 4–5 appears to be the mode. The pattern is often an overlay to actual or past illness, and there is evidence that the child victims may begin to participate in the deception as they get older.

Chapter 6

PSYCHOPHARMACOLOGY AND THE PSYCHOLOGIST

Psychopharmacology is an increasingly important topic for psychologists. I first discuss the issue of prescription privileges for psychologists, a common question in exams, and then provide an overview of the psychopharmacology categories—concepts that may be of importance to the individual psychologist, or in an examination case.

PRESCRIPTION PRIVILEGES FOR PSYCHOLOGISTS

Whether or not psychologists should have or seek prescription privileges is such a visible and important issue that it is very possible that you will be asked about it in a licensing or board exam. As with most issues, it is worthwhile to be able to present some arguments on each side of the issue, and to be prepared to present your own opinion if asked, as well as your rationale. Following are the major pro and con arguments. For more detailed information, see M. Smyer et al., "Summary of the Report of the Ad Hoc Task Force on Psychopharmacology of APA" (*Professional Psychology*, 1993, *24*(4), 394–403), or *The Legal and Legislative Considerations of Prescription Privileges for Psychologists* (January 1994), published by and available from the Office of Legal and Regulatory Affairs of the Practice Directorate of the American Psychological Association. See also *Dent v. West Virginia* (1889), in Chapter 2.

Con Arguments

- It will be very divisive for the profession. Many psychologists presently oppose it, for a variety of reasons. Older psychologists will be reluctant to go through substantial "retreading," thus are likely to oppose such a move, as they may perceive it as making them second-class citizens. In any case, two tiers of psychologists would be created, with two classes of advocacy, reimbursement, etc.

- Guild issues, such as increased liability insurance costs, state licensure changes, and division of labor within treatment settings would cause further dissension and hostility within the ranks of psychology.
- Psychologists will move further away from their traditional unique strengths, relative to other mental health professionals, of skills in psychological testing and in research sophistication.
- Psychologists would change their professional identity by opting for "nature" versus "nurture" in endorsing the biological bases of behavior over drug-free treatment.
- The efficacy of medication is questionable, at best, in many patients, and may allow the client, or therapist, or society to avoid the challenge of a true cure. Why sell out?
- With more prescribers, there would be an increase, not a decrease, in the use and abuse of medications.
- There would be enormous political costs: confrontation with the entire medical community (not just psychiatry), costly legislative initiatives, and the risk that the losses overall may eventually outweigh the gains that psychology has recently achieved.
- Arguments for prescribing privileges conflict with the arguments for hospital privileges; haven't we been saying, "We just want more settings in which to practice psychology."
- Psychology training programs are already too competitive and overloaded to handle further specialization.

Pro Arguments

- With their traditional orientation, psychologists would be motivated to reduce medications to prevent patients from being overmedicated.
- One probable result would be decreased consumer costs, since psychologists charge less for services than do physicians (at least presently), and the increased competition on this variable would likely keep costs down.
- Since patients could receive treatment from a single provider, services would be better integrated as well as less expensive; freestanding programs for treatment of smoking cessation and substance abuse, for example, will no longer need psychiatric consultation.
- Prescription privileges would allow psychologists to assist in reaching underserved populations with scarce access to mental health services, e.g., military personnel, rural residents, and patients in public institutions.

- Psychologists can provide better comprehensive treatment than psychiatrists in many areas, such as cognitive deficit side effects, by coupling medication more imaginatively with therapeutic activities.
- Considering psychologists' thorough research background, there would be improved research in psychopharmacology.
- Psychologists already "quasi-prescribe" medication, as they frequently serve as consultants to family physicians and other medical specialists concerning patient care.
- In terms of practice issues, prescribing is a logical extension of services as psychologists compete in the marketplace for parity with physicians.
- Other nonphysicians already prescribe medications, e.g., dentists, optometrists, and nurse practitioners.
- Psychologists already are prescribing other modes of treatment, e.g., exercises, diets, and biofeedback.

I believe that one of the most compelling "pro" arguments, yet one that is not often discussed, is the fact that the psychiatric pharmacopeia is not that complex. It is absurd to argue that psychiatrists should be licensed in and thus be assumed to have active competence in the vast array of pharmacopeias that are included in the practice of medicine, and at the same time argue that psychologists with some additional training can't practice the minor subset of the pharmacopeia needed for the great majority of their clients.

When I was an intern and then staff psychologist at the Psychiatric Clinic of the State Prison of Southern Michigan at Jackson around 1968–69, it was standard practice for me and another psychologist (who now works in research on psychotropics) to write a one-paragraph case summary with a prescription note like, "I believe it would help Mr. Smith if he were placed on Thorazine 200 mg. b.i.d." Sometimes our consulting psychiatrist saw the inmate for a short period, most of the time he just scanned the case file, and sometimes he did neither. But he virtually always signed it as his prescription, and almost never changed it. And, though it wasn't good medical practice, it worked very well. It simply didn't take very long to learn the required pharmacopeia.

It is interesting that most of the curriculum proposals drift toward what I believe are two errors: a) too closely mimicking a medical school curriculum and b) going toward overkill in the amount of required training. No doubt, both are a product of the desire to make it easier to get such proposals past legislators, who are not likely to be very sophisticated about these issues.

Most who have advocated prescription privileges for psychologists have proposed a "limited formulary" idea, i.e., prescribing only certain "classes" of medications that are appropriate for mental health treatment. Herein lies a critical issue. How can this limited formulary be identified, in view of the fact that certain classes of medication must be excluded? Some possibilities are:

- Exclude the major psychotropics, i.e., those for the psychotic disorders. But, this would eliminate drug treatment for the very populations that are already underserved, and there is really no logical reason for this exclusion.

- Exclude controlled substances. But, this would presently exclude benzodiazepines, those medications such as Valium, Librium, and Xanax that are useful to control anxiety disorders, which are often seen in outpatient settings.
- Exclude all nonpsychiatric drugs, the most common proposal. But this could eliminate drugs such as Cogentin that are used to control the side effects of antipsychotic medications. Moreover, many patients present with mental illness exacerbated by other physical disorders, leading to situations where comprehensive treatment and drug interactions become major issues.

As is evident, the issue is complex. But then, most issues in this field are complex. Let us now turn to a consideration of the various categories of psychopharmacology.

The introduction of the antipsychotic and antidepressant drugs in the 1960s revolutionized mental health treatment. Though the side effects can be problematic, their use has resulted in decreased hospital stays, an increased emphasis on outpatient treatment, and an overall increase in the level of functioning for individuals with such disorders.

The term *psychotropic* broadly refers to medications that have an effect on the central nervous system to produce changes in aberrant behavior. These medications are divided into several groups based on their behavioral effect. However, psychotropic medications can have other uses, some of which will be discussed in this chapter, and there are drugs currently not classified as psychotropic medications that can also have behavioral effects. For example, Reserpine, developed as an antihypertensive in the 1950s, was routinely found to cause depression. In fact, reserpine-induced depression in laboratory animals has often been used as a model in the early development and testing of antidepressants.

As in many aspects of medicine, the early psychotropics were found by serendipity or were related to drugs that were being used for other purposes and were then refined for use as psychopharmacologic agents. Imipramine, for example, was originally being studied as an antihistamine. MAO inhibitors had originally been used as antituberculin drugs. From observations that patients on these or similar compounds improved their functioning and/or moods was born the field of psychopharmacology.

Familiarity with psychotropic medications is important for all psychologists to enable them to provide clients with informed judgments in a variety of intervention and case situations.

PHARMACOKINETICS

The term *pharmacokinetics* refers to how the body handles a drug that has been administered. In other words, what happens to the drug once a person takes it? There are four major components to the concept of pharmacokinetics: (1) *absorp-*

tion—where the drug is taken into the body and how rapidly it is taken in; (2) *distribution*—how the drug gets to its intended site of action, and exactly what bodily system it affects; (3) *metabolism*—where the drug is broken down in the body and how rapidly this takes place; and (4) *excretion*—how the breakdown products from metabolism are eliminated from the body. Let us consider these areas in more detail.

Obviously, getting the drug into the body is the most important first step; this represents *absorption*. Most drugs are given orally. When taken by this route, the drug is swallowed and absorbed into the bloodstream somewhere in the gastrointestinal (GI) tract. Usually, this occurs in either the stomach or the upper portion of the small intestine. A number of factors influence this process. The chemical composition of the drug, for example, will determine how rapidly it dissolves and also how quickly it passes through the gastrointestinal mucosa. The acid-base composition of the drug, referred to as its pH, will also affect rate absorption, as will the pH of the GI tract. Drugs that are lipid soluble tend to be absorbed more rapidly; lipid solubility simply refers to whether or not a given drug is chemically similar or dissimilar to most fluids and molecules in the body. The more similar it is, the greater its degree of lipid solubility and the faster its rate of absorption.

Two other routes of absorption exist for psychotropic medications. One is the intravenous route, where the drug is injected directly into the blood system, the fastest route of absorption. Obviously, the faster the absorption, the earlier the onset of therapeutic action. The other route is intramuscularly, i.e., injected directly into muscle tissue, where the drug binds with certain molecules and is released into the blood slowly over a period of days or weeks. This latter method has the advantage of eliminating the need for daily medication ingestion or injection.

Distribution refers to what happens to a drug after it gets into the blood stream. In general, one of three things can happen: 1) the drug is freely dissolved in the blood; 2) it is bound to plasma proteins, which circulate throughout the bloodstream; or 3) the drug is carried within the blood cells. How quickly the drug dissolves in the blood, binds to proteins, or gets absorbed and then released from the blood cells determines, in part, how quickly the therapeutic action of the drug begins. Obviously, the psychotropic medications exert a large part of their action on the brain, so they must cross something called the blood-brain barrier. Not all of the blood vessels in the brain can release substances directly into brain tissue. In order for psychotropic medications to be effective in the brain, they must be able to gain access to those blood vessels that directly communicate with brain tissue. This requires that the drug molecules be of a certain size (i.e., very small), have a high degree of lipid solubility, and have affinity for certain neuroreceptors. If the drug has all of those characteristics, then it can pass through the blood-brain barrier, where it can exert its effects.

Once in the body, or specifically in the brain, the drug begins to undergo a series of chemical changes, which ultimately result in its degradation, or breakdown; this process is referred to as *metabolism*. If metabolism did not take place, the drug would remain in its original form and exert its action indefinitely. In other words, there would be no way to control the action of the drug. The blood circulates through-out the body constantly, meaning that the drugs carried in the blood do the same thing. As a result, no psychotropic drug remains in the brain forever. One organ that the blood continually passes through is the liver, and it is here that most drug me-tabolism takes place. While some drugs are metabolized by other organs, the liver is of primary importance. Metabolism simply involves a series of chemical reactions, facilitated by enzymes in the body, that transform the drug into a number of related compounds. Some of these compounds retain the actions of the original drug, and are called "active metabolites." Others lose the therapeutic action of the drug and become inactive. It is the rate of metabolism and the number of active metabolites for each drug that determines how long the therapeutic effect lasts.

The metabolic products from the drug are then eliminated, or *excreted*, from the body. For most drugs this occurs via the kidney, with the drug metabolites being eliminated in the urine. Other routes of excretion include tears, saliva, sweat, feces, and breast milk. Excretion, then, is the final step in removing a drug from the body.

CLASSIFICATION

The psychotropic medications are typically divided into five groups based on their predominant behavioral effect: 1) antipsychotic agents, 2) antidepressants, 3) antimanic drugs, 4) antianxiety agents, and 5) sedative-hypnotics. Many of these drugs have secondary actions such as the control of violent and agitated behavior, and some are utilized as "truth serums." Each group is discussed later. Also, note that prescribing conditions and issues differ considerably for children. For an excel-lent review, see Sylvester and Kreusi (1994).

Each group of drugs is useful in the treatment of specific mental disorders. For example, the antipsychotic drugs, often referred to as neuroleptics, have their greatest application in the treatment of schizophrenia and other disorders accompanied by psychotic symptoms (e.g., psychotic depressions). Mood-altering agents such as the antimanic and antidepressant medications are useful in the treatment of severe de-pressions and bipolar (manic-depressive) illness. The antianxiety agents produce a gen-eralized calming effect and are useful in any condition in which anxiety is a prominent symptom (e.g., phobias or generalized anxiety). The sedative-hypnotics tend to in-duce drowsiness and alter consciousness, and are used in the treatment of sleep disturbances such as insomnia.

There are a large number of specific drugs within each of the effect groups. The proper selection of an appropriate class of drug, as well as the selection within a classification of the specific drug for the actions desired or to be avoided, if pos-sible, depends on the clinician's skills in a number of areas. Most importantly, it depends on the ability to understand the specific etiology of the behavior to be treated; the ability to accurately define behavior in terms of target symptoms; the need to understand how specific drugs can be used to affect specific symptoms; the ability to understand delay of onset and length of action; and an understanding of drug interactions and possible side effects. Each drug has both a trade name, assigned by the manufacturer, and a generic or chemical name. In the sections that follow, both names will usually be listed for each specific agent.

Because of their potential to alter behavior, and because some of these drugs are addicting, a number of the psychotropic agents are classified as controlled substances by the Drug Enforcement Administration (DEA). Drugs are classified as controlled according to their potential for abuse; the greater the potential, the more limitations are placed on their use. Only the antianxiety agents and the sedative-hypnotics are presently classified as controlled. Table 6A lists examples of controlled substances and the DEA classification system.

The psychologist must be ever mindful that dependency and abuse are also a function of personality factors as well as of the substance itself. This is especially true for the anxiolytic drugs. Individuals who use increasing dosages of anxiolytics as a way of "feeling better," "taking off the edge," or "getting through a tough day," or who have a history of drug-seeking behavior with abuse or dependency in other areas, are likely to abuse anxiolytics. Such individuals need to be carefully monitored by the prescribing physician, any related therapists, and the dispensing pharmacy.

A related concept is that of mind-altering versus mood-altering drugs. A mind-altering drug is a substance that will have a similar effect given to a general population of individuals. Stimulants, for instance, if given to 100 people at large,

TABLE 6A
Controlled Substances

DEA Class	Characteristics	Examples
I	High abuse potential No accepted medical use	LSD, heroin, marijuana
II	High abuse potential with severe physical and psychological dependence	Amphetamines, opium, morphine, codeine, barbiturates, cocaine
III	High abuse potential with low to moderate physical dependence and high psychological dependence	Compounds containing codeine, morphine (e.g., narcotic analgesics)
IV	Low abuse potential with limited physical and psychological dependence	Benzodiazepines, certain barbiturates, other sedative-hypnotics
V	Lowest abuse potential	Narcotic preparations containing non-narcotic active ingredients (e.g., cough medicines with codeine)

will have a stimulating effect on virtually all. Antidepressants (which are mood-altering), as an example, when given to 100 people selected at random, are likely to have a positive effect only on a subgroup of those individuals suffering from an affective disorder. Even then, it may take weeks, and the effect of the drug is not superimposed over the existing mood. Rather, it reestablishes a normal range of appropriate mood. Mind-altering drugs, on the other hand, limit the range and superimpose the effect in almost anyone taking that type of substance.

ANTIPSYCHOTIC DRUGS

The antipsychotic medications are a large class of drugs that are useful in the treatment of psychotic disorders such as schizophrenia. A number of mental disorders, in addition to schizophrenia, may be accompanied by psychotic features. These include severe mood disorders such as psychotic depressions and mania. Transient psychoses may also be seen in certain of the personality disorders.

Antipsychotic medications are usually effective in correcting the thought disturbances, delusional thinking, and hallucinations seen in psychotic disorders. They are not directly effective with apathy, social withdrawal, and blunted affect. A widely held theory asserts that many psychoses are caused by an overabundance of the neurotransmitter dopamine in the brain. Dopamine is believed to play an important regulatory role in thought and perception, and is also important in coordinating fine motor movements. When imbalances in dopamine occur in the brain, the characteristic symptoms of psychosis (thought disorder, delusions, and hallucinations) are likely to occur. The antipsychotic agents appear to act by blocking dopamine receptors in the brain, thereby decreasing the functional availability of the neurotransmitter. This corrects the imbalance and restores thought and perception to its normal state.

In addition to their action on psychotic symptoms, most of the antipsychotic medications cause some degree of sedation. This effect is useful in decreasing agitation that often accompanies a psychosis. As will be discussed later in the chapter, the sedating properties of these drugs also make them useful in the treatment of violent behavior. The phenothiazines (e.g., chlorpromazine and thioridazine), the largest group of antipsychotic drugs, tend to produce the most sedation.

In addition to their therapeutic properties, all medications have certain side effects and adverse reactions. As a group, the antipsychotics are noteworthy because of the large number of side effects that may occur. These are potent drugs; as such, they affect a variety of systems in the body. A common side effect is muscular stiffness and rigidity, referred to as dystonia. These drugs may also cause a vague feeling of restlessness and an inability to sit still, referred to as akathesia. The shuffling gait perceived by many as a hallmark behavior of the chronically ill patient who has been overmedicated is the result of akathesia. Some patients on high doses of these drugs for extended periods of time will develop involuntary movements of the face, mouth, and tongue, known as tardive dyskinesia. All of the neuromuscular side effects are described under the general heading of extrapyramidal symptoms. This term derives from the areas of the brain and central nervous system that control movement, the extrapyramidal tracts. These symptoms are also often referred to as Parkinsonian side effects because they clinically resemble the symptoms of Parkinson's disease.

The antipsychotic drugs exert an influence on other neurotransmitters in addition to dopamine. One of these is acetylcholine, a muscarinic transmitter that is involved in the regulation of many bodily functions. The antipsychotics block the action of acetylcholine, with the result that this group of side effects is often referred to as anticholinergic effects. Specific symptoms include dry mouth, intolerance to heat, constipation, and blurred vision. In extreme cases, an anticholinergic delirium may occur, characterized by confusion, disorientation, and agitation. These drugs also may temporarily cause a drop in blood pressure, especially when one is arising from a sitting or supine position. This phenomenon, called postural hypotension, may lead to dizziness. These symptoms can serve to complicate the already complex clinical picture and often require the administration of medication to offset the effects.

Other side effects seen with the antipsychotic medications include photosensitivity to sunlight, liver damage, cardiotoxicity, a depression of blood cell production, leading to anemia (agranulocytosis), and seizures. A very serious and potentially life-threatening side effect is the neuroleptic malignant syndrome, characterized by high fever, convulsions, muscular rigidity, and rapid progression to coma and death. With such side effects as these, it is not surprising that the antipsychotics have a low potential for abuse, dependence, or addiction.

A large number of specific drugs are available in this group. These are listed in Table 6B. Despite their numbers, virtually all of these agents are thought to primarily act by blocking dopamine receptors in the brain, and many of the specific agents are chemically related to each other. The main features that differentiate the individual medications are dose range, degree of sedation, duration of action, and intensity of side effects. All of these drugs are metabolized, or broken down, by the liver, so caution is required in persons with preexisting liver disease.

Three major classes of antipsychotic drugs exist: 1) the phenothiazines; 2) the thioxanthenes, e.g., thiothixine (Navane); and 3) the butyrophenones, e.g., haloperidol (Haldol). Several other antipsychotics are also in clinical use that do not belong to any of these groups. The phenothiazines may be further subdivided into drugs with low potency that are used at relatively high doses (e.g., Thorazine and Mellaril) and those with high potency that are used at lower doses (e.g., Stelazine and Prolixin). As a general rule, the low-potency, high-dose drugs cause more sedation, whereas the high-potency, low-dose preparations have less sedation but more tendency to cause extrapyramidal reactions.

The two most commonly used antipsychotics are chlorpromazine (Thorazine) and haloperidol (Haldol). There is some evidence that haloperidol is typically prescribed at higher dosages than is necessary to gain the desired effect. Long-acting (decanoate) preparations are available for haloperidol (Haldol decanoate) and

TABLE 6B
Antipsychotic Drugs

Name (Generic/Trade)	Dose Range*
Phenothiazines	
chlorpromazine (Thorazine)	50–1500 mg/day
thioridazine (Mellaril)	50–800 mg/day
fluphenazine (Prolixin)	5–40 mg/day
fluphenazine decanoate (Prolixin D)	25–100 mg IM Q1-4 weeks
perphenazine (Trilafon)	4–64 mg/day
trifluoperazine (Stelazine)	5–40 mg/day
Butyrophenones	
haloperidol (Haldol)	5–100 mg/day
haloperidol decanoate (Haldol D)	50–200 mg IM Q2-4 weeks
Thioxanthenes	
thiothixine (Navane)	5–60 mg/day
Other Antipsychotic Drugs	
loxapine (Loxitane)	20–250 mg/day
molindone (Moban)	20–225 mg/day
clozapine (Clozaril)	300–500 mg/day
risperidone (Risperdal)	3–6 mg/day

* Average therapeutic dose range.
IM—Intramuscular administration.

fluphenazine (Prolixin decanoate). Both of these are given intramuscularly by injection and have a duration of action of from two to four weeks. The duration of action for orally administered antipsychotics ranges from 4 to 12 hours, depending in part on how quickly the drug is metabolized.

The first therapeutic effect that occurs 30 to 60 minutes after ingestion is a generalized calming effect, often accompanied by some degree of sedation. A person on antipsychotics is also likely to appear rather stiff and clumsy, due to the extrapyramidal effects mentioned above. Although the person is fully alert while on these drugs, he may often appear emotionless and possess a rather blank stare, due also to the extrapyramidal effects. The full antipsychotic action on hallucinations and delusions may take from several days to several weeks to appear, depending on the severity and intensity of the symptoms. Unless the situation is acute, it is prudent to give low doses in increasing frequency until one has titrated the dose of medication against behavior and side effects. Some psychotic patients do not respond significantly to these medications, for reasons that are not completely clear.

Two of the newer antipsychotics, clozapine (Clozaril) and risperidone (Risperdal), seem to be effective with treatment-resistant patients, and also have much less potential for extrapyramidal side effects and tardive dyskinesia. Clozapine (Clozaril) blocks a number of receptors in the brain: dopamine, serotonin, adrenergic, and muscarinic. Its specific mechanism of therapeutic action, however, is not known, though it is a weak D_2-receptor antagonist. Side effects include a potentially fatal agranulocytosis (primarily in the six-week to six-month clozapine exposure period) in 1 to 2% of patients receiving the drug (hence, consistent blood monitoring is necessary), as well as seizures, sedation, tachycardia, hypotension, hyperthermia, nausea, excessive salivation, and drooling. The dose range for clozapine is 300 to 500 mg/day (not to exceed 900 mg/day), but the risk of seizures increases dramatically at doses greater than 500–600 mg/day. Side effects for risperidone include insomnia, fatigue, somnolence, agitation, and increased saliva.

ANTIDEPRESSANTS

Depression, described earlier in Chapter 4, is one of the most frequently encountered psychiatric symptoms. Most depressions occur in response to some trauma or loss that the individual can identify. In many cases, this type of depression is self-limiting and does not require treatment. In those cases that persist, psychological treatments are usually effective in alleviating the depression. Some people, however, experience severe depressions that are seemingly unrelated to any external event, and apparently reflect abnormalities in the neurotransmitters that regulate mood.

The antidepressant medications consist of four broad groups of drugs: 1) The tricyclic and tetracyclic antidepressants (TCAs), which generally act on both serotonin and norepinephrine. Examples of tricyclic antidepressants are amitriptyline (Elavil) and imipramine (Tofranil). 2) The monoamine oxidase inhibitors (MAOIs), which act primarily on norepinephrine. 3) The nontricyclic antidepressants, consist of drugs that act on serotonin and norepinephrine by unknown mechanisms and are structurally unrelated to the other antidepressants. This group includes bupropion (Wellbutrin), which is thought to act by blocking norepinephrine reuptake. Another member of this group is venlafaxine (Effexor), which acts on both norepinephrine and serotonin. 4) Finally, the selective serotonin reuptake inhibitors (SSRIs) act by blocking reuptake of serotonin, thus increasing its concentration at postsynaptic neuroreceptors. Drugs in this class include fluoxetine (Prozac), sertraline (Zoloft), paroxetine (Paxil), and trazodone (Desyrel).

For example, one of the newer antidepressants, a unicyclic, bupropion (Wellbutrin), has an unknown mechanism of action, but is thought to act by blocking norepinephrine reuptake. It is not anticholinergic, but it can be too "activating" for some patients. Buproprion's release for use as an antidepressant was delayed when it was discovered, late in clinical trials, to have a higher seizure potential than the tricyclics to which it was being compared. Closer analysis of the data revealed that its increased seizuregenic potential was limited primarily to its use with a particular subgroup being studied—bulimic women. Because this increased the overall side effect profile of the drug, Wellbutrin has been approved only for use in dosages of approximately one-half that found to be effective for use in depression.

Most of the antidepressants require a period of from 10 days to two weeks before they begin to exert their therapeutic action. This poses a problem when a client presents with a high risk of suicide. Control and monitoring must be exerted until the medications or other treatments apparently take effect. During this lag period, blood levels of the drug are rising into a therapeutic range. These levels can be measured and the dosage adjusted accordingly to obtain an optimal clinical response. Monitoring of blood levels also decreases the likelihood of toxic reactions. Amoxapine (Asendin), with a four-ringed structure, can be helpful because of its rapid onset of effect, sometimes within 4 to 7 days.

Table 6C lists the antidepressant medications. The most commonly used tricyclics have traditionally been amitriptyline (Elavil), imipramine (Tofranil), and desipramine (Norpramin). Predictors of positive response to tricyclics include high socioeconomic class, good treatment motivation, insidious onset, anorexia, weight loss, middle and late insomnia, and psychomotor disturbance. Predictors of poor response to tricyclics include hypochondriasis, hysterical traits, multiple prior episodes, and delusions, and tricyclics are more likely to be abused effectively as a suicide agent. The MAO inhibitors, on the other hand, are used less often because of their side effects (mentioned below).

The initial effect experienced after taking an antidepressant is sedation. The severity of this effect varies with the drug; amitriptyline, for example, is very sedating, whereas desipramine has relatively little sedation. Thus, a depressed patient with insomnia might benefit from amitriptyline.

Antidepressants also often generate feelings of dizziness or lightheadedness. This occurs because norepinephrine exerts an effect not only on mood but on other organ systems such as the cardiovascular system. Most clients will also experience a calming effect, related to either the sedative effect of the drugs or to the direct action on serotonin. Depending on the degree of sedation and calming, the person may appear either drowsy or detached and disinterested; it is unlikely, however, that the person would appear intoxicated. Once the antidepressant action of the drug takes effect, the person will probably not notice any major effect from the medication; mood will simply appear to be normal. In some persons, however, the mood will become somewhat agitated as a result of too much stimulation of the norepinephrine system. In fact, persons with a bipolar disorder who take antidepressants may cycle into a manic episode.

The antidepressants have a number of side effects, many of which are potentially dangerous. Nearly all of the drugs in this class cause some degree of drowsiness and sedation. Like the antipsychotics, many also cause anticholinergic side effects. Other side effects include feelings of restlessness and agitation, sleep disturbances, nightmares, seizures, and exacerbation of psychosis in susceptible persons. The monoamine oxidase inhibitors may cause an interaction with certain foods and alcohol to produce a sudden rise in blood pressure (hypertensive crisis). Because of this effect, certain dietary restrictions (especially for foods containing tyramine, such as beer, red wine, certain cheeses, liver, and pickled or smoked meats and fish) apply for MAOI use.

TABLE 6C
Antidepressant Drugs

Name(Generic/Trade)	Dose Range*
Tricyclic and Tetracyclic Antidepressants	
amitriptyline (Elavil)	75–300 mg/day
imipramine (Tofranil)	75–300 mg/day
desipramine (Norpramin)	75–300 mg/day
nortriptyline (Pamelor)	30–100 mg/day
protriptyline (Vivactil)	15–40 mg/day
doxepine (Sinequan)	50–300 mg/day
maprotiline (Ludiomil)	75–150 mg/day
amoxapine (Asendin)	50–300 mg/day
clomipramine (Anafranil)**	150–250 mg/day
MAO Inhibitors	
tranylcypromine (Parnate)	20–60 mg/day
phenelzine (Nardil)	60–90 mg/day
Other Antidepressants	
fluoxetine (Prozac)	20–80 mg/day
bupropion (Wellbutrin)	200–450 mg/day
trazodone (Desyrel)	100–400 mg/day
sertraline (Zoloft)	20–200 mg/day
paroxetine (Paxil)	50–200 mg/day
venlafaxine (Effexor)	75–225 mg/day

* Average therapeutic dose range.
** Used also for treatment of obsessive-compulsive disorder.

Several antidepressants, including maprotiline (Ludiomil) and bupropion (Wellbutrin), are associated with an increased risk of seizures, particularly when taken in high doses. The tricyclic antidepressants may cause a number of cardiac effects. At therapeutic doses these effects include tachycardia (rapid heart rate) and a decreased conduction time, which causes electrocardiogram (ECG) changes. At very high doses, as seen in overdoses, these drugs cause cardiac arrhythmias, which may be potentially fatal, and slow heart rate. This effect presents a significant risk for persons with preexisting heart disease or who overdose on these medications as part of a suicide attempt. Thus, the tricyclics and tetracyclics should be prescribed in limited amounts to minimize the risk of overdose. Blood levels of the drugs should also be monitored to prevent toxicity. There is low potential for abuse or dependence in this group of drugs.

The Prozac Controversy

The most controversial newer-generation antidepressant is certainly fluoxetine (Prozac). This versatile compound (like sertraline [Zoloft], a "selective serotonin reuptake inhibitor" [SSSR]) was initially accepted with great hopes for the treatment of depressed patients, and quickly became highly controversial. Despite its demonstrated lack of toxic physiologic side effects, the drug was accused of creating some of the very conditions that it was supposed to treat. Reports surfaced of individuals on Prozac increasing their suicidal or homicidal ideation, and sometimes going so far as to act on those impulses. As of the date of the writing of this chapter, many of those controversies continue despite the fact that there are only a few hundred reported cases of this kind of behavior in a population of almost five million people worldwide who have taken the drug. The latest controversy centers around the overprescription of such drugs, in part because they are so effective but abused in the Orwellian sense of placating everyday anxieties.

ANTIMANIC DRUGS

Manic episodes often cycle with recurrent depressions, forming what is referred to as a bipolar disorder (previously called manic-depressive illness). Lithium, a psychotropic medication that functions as a mood-stabilizing agent, remains the first line of treatment for the manic phase of a bipolar disorder. Certain schizophrenic individuals may also respond favorably to lithium used in combination with an antipsychotic medication.

The exact mechanism of action for lithium is not clear. It is generally thought that manic episodes result from an excess of the neurotransmitter norepinephrine, just the opposite situation from depressive episodes. Lithium is believed to act by stabilizing the membranes of neuronal cells in the central nervous system, resulting in a decrease in the amount of norepinephrine released from the cells. There is also a probable increase in the reuptake of norepinephrine by the cells, decreasing the overall concentration of the neurotransmitter. Lithium is metabolized and excreted by the kidney.

Because it is a salt that occurs naturally in the body, unlike many of the other psychotropic medications, lithium has a therapeutic dose range that can be measured in the blood. Dosage of the medication, beginning with divided doses of 300 mg two to three times per day, is increased until the blood levels reach a range of 0.5 to 1.5 mEq per liter. Within 7 to 10 days on a therapeutic dose, the manic patient should be observed to become calmer, less agitated, have a general slowing of speech and thought processes, and return to a normal, or euthymic, mood.

The monitoring of lithium blood levels is necessary to prevent toxicity, which is caused by doses of lithium that are too high. Lithium toxicity is characterized by nausea and vomiting, muscle cramps, diarrhea, excessive thirst, and increased urination at blood levels between 1.5 and 2.0 mEq per liter. At levels above 2.0 mEq per liter, the individual experiences confusion, lethargy, tremor of the extremities, muscle spasms, ataxia (unsteady gait), slurred speech, convulsions, and ultimately coma. When maintained at therapeutic blood levels, however, lithium is notably free of day-to-day side effects. It is unlikely to cause sedation, and has little or no potential for abuse or dependence. The most common side effects on therapeutic doses are fine tremor of the hand and skin rash. The long-term use of lithium virtually guarantees the eventual production of hyperthyroidism. Likewise, over time, there is a potentially reversible alteration of the basement membrane in the kidney, which requires careful scrutiny.

Lithium, when combined with certain other drugs, can have problematic effects. Many diuretics (drugs that remove water from the body) increase the level of lithium and can cause toxicity. Other diuretics, like coffee and tea, can lower the level of lithium. Problems may occur when lithium is combined with hydroxyzine (Atarax, Vistaril), antipsychotic drugs, or methyldopa (Aldomet and others). A patient who is taking lithium should tell all the physicians he sees about all other medication he is taking.

Because it is a salt and is turned over fairly rapidly in the body, lithium has to be administered two to three times a day to maintain blood levels. There are some patients who are so precariously balanced with regard to their blood levels that missing one or two doses can be enough to initiate hypomanic behavior and thinking.

The evolution of lithium as an effective treatment is a good example of the driving force of the profit motive in pharmacological research. Lithium is a chemical element that was first isolated in 1817 by John Arfwedson, a young Swedish chemistry student. He named it lithium because he found it in stone (*lithos* in Greek). John Cade, an Australian psychiatrist, discovered the positive effect of lithium on mania by chance in the 1940s, while studying whether an excess of uric acid might be the cause of manic-depressive episodes. Cade injected humans with urea from the urine of guinea pigs. Expecting to learn that uric acid (a compound containing urea) increased the toxicity of urea, he added the most soluble salt of uric acid, lithium urate, and was surprised to find instead that the urea was less toxic as a result. Further experiments isolating lithium eventually indicated its curative properties.

However, it was a long time between initial discovery and the recent widespread marketing and use of lithium. In general, there had been little research on lithium, while more exotic, less widely available compounds have received much attention. Two explanations for this seem plausible. First, there was warranted concern about the significant side effects of lithium. Second, since lithium is a naturally occurring element, it cannot be patented. Drug companies are much more interested in researching new synthetic compounds that they can patent, so that they can control the market and gain substantial profits.

Unfortunately, as noted, lithium is not always effective with mania. Until the 1970s, there were no alternatives to the use of lithium and/or neuroleptics for the treatment of mania. In the 1970s, Robert Post first described the possible application of carbamazepine (Tegretol), an anticonvulsant previously used to treat temporal lobe epilepsy, for the treatment of mania. Bipolars who cycle rapidly—that is, they change from mania to depression and back again over the course of hours or days, rather than months—seem to respond particularly well to carbamazepine. While Tegretol does not produce the hypothyroidism common to lithium, it has significant side effects of its own, including blood dyscrasias such as agranulocytosis and leukopenia. It can also disturb iron metabolism. Therefore, like lithium, Tegretol has a therapeutic dose level that needs to be carefully monitored. Following the discovery of Tegretol's value in the treatment of mania, other anticonvulsants used to treat temporal lobe epilepsy have been tried and found to be useful as well, including valporic acid (Depakote) and clonazepam (Klonopin). About one-third of nonresponders show a 50% symptom reduction with divalproex sodium, the same rate of reduction obtained in those who do respond to lithium.

ANTIANXIETY MEDICATIONS

Anxiety is one of the most frequent complaints among persons requiring mental health consultation. The antianxiety medications exert a calming and sedating effect to counteract the effects of anxiety. Originally, this class of drugs consisted primarily of the barbiturates, which had high potential for dependence and addiction as well as for a variety of other side effects. Since the mid-1960s, however, a large number of drugs belonging to the benzodiazepine family have been introduced. For the treatment of anxiety, these drugs are more effective and safer, have less addiction potential, and generally produce less sedation than the barbiturates. Consequently, benzodiazepines have become some of the most frequently prescribed medications in the United States. In addition to their antianxiety effects, they are also useful as sedative-hypnotics. The introduction of chlordiazepoxide (Librium) and diazepam (Valium) heralded the benzodiazepine age. Both of these agents still have considerable clinical utility, but are also often drugs of abuse.

Benzodiazepines, because of their varying half-lives, end up contributing to the problems they were prescribed to solve. The term *half-life* refers to the length of time it takes for one-half of a drug dose to be metabolized, i.e., how long it remains active in the body. The longer the half-life, the longer the overall duration of the drug's effect. The more recent benzodiazepines, such as alprazolam (Xanax), differ from those introduced earlier primarily in the length of their half-life. Xanax has rapidly grown to be the most widely prescribed benzodiazepine and, consequently, the most widely abused. A sister compound, triazolam (Halcion), was banned in 1991 in Great Britain because of its reported production of amnestic states, with several reports of individuals committing serious crimes while in that state.

These shorter-acting benzodiazepines can create what is referred to as "breakthrough anxiety states" or mini-withdrawal states as their serum level in the body falls. For this reason, a behavioral paradigm can be created whereby individuals who are feeling anxious develop drug-seeking behaviors in an attempt to ameliorate these feelings. This drug-seeking behavior reinforces the further use of the drug and begins the process of abuse by putting the patient in a constant state of anticipatory anxiety and, therefore, of anticipating the next dose of relief (the drug). Longer-acting benzodiazepines, or timed-release medications of this class, should, theoretically, have less abuse potential but may have no less potential for addiction, since true physiological states of withdrawal are created when these drugs are used at therapeutic doses for extended periods of time. All of the benzodiazepines are metabolized by the liver. The currently used antianxiety agents are listed in Table 6D.

In addition to their clinical action on anxiety and their sedative effects, the benzodiazepines are also cross-tolerant with alcohol and other drugs such as the barbiturates. In other words, they may potentiate the effects of alcohol or other sedative drugs, making the concurrent use of antianxiety drugs and alcohol or other sedatives contraindicated. The clinical benefit that is derived from this finding, however, is that the benzodiazepines can be used to detoxify and withdraw individuals who are addicted to either alcohol or the barbiturates. Chlordiazepoxide (Librium), for example, is often used to withdraw persons from alcohol and to treat alcohol withdrawal delirium (delirium tremens, or the DTs). Of course, one has to be careful with this population that a secondary addiction to the benzodiazepine does not occur.

Because of the cross-tolerance with alcohol, a person who drinks while taking benzodiazepines will appear more intoxicated than a person using either drug alone. In fact, the sedating and tranquilizing effect of this class of drugs causes many person taking them to appear drunk, even in the absence of alcohol consumption. Accompanying features sometimes seen with the benzodiazepines include slurred speech, ataxia (unsteady gait), impaired coordination, slowed reflexes, and impaired judgment. As a result of these effects, persons taking benzodiazepines need to exercise considerable caution when driving or operating machinery. These drugs have a relatively rapid onset of action, usually within 30 minutes. Their duration of action ranges from 4 to 6 hours for the short-acting preparations (e.g., lorazepam) to more than 20 hours for the longer-acting drugs (e.g., diazepam).

TABLE 6D
Antianxiety Drugs

Name (Generic/Trade)	Dose Range*
Benzodiazepines	
diazepam (Valium)	2–40 mg/day
chlordiazepoxide (Librium)	15–100 mg/day
chlorazepate (Tranxene)	15–60 mg/day
prazepam (Centrax)	20–60 mg/day
halazepam (Paxipam)	60–120 mg/day
lorazepam (Ativan)	2–6 mg/day
alprazolam (Xanax)	0.5–6.0 mg/day
oxazepam (Serax)	30–120 mg/day
clonazepam (Klonipin)	0.5–6.0 mg/day
Non-benzodiazepine	
buspirone (Buspar)	5–20 mg/day

* Average therapeutic dose range.

A new generation antianxiety drug of a non-benzodiazepine class, considered to be a partial serotonin agonist, was released in 1985. This drug, buspirone (Buspar), has generated a good deal of controversy regarding its usefulness in the treatment of anxiety. Because of its extended onset of action, requiring up to two to three weeks to become effective, anxious patients previously disposed to the faster-acting benzodiazepines may be less tolerant of waiting for the drug to take effect. As a result, patients often discontinue use of this drug or fail to comply with its thrice-daily dosing requirement. Although its antianxiety effects are not as potent as the benzodiazepines, it has the advantage of having a very low potential for addiction or abuse.

While the benzodiazepines and related compounds are used primarily in the treatment of anxiety disorders, other treatments such as biofeedback, relaxation training, and other forms of psychotherapy are also effective. Since these latter treatments are less intrusive and do not pose the problem of side effects, and yet are effective, they should be employed first.

A number of other drugs have been used to treat anxiety, although none are as effective as the ones described above. Antihistamines, such as diphenhydramine (Benadryl) and hydroxyzine (Vistaril), have been used. Their antianxiety effect is largely a function of their sedating properties, and they are not thought to exert any direct effect on GABA. These drugs are also sometimes used to treat the extrapyramidal side effects associated with antipsychotic drug therapy. Propranolol (Inderal) acts to block receptors for beta-adrenergic neurotransmitters, a large group of transmitters that exert a number of effects throughout the body. Inderal, as well as the earlier mentioned SSRIs, have been reported to be effective in the treatment of certain anxiety disorders such as panic disorder. Clomipramine (Anafranil), a tricyclic antidepressant, was introduced specifically for the treatment of obsessive-compulsive disorder, and sertraline (Zoloft) is also used with OCD.

SEDATIVE-HYPNOTIC MEDICATIONS

Sleep disturbances are common complaints, but in most cases are transient and thus do not warrant treatment. These difficulties may also be related to some other disease process, such as a medical condition or depression. Many individuals, however, have chronic problems with sleep. This has led to the development of a group of medications, the sedative-hypnotic drugs, whose primary action is the induction of sleep. Most of these agents act on serotonin and GABA in the brain, both of which exert a natural calming and sedating effect.

Most of the commonly used commercially available sedative-hypnotic agents are actually antianxiety drugs whose sedating properties are stronger than their antianxiety properties. As a result, many of the sedative-hypnotics currently available are either benzodiazepines or barbiturates. As with the other members of these groups, there is a definite potential for abuse and dependence. These drugs also tend to lose their effectiveness in inducing sleep when taken for extended periods of time, a process referred to as tolerance or habituation. The result is that higher doses are required over time to exert the same therapeutic effect, a consequence that facilitates addiction and dependence. Table 6E lists the sedative-hypnotic drugs currently in clinical use.

The side effects for these drugs are similar to those for the other benzodiazepines and barbiturates. The most common side effect is excessive drowsiness upon awakening. In very high doses, respiratory depression may occur, particularly with the barbiturates. Tolerance and addiction, however, are the most serious long-term side effects for these drugs.

There are several other drugs that have 1) a secondary sedative effect, 2) low addiction and abuse potential, and 3) a low ratio of side effects. One good example is the antihistamines, such as the over-the-counter medication Benadryl (diphenhydramine). Another is the group of drugs sometimes referred to as the ataraxics, such as Vistaril (hydroxyzine pamoate) and Atarax (hydroxyzine hydrochloride), which are primarily intended to reduce anxiety, especially where accompanied by physical conditions, e.g., dermatological and/or gastrointestinal distress.

It is good policy to first try to cure a sleep problem with something like Benadryl. Another option is a low-dose regimen of melatonin (which, like Benadryl, is available without prescription). This latter option appears especially useful for older persons with a sleep problem, or for those who show evidence of dysfunction (possibly with depression) from a disruption of diurnal rhythms. Then, if these are unsuccessful, move to a prescribed drug such as an ataraxic, especially if agitation from the stress of living is a factor, or trazodone (Desyrel) if depression and early morning awakening are factors. Then, if these are unsuccessful and manipulation or an addictive personality component are ruled out, one can move to the traditional sedative-hypnotics.

ANTI-PARKINSONIAN MEDICATIONS

Earlier, it was mentioned that the antipsychotic medications cause a variety of "extrapyramidal" side effects characterized by muscular stiffness and rigidity, feelings of restlessness (akathesia), involuntary movements (dystonias), and a general slowing of movements (Parkinsonian effects). They occur most frequently in young adult males and in persons recently started on antipsychotic medications. These effects are naturally quite bothersome to clients and are frequently responsible for poor medication compliance. Since the apparent mechanism of action is the blocking of dopamine, the same action that leads to a diminishing of psychotic symptoms also leads to neuromuscular disturbances.

Fortunately, several medications exist that have the ability to lessen the degree of the extrapyramidal symptoms. Collectively, these drugs are often referred to as anti-Parkinsonian agents. The two most commonly used drugs in this group are trihexyphenidl (Artane) and benztropine (Cogentin). Both are administered orally in doses of 2 mg, up to three times a day. They may also be used either intravenously

TABLE 6E
Sedative-Hypnotic Drugs

Name (Generic/Trade)	Dose Range*
Benzodiazepines	
flurazepam (Dalmane)	15–30 mg/day
temazepam (Restoril)	15–30 mg/day
triazolam (Halcion)	0.25–0.5 mg/day
estazolam (ProSom)	1.0–2.0 mg/day
quazepam (Doral)	7.5–15 mg/day
Barbiturates	
secobarbital (Seconal)	100–200 mg/day
Other Sedative-Hypnotics	
chloral hydrate (Noctec)	500–1000 mg/day
zolpidem tartrate (Ambien)	5–10 mg/day

* Average therapeutic dose range.

or intramuscularly. Although neither Cogentin nor Artane cause classic addiction, they are frequently abused because persons taking these medications often experience a temporary "high" immediately after ingesting the drug.

CENTRAL NERVOUS SYSTEM STIMULANTS

Certain central nervous system stimulants are effective in dealing with disorders such as hyperactivity, and also in some forms of apathy-depression. For example, methylphenidate (Ritalin), one of the piperidyls, is commonly used to control hyperactive patterns, especially in children and adolescents. Other types of drugs that may be used to control these symptoms are diphenhydramine (Benadryl) or diazepam (Valium), both of which are used intravenously in acute situations.

MEDICATIONS FOR CONTROL OF VIOLENT AND AGGRESSIVE BEHAVIOR

Psychologists often deal with violent behavior when it occurs in association with mental illness. A variety of psychotropic medications have been found to be effective in controlling or diminishing this type of behavior. Such management is often complicated by the person's use of alcohol or drugs, i.e., both inhibitions and good intentions are soluble in alcohol.

Violence and aggression are generally caused by a complex interaction of biological, psychological, and environmental factors. The management of violent behavior with medication relies on an appreciation of the biological factors that underlie violence. As with other symptoms, the biological explanation of violence rests with the neurotransmitters. In general, violence is correlated with an interaction of three factors in the brain: (1) an overabundance of certain neurotransmitters (e.g., dopamine and norepinephrine); (2) a relative deficiency of other neurotransmitters (e.g., serotonin and GABA); and (3) excess electrical activity in the brain, leading to seizures. Drugs that control violent behavior act by correcting the neurotransmitter imbalance or by decreasing the electrical activity in the brain.

Table 6F lists the medications useful in controlling violent or aggressive behavior. These drugs are members of several of the groups already described. When violent behavior is associated with a psychotic disorder such as schizophrenia, the antipsychotic medications are clearly indicated. Violent tendencies in nonpsychotic persons may also be controlled by these medications because of their dopamine-blocking action. Antidepressants that increase the action of serotonin, such as trazodone (Desyrel), may also be useful. One of the actions of serotonin in the brain is a calming influence on behavior. Those drugs that increase levels of norepinephrine, however, may actually facilitate violent or aggressive behavior. Lithium, through its action to decrease norepinephrine activity, may be useful in controlling aggression in some clients. Norepinephrine-blocking agents such as propranolol (Inderal) have also been shown to be effective.

The benzodiazepines, by increasing levels of GABA in the brain, which exerts a calming effect similar to that of serotonin, may also decrease violence. These drugs must be used cautiously, however, not only because of their potential for abuse but also because they cause a paradoxical increase in violence in some individuals. Finally, carbamazepine (Tegretol), an anticonvulsant medication, is useful especially when violence occurs in association with seizure activity.

DRUGS USED FOR ASSESSMENT

Certain psychotropic drugs are used to induce a light sleep or trancelike state during which the person remains conscious and able to talk, akin to the altered level of consciousness achieved during hypnosis. During this period, it is possible to interview the patient and obtain important diagnostic information, including previously repressed or forgotten memories. Drugs that promote such a state have often been referred to as "truth serums." However, it is a common misconception that these drugs make people reveal information that they would otherwise withhold; this seldom occurs. It is also not possible to be sure that the information obtained from such an interview is entirely factual.

Currently, two drugs are most commonly used for this type of interview, often referred to as narcotherapy or narcoanalysis. One of these is the short-acting barbiturate, sodium amobarbital (Amytal). The other is a short-acting benzodiazepine, lorazepam (Ativan). The primary use of these agents is for diagnostic purposes, although lorazepam is also a frequently prescribed antianxiety agent when taken orally. For example, interviews using these drugs are useful for clarifying the diagnosis of catatonic schizophrenia, in which patients are often mute, and with certain disorders characterized by dissociative symptoms.

For this type of interview, both sodium amobarbitaltal and lorazepam are administered intravenously. Small doses are injected at one-to-two-minute intervals until the patient becomes drowsy but not completely asleep. Blood pressure and respirations must be monitored throughout the interview. Injection of the medication too rapidly will produce sleep, and using doses that are too high may cause respiratory depression or arrest. As the person becomes drowsy, a series of generalized questions are asked, proceeding then to more specific questions. If the person appears to resist questioning, additional medication is gradually infused until the person becomes more open. Because the duration of action of these drugs is brief, additional medication must be infused periodically throughout the interview. The client will be aware of information disclosed following the interview. How long this awareness remains depends on the underlying condition the client suffers from. Many neurotic individuals will remain aware of the contents of the interview, while catatonic patients are likely to lapse back into a psychotic state.

TABLE 6F
Medications Used to Control Violent Behavior

Name(Generic/Trade)	Dose Range*
Benzodiazepines	
lorazepam (Ativan)	1–2 mg PO or IM Q2–4hr. PRN
oxazepam (Serax)	15–120 mg/day
Mood-Altering Drugs	
lithium carbonate	300 mg in divided doses to attain a therapeutic blood level
trazodone (Desyrel)	100–400 mg/day
Adrenergic Blocking Agents	
propranolol (Inderal)	200–600 mg/day
Anticonvulsants	
carbamazepine (Tegretol)	200 mg in divided doses to attain a therapeutic blood level
Antipsychotics	
haloperidol (Haldol)	2–5mg PO or IM Q2–4 hr. PRN
chlorpromazine (Thorazine)	50–100 mg. PO or IM Q2–4hr. PRN

* Average therapeutic dose range.
PO— Oral administration.
IM—Intramuscular administration.

OTHER DRUGS USED IN MENTAL TREATMENT

Many drugs, from a variety of classes, have been found to be effective for certain conditions where traditional drug therapy has been ineffective. One example of this is the calcium channel blocker verapamil (Calan, Isoptin). The calcium ion is an important intracellular messenger that exerts an effect on many neurons. An overactivity of this ion may result in signals being sent to neurons that are firing excessively or sporadically. By blocking calcium in the brain, the neurons are restored to normal rates of firing. Verapamil has been found to be effective in the treatment of some types of bipolar disorder, tardive dyskinesia, and certain other movement disorders that are accompanied by psychiatric symptoms (e.g., Tourette's disorder).

Clonidine (Catapres) is an alpha-adrenergic receptor agonist, i.e., it facilitates the action of the alpha-adrenergic transmitters. This drug has been widely used to treat hypertension, but has also been found to be effective in treating Tourette's disorder and in helping clients to withdraw from opioids.

For an excellent review of psychopharmacology as it relates to children, see Sylvester and Kreusi (1994).

LEGAL ISSUES IN THE USE OF PSYCHOTROPIC MEDICATIONS

Because the psychotropic medications exert powerful effects on behavior, mood, and thought, it is not surprising that a number of legal issues are associated with their use. Specific issues include informed consent, malpractice, the right to refuse treatment, the right to treatment, and the role of medications in criminal proceedings (see Chapter 2).

As noted previously, one important legal concept involved in the use of psychotropic medications is informed consent. The basic principle underlying informed consent is that the patient has a right to determine what should be done to his body and cannot be forced to accept treatment that is not wanted. Informed consent requires that the client be apprised of the potential benefits and major risks of any proposed treatments, as well as of all alternative treatments available. In order to give consent for treatment, the client must be competent, possess adequate information, and make the decision for treatment voluntarily. With respect to psychotropic medications, for example, the client must be informed about all potential major side effects and their relative risk, drug interactions, and any special precautions that should be taken. Common examples of risks that need to be explained thoroughly are tardive dyskinesia and the neuroleptic malignant syndrome associated with the antipsychotic drugs.

Related to the concept of informed consent is the right to refuse treatment. This concept basically says that a competent adult has the right to refuse treatment if the perceived risks or consequences are viewed as intolerable. Even though the decision may be ill-advised or have negative consequences for the person, the competent (and nonincarcerated) client retains the right of refusal.

REFERENCES

American Psychiatric Association. (1994). *Diagnostic and Statistical Manual of Mental Disorders (DSM-IV)*, 4th ed. Washington, DC: Author.

Beaber, R., Marston, A., Michelli, J., and Mills, M. (1985). A brief test for measuring malingering in schizophrenic individuals. *American Journal of Psychiatry, 142*, 1478–1481.

Bersoff, D., Glass, D., and Blain, N. (1994). Legal issues in the assessment and treatment of individuals with dual diagnoses. *Journal of Consulting and Clinical Psychology, 62*, 55–62.

Bongar, B. (1991). *The Suicidal Patient*. Washington, DC: American Psychological Association.

Boyer, J. (1990). Fatal attraction: The borderline personality and psychotherapy. *National Register Report, 16* (2), 5–7.

Camara, W., and Schneider, D. (1994). Integrity tests: Facts and unresolved issues. *American Psychologist, 49*, 112–119.

Carr, C. (1994). *The Alienist*. New York: Random House.

Cassini, J., and Workman, D. (1992). The detection of malingering and deception with a short form of the MMPI-2 based on L, F, and K scales. *Journal of Clinical Psychology, 48*, 54–63.

Conn, S., and Rieke, M. (Eds.). (1994). *The 16PF Fifth Edition Technical Manual*. Champaign, IL: IPAT.

Dar, R., Serlin, R., and Omer, H. (1994). Misuse of statistical tests in three decades of psychotherapy research. *Journal of Consulting and Clinical Psychology, 62*, 75–82.

Davis, K., and Sines, J. (1971). An antisocial behavior pattern associated with a specific MMPI profile. *Journal of Consulting and Clinical Psychology, 36*, 229–234.

Dunn, G. (1992). Multiple personality disorder. *Professional Psychology: Research and Practice, 23*, 18–23.

Ekman, P., and O'Sullivan, M. (1991). Who can catch a liar? *American Psychologist, 46*, 913–920.

Ellis, A. (1992). Group rational-emotive and cognitive-behavior therapy. *International Journal of Group Psychotherapy, 42*, 63–80.

Everson, M., and Boat, B. (1994). Putting the anatomical doll controversy in perspective: An examination of the major uses and criticisms of the dolls in child sexual abuse examinations. *Child Abuse and Neglect, 18*, 113–129.

Exner, J. (1978). *The Rorschach: A Comprehensive System*, Vol. 2: *Current Research and Advanced Interpretation*. New York: Wiley.

Exner, J. (1988). *Rorschach: A Comprehensive System: Assessment of Personality and Psychopathology*, 2nd ed. New York: Wiley.

Federal Rules of Evidence for United States Courts and Magistrates with Amendments Effective December 1, 1991. (1992). St. Paul, MN: West Publishing.

Gilmore, J. (1991). Murdering while asleep. *Forensic Reports, 4*, 455–459.

Graham, J. (1991). *MMPI-2: Assessing Personality and Psychopathology*. New York: Oxford University Press.

Grisso, T. (1986). *Evaluating Competencies*. New York: Plenum.

Hare, R., Hart, S., and Forth, A. (1992). Workshop on the assessment of psychopathy. Biennial meeting of the American Psychology-Law Society, San Diego, CA.

Hersen, M., Ammerman, R., and Sisson, L. (1994). *Handbook of Aggressive and Destructive Behavior in Psychiatric Patients*. New York: Plenum.

Honts, C., and Perry, M. (1992). Polygraph admissability. *Law and Human Behavior, 16*, 357–379.

Jacob, S., and Hartshorne, T. (1991). *Ethics and Law for School Psychologists*. Brandon, VT: Clinical Psychology Publishing.

Jones, R., Sevilla, C., and Uelman, G. (1989). *Disorderly Conduct: Verbatim Excerpts from Actual Court Cases*. New York: W. W. Norton.

Kalichman, S. (1993). *Mandated Reporting of Suspected Child Abuse*. Washington, DC: American Psychological Association.

Kempe, C., Silverman, F., Steele, B., Droegemueller, W., and Silver, H. (1962). The battered child syndrome. *Journal of the American Medical Association, 181*, 17–24.

Krug, S. (1978). Further evidence on the 16PF distortion scales. *Journal of Personality Assessment, 42*, 513–518.

Kurtz, R., Meyer, R., and Barnes, J. (1994). Biennial Meeting of the American Psychology-Law Society. Santa Fe, NM.

Laurence, J., and Perry, C. (1988). *Hypnosis, Will and Memory: A Psycholegal History*. New York: Guilford.

Lykken, D. (1981). *A Tremor in the Blood*. New York: Macmillan.

Marlowe, D., and Crowne, D. (1964). *The Approval Motive*. New York: Wiley.

Martell, D. (1992). Forensic Neuropsychology and the Criminal Law. *Law and Human Behavior, 16*, 313–337.

McGarry, A., Curran, W., Lipsitt, P., Lelos, D., et al. (1983) *Competency to Stand Trial and Mental Illness*. Rockville, MD: NIMH.

Meyer, R. (1992). *Abnormal Behavior and the Criminal Justice System*. Lexington, MA: Lexington Books.

Meyer, R. (1992). *Practical Clinical Hypnosis*. New York: Lexington Books.

Meyer, R. (1995). *The Clinician's Handbook*, 4th ed. Boston: Allyn & Bacon.

Meyer, R., Deitsch, S., and Wolverton, D. (1994). Antisocial personality disorder. In V. Ramachandran (Ed.), *Encyclopedia of Human Behavior*. San Diego: Academic Press.

Milner, J. (1991). Physical child abuse perpetrator screening and evalution. *Criminal Justice and Behavior, 18*, 47–63.

Monahan, J. (1981). *Predicting Violent Behavior*. Beverly Hills, CA: Sage.

Paulhus, D. L. (1991). *BIDR Reference Manual for Version 6*. Unpublished manual. University of British Columbia.

Resnick, P. (1989). The detection of malingered mental illness. Symposium on the Mental Health Professional and Forensic Issues. Costa Mesa, CA.

Robins, L., and Regier, D. (1990). *Psychiatric Disorders in America*. New York: The Free Press.

Roesch, R., et al. (1984). Fitness to stand trial. *International Journal of Law and Psychiatry, 7*, 115–126.

Rogers, R. (Ed.). (1988). *Clinical Assessment of Malingering and Deception*. New York: Guilford.

Schretlen, D., Wilkins, S., Van Gorp, W., and Bobholz, V. (1992). Cross-validation of a psychological test battery to detect faked insanity. *Psychological Assessment, 4*, 77–83.

Schwartz, D., and Goodman, J. (1992). Expert testimony on decision processes in employment cases. *Law and Human Behavior, 16*, 337–355.

Shapiro, D. (1984). *Psychological Evaluation and Expert Testimony*. New York: Van Nostrand Reinhold.

Smith, S., and Meyer, R. (1987). *Law, Behavior and Mental Health: Policy and Practice*. New York: New York University Press.

Spitzer, R., and Endicott, J. (1978). *Schedule of Affective Disorders and Schizophrenia*. New York: Biometrics Research.

Steadman, H., McGreevy, M., Morrissey, J., Callahan, L., Robbins, P., and Cirincione, C. (1993). *Before and After Hinckley: Evaluating Insanity Defense Reform*. New York: Guilford.

Summit, R. (1983). The child sexual abuse accommodation syndrome. *Child Abuse and Neglect, 7*, 177–193.

Sylvester, C., and Kreusi, M. (1994). Child and adolescent psychopharmacotherapy: Progress and pitfalls. *Psychiatric Annals, 24*, 83–90.

Ziskin, J., and Faust, D. (1988). *Coping with Psychiatric and Psychological Testimony,* 4th ed. Marina del Rey, CA: Law and Psychology Press.

Zook, A., and Sipps, G. (1985). Cross-validation of a short form of the Marlowe-Crowne social desirability scale. *Journal of Clinical Psychology, 41*, 236–238.

CASE CITATION LIST

INDEX

ABOUT THE AUTHOR

For a number of years Dr. Meyer has offered licensing and board preparation exams for various states, as well as for the American Board of Professional Psychology (ABPP) and the American Board of Forensic Psychology (ABFP). He has been an examiner for ABPP and ABFP as well as for the Kentucky state licensing board and has been on the Board of Directors of ABFP and the Southeastern Regional Board of ABPP.

After receiving his Ph.D. in psychology from Michigan State University in 1967, he was chief psychologist at the Psychiatric Clinic of the State Prison of Southern Michigan during 1968. He then became an Assistant Professor in the Department of Psychiatry at the Medical School of the University of North Carolina at Chapel Hill, came to the University of Louisville in 1969 as Psychology Clinic Director and Assistant Professor, and is now a full Professor there in the Department of Psychology.

As implied, he is board certified in clinical psychology and in forensic psychology by the American Board of Professional Psychology, and he is also a fellow in both Division 12 (*Clinical*) and Division 41 (*Law and Psychology*) of the American Psychological Association. He is or has been a member or fellow of the International Neuropsychological Society, the American Society of Clinical Hypnosis, the Society for Clinical and Experimental Hypnosis, Divisions 30 (*Psychological Hypnosis*) and 31 (*State Psychological Associations*) of the American Psychological Association, the American Psychological Society, the American Academy of Forensic Psychology, and the Kentucky Psychological Association, of which he is a past president.

In addition to over 50 journal articles, a number of book chapters, and a number of other books, he has authored *Law, Behavior and Mental Health* (with Dean Steven Smith of the Cleveland Marshall School of Law), *Law for the Psychotherapist* (with Rhett Landis and J. Ray Hays), *The Clinician's Handbook* (4th Edition, 1995), *Abnormal Psychology*, and *Practical Clinical Hypnosis*; is editor of the Bulletin of the American Academy of Forensic Psychology; and received the Grawemeyer Award for innovative curriculum development for the course he developed in Law and Psychology with Dean Smith. In a lighter vein, he wrote *The Complete Book of Softball: The Loonies' Guide to Playing and Enjoying the Game* (Human Kinetics), and has coauthored a Sunday column, "Parent Talk," in the *Louisville Courier-Journal*.